YOU'RE NICKED MY SON

A True Account of 30 Years Policing

by
Andy Vick

authorHOUSE®

AuthorHouse™ UK Ltd.
500 Avebury Boulevard
Central Milton Keynes, MK9 2BE
www.authorhouse.co.uk
Phone: 08001974150

©2008 Andy Vick. All rights reserved.

No part of this book may be reproduced, stored in a retrieval system, or transmitted by any means without the written permission of the author.

First published by AuthorHouse 10/23/2008

ISBN: 978-1-4343-7800-2 (sc)
ISBN: 978-1-4343-7801-9 (hc)

Printed in the United States of America
Bloomington, Indiana

This book is printed on acid-free paper.

Heathrow Airport Bullion Robbery photographs reproduced with the permission of Mirrorpix, Trinity Mirror Print, UK.

IN MEMORY OF

PC JOHN CAPLIN
Gwent police and Metropolitan Police

PS PAUL THOMAS
Gwent Police

PC ANDY TOOLE
Royal Marine Commando and
Metropolitan police

PC CHRIS ROBERTS
Metropolitan Police

This book is dedicated to

My wife, Paula for all your love, strength and support in everything I did – it was immense. I cannot express how much I love you.

To both of our families: thank you for allowing us to lead our lives away from you without guilt and with your total love and support.

My daughter Natalie: I love you dearly.

Contents

Foreword	xiii
How it all started	1
The beginning	4
How not to impress the boss	9
Reality strikes	11
No longer the new boy	13
The skills of a police driver	16
'A' Division Maindee	20
Walking the beat	23
Murder. Chepstow Road	25
Close to home	27
My driving career finally takes off	31
Why do I always pick the big one?	34
The petrol shortage	42
The Old Barn arsonist	43
A scary horse box story!	46
Lost in translation	48
It's not big and it's not clever!	50
Complaints against the police	53
Taxi, gentlemen	58

What good is a piece of wood?	60
The boss is always right!	63
How do you cope with this?	68
Nearly a watery grave	70
Time to move on	74
Off to the Met	76
My first transvestite!	83
The football yob	85
Another lucky escape	87
Definitely the wrong move	89
Almost a deadly mistake	93
Advanced course here I come	96
Terrorism	101
Oh no, not Heathrow	105
Political incident	107
And so to West Drayton	111
Firearms incident	115
Fatal road crash, M4: how money talks	118
The Cosworth crowd	124
An arrest at last	127
A return to Gwent	129
The builder's skip	132
A very stormy night ahead	135
Harmondsworth immigration centre	138
The traffic car	140
M4 motorway crash	142
Please can we drive a little slower?	145
My slowest chase ever	147
One that did get away	149

Yet another injury	151
Now I know I am getting old	153
Inspector Gumbleton	155
Don't jump	158
The dog section years	161
I'm in	163
The wrong dog	168
Close to home	170
Conan the destroyer	173
Don't mess with me	175
How embarrassing	177
Tegan to the rescue	192
Tegan's finest hour	196
Windsor Castle	200
Firearms support dogs	202
Central demonstration team	212
A man to be admired	215
Time to leave	218
Return to Hammersmith	230
The kung fu vicar	233
We finally catch one!	237
You always get one	240
My biggest regret	243
Summary justice	251
A very tragic time	256
Driving for the Flying Squad	259
Long service and good conduct medal	261
A major change	263

The Flying Squad	271
Firearms training	273
Even more work to do	278
Operation Juneberry	281
Operation Magician – The Millennium Dome Robbery	285
Operation Rockley	291
The great train robber returns	296
Now this was a scary one!	306
The skull cracker – Operation Rockley	311
Heathrow airport (better known to police as thief row) – Operation Cartwright	316
A slightly different story	324
Operation Poe	329
The murder squad	332
Operation Achor	343
An ending I just did not want	351

Foreword

THERE HAVE BEEN MANY BOOKS written over the years by police officers. Some have been excellent and some have been so over the top they were like scripts from a television programme like *The Bill*. I have tried to tell my story of thirty years' police service as I saw it: through the eyes of a frontline police officer. It is a view from my position as an officer who has dealt with probably every sort of incident a police officer could come across, and I have tried to show exactly what being a police officer can be like – good and bad, funny, sad and tragic. They are my memories as I remember them.

The mere mention at a non-police social gathering that you were a policeman could bring entire conversations to a stop and cause people to walk away from you. On the other hand, it could also kick-start good conversation and serious debate. It was something you got used to and made you realise how much you relied on your colleagues. The police service itself is so full of strong characters and individuals that at times things can boil over with fellow officers. There are many police officers I have worked with who I think were absolute knob heads and there will be many officers who I have worked with who think the same of me. But what the police used to have is the strength of unity; it did not matter if the officer in trouble was someone you disliked intensely – if he was in trouble and required urgent assistance, you went as fast as you dared to get there and help him. That was the police family you were in. Things are in an awful state now and are continually getting worse as the years go by.

I hope this book gives people an insight into everyday policing and helps them realise that police officers are just as normal as everyday people. The vast majority put their lives at risk every day to police the country for everyone who lives here. The police are constantly berated for things they do. Every so often something bad happens, for instance an innocent person gets shot by police. Unfortunately, mistakes happen, but for every one mistake there are hundreds of times when a police officer draws his firearm and prevents a serious offence from taking place. Police officers are only human and are trying to do the right thing for the community they work for, and they are always the first people you look for when you are in trouble. Give them the respect and help they deserve. You will need them one day.

AT 4.20 A.M. ON A Monday morning the 21st June 2004, a large group of police officers comprised of Flying Squad from Barnes, surveillance officers and SO19 firearms officers attended a briefing at Croydon Police Station. This was the culmination of over twelve months' work by DS Charlie Cairns and the intelligence team he was in charge of at Barnes Flying Squad. They had been desperately trying to identify a prolific armed robber who had been targeting betting shops in and around London and the Home Counties. His total so far was 28 offences that police knew of; there could well have been more.

The offender was a lone male who would enter a premises shortly after they opened up for the day, produce a firearm or intimate that he had one, and force the staff to hand over cash. He would sometimes spend a little time in the shop posing as a customer. After a year of committing offences, and despite rigorous attempts to identify him, police were struggling to find the male responsible.

The police did have a couple of CCTV pictures of the suspect but efforts to identify him struggled on. Then they got a breakthrough. Two prison officers contacted the flying squad after seeing the latest CCTV pictures and said that the male could be a Malcolm Leferve.

Leferve had been sentenced to eighteen years' imprisonment following an armed robbery in 1989 when he fired a shot from a sawn-off shotgun and killed a female cashier. He was on the run for a week and was eventually arrested in London by Finchley flying squad after a siege. He claimed the gun went off by accident and somehow got away with being found guilty of manslaughter. The prison informed the squad that Leferve had changed his name whilst in prison and that he was now called Malcolm Parker. Copies of his prison photograph were quickly obtained and he certainly looked good as the suspect. This started a mad week of trying to locate the current whereabouts of Parker. DS Cairns set his team tasks to carry out in order to try and locate the current whereabouts of the suspect; all the usual intelligence enquiries were made and it led the team to the New Addington area of Croydon in south London. They had no definite address, but intelligence told them that he may have been living in that area.

The next couple of days saw the team running around the Croydon area in an attempt to track him down. On Thursday 17 June 2004, DS Charlie Cairns was out in one vehicle and DC Neil Hanchett and DC Andy Vick were in another when DS Cairns rang the others and told them that he had just seen a male in a red BMW who may have been the suspect. As he said it, DC Hanchett spotted a red BMW convertible turning into Featherbed Lane. Unfortunately, they were out of the car at the time and not close enough to it to see the driver. It drove away out of their sight.

DS Cairns joined them and they searched the estate for the red BMW without success; he had, however, managed to get the registration number. They were finally getting close to their man and so they headed back to Barnes. The next morning DS Cairns struck gold. He checked on the registration number of the car and it came back to a female living on the housing estate they had seen the car drive onto. Even better, a further check on the vehicle insurance details showed a named driver as being Malcolm Parker. Bingo: they had him! Now all they had to do was confirm he was the right man.

This was the start of a very long weekend. The officers went back to Croydon on Friday and managed to find an observation post giving them a view of the address where it was believed Parker was living. DS Cairns worked miracles and got cameras fitted on the address (you would not believe the amount of paperwork this takes). The observation post was manned by the three officers all weekend. Then at about 6 p.m. on Sunday night DS Cairns spotted the male coming back to the address and was 90 per cent sure it was the suspect. Suddenly, as quickly as he had arrived, he was out again with the female from the address, who turned out to be his wife.

DC Vick was positioned a short distance from the address and got himself out to the junction to try and have a look at the male to confirm the identification. He timed it just right and was crossing the junction as the suspect pulled out from the estate onto the main road. DC Vick was positive it was the right man. This was it: they were in.

DS Cairns again worked miracles, getting a surveillance team and SO19 together and this is how the whole of the Barnes Flying Squad found themselves at Croydon police station at 4.20 a.m. the next morning. The Flying Squad has its own firearms capability and would normally have carried out this operation themselves, but because Parker had previous convictions for offences with shotguns, 'the powers that be' decided that SO19 had to be used, much to the disappointment of all the squad officers. They really preferred doing the job themselves and it annoyed them that even though they were highly trained to carry out armed vehicle ambushes, it was felt that SO19 had to be used. This was a constant bone of contention in all the squad offices.

The briefing covered the fact that the suspect always commits the offence just after opening time, usually on a lone member of staff. He always wore a baseball cap and sometimes sunglasses, along with a dark-coloured plastic-style jacket. He also nearly always carried a copy of the *Sun* newspaper under which he would hide the gun.

Following the briefing, everyone headed off to take up their relevant standby positions, with the surveillance team being the closest, ready to pick up the suspect. They were all in position just prior to 6.00 a.m. and within ten minutes of being in place DS Cairns put it out on the radio that the suspect was out of his address, in the red BMW and away from the premises. He was picked up by the surveillance team and, after stopping at a nearby petrol station where he purchased a copy of the *Sun*, off they went on a drive that took them eventually to a trading estate in East Molsey, south west of London, close to Hampton Court. Parker was observed entering the premises of a large well-known company. It was assumed and later confirmed, that this was his place of work.

Fifteen minutes later he was spotted coming back out of the premises. He had changed his clothes and was now wearing a dark blue plastic jacket and a baseball cap. Game on: everyone's expectations suddenly lifted and off they went, around the M25 onto the M40, westbound out of London and about thirty minutes later he eventually came off the M40 towards Oxford on the London Road. Parker stopped in a little village called Headington and parked his car in a side road. On the corner of this road was a Ladbrokes betting office, the time was just after 9.00 a.m. He walked to the front of the shop, had a good look inside, then walked off and went around the area several times before entering a nearby park.

The surveillance team did a fantastic job. They had Parker completely under control without him knowing. He was seen popping his head over a hedge several times to look at Ladbrokes. Eventually, he entered a public toilet within the park where he remained for some considerable time. SO19 had three armed vehicles nearby and the flying squad had another four plotted up away from the street waiting.

Just after 10.00 a.m., one of the surveillance officers put out on the radio that a male member of staff was now in the premises and that he had locked the door behind him. There was no sign of Parker. Ten minutes later, the surveillance officer stated the betting shop was now open for business. Shortly after, on the radio came the message:

'Subject 1 is out of the toilet block, he is wearing the dark jacket, baseball cap and sunglasses. He has the newspaper in his hands. He is towards the premises; he is now in the premises.' Game definitely on.

The squad was instructed by the DI, Andy Dunn, to move closer ready for the attack and 'state amber' was called. Then the surveillance team put Parker up as coming out of the front of the betting shop and looking around. He walked up and down as if looking for signs of police, and then turned around and re-entered Ladbrokes.

A surveillance officer positioned across the road told us via the radio that Parker was up at the counter and something appeared to be happening. Suddenly Parker was running out of the premises and down the street towards his car. All three SO19 cars moved up and entered the one-way street he was parked in. DC Vick was driving the car containing DS Cairns and DC Hanchett and he moved to the top of the street.

The road was a one-way system. At the bottom cars could turn left or right. The left bringing you back up to the main London Road, one block away from Ladbrokes.

DC Vick held at the top of the road and saw the surveillance officers running into the betting shop. Within seconds the words 'Robbery,

Robbery, Robbery' came over the secure radios to confirm to everyone that an offence had taken place. 'State red' was called by the DI and this gave SO19 the authority to put an ambush in on the vehicle as soon as they felt it was safe to do so.

From the junction DC Vick saw the red BMW force its way out and turn right on to London Road back towards London. He then drove slowly forward effectively holding back traffic. This allowed the SO19 and surveillance vehicles to also get out of the junction quickly and off they went, just waiting for the hit to take place on the BMW. As the road became dual carriageway on the London Road, SO19 put the hit in.

Knowing that the hit was about to go in, the flying squad cars were used to slow down all the traffic behind them to give the SO19 guys a clear run at the BMW without endangering members of the public in any way. One car cut across the front of the BMW. Another one went up tight behind it and a third vehicle came alongside. The vehicle was immediately brought to a sudden stop and surrounded by armed officers. Several loud bangs were heard and the squad guys knew that Hatton rounds had been fired into the tyres to immobilise the car. Parker could then be seen being dragged out of the driver's seat, forced face down into the road and be plasti-cuffed with his hands behind his back.

DS Cairns, DC Hanchett and DC Vick went across to Parker. The look on his face was a picture! He had not known what had hit him. DS Cairns told him who they were and that he was under arrest for armed robbery at the Ladbrokes betting shop. He was in a state of shock. DC Vick searched him and in the zipped front of his plastic coat he found an the gun and all the cash stolen from the betting shop, along with a mobile phone taken from the member of staff. After removing the items the officers stood him up so that he could be videoed for evidential purposes. As the photographer was videoing him, he looked straight at the camera and said: 'The flying squad mate. All I can say is ten out of ten, definitely ten out of ten.'

I was one of those officers and I was doing the work I really loved. I was in the last three years of my police career and loving every minute of it. This is my story of how, from the time I had spent watching *Z Cars* on TV as a kid, I had longed to join the police force. At eighteen years of age I joined my home force (Gwent) and then twenty-three years later I had reached the dizzy heights of being part of the world famous flying squad. I hope you enjoy reading about it as much as I enjoyed doing it.

How it all started

My career in the police force commenced on 21 February 1977. I attended Gwent police HQ in the morning and sat an exam which I passed, and this was swiftly followed by a full medical examination. In the afternoon, those who were left were then interviewed by the Assistant Chief Constable (ACC), Mr Rostron.

I was one of twelve candidates on that day. I was, to say the least, very uneasy about the situation. I was the only one who had not continued on in school after taking my CSE exams. I had left school at sixteen years of age with mediocre CSE results. All the others had stayed on to do O-levels. Some had even been to university. I felt that I had no chance of getting one of the vacancies ahead of any of the other candidates.

The interview was a very stern, blunt and rude event. My lasting memory is of being admonished by the ACC for not calling him 'Sir' when I addressed him or answered a question. I left the room shell-shocked and shaken by the whole experience. I desperately wanted to be a police officer and I was prepared to take a very large drop in wages to do so. I did not know if I was prepared to be spoken to like an idiot, and on a couple of occasions during the interview I had very nearly told the ACC exactly what I thought of him. I managed to hold my tongue; this was to be a problem to me all through my career. I have always stood up for what I believed to be right, against all ranks and it has not always been the right thing to do!

I then sat and waited for what seemed like hours while all the others were interviewed. Finally, I was called back into the ACC's office. I walked in and stood to attention before Mr Rostron. He looked at me and I thought I was about to be ripped up into little pieces.

Without an emotion on his face he suddenly said: 'Congratulations, you are now a member of Gwent constabulary.'

I can remember nothing else except leaving the room and following a member of personnel to their office and signing a load of forms. It was not until I found myself at the stores collecting a great big pile of uniforms, handcuffs and a truncheon, did it finally start to sink in.

I then had the biggest grin you can imagine and on my face I was absolutely chuffed with myself. I was allocated the shoulder number 520 and sent home loaded down with uniform, and given instructions to return the following week for my full joining details and also my warrant card. I drove home to my parent's house elated. Now came the hard bit…

My father was a stevedore at Newport Docks. He was not happy about me joining the police and had refused to sign for me to apply for the cadet force when I was 16. I was very unsure of how he would take the news. I arrived home bursting with the feeling of having done something that would set me off for the rest of my life, but also a little apprehensive of what my parents were going to say. My mother was very pleased but a little unsure of what I had let myself in for. My father appeared pleased but did not make too much fuss.

The following Monday I returned to police HQ in Cwmbran. I was amazed to discover I was the only one of the twelve to get through. I was told by the training sergeant that the fact that I had some experience of life away from a school or college environment, and because I was prepared to take a big drop in wages, that had got me the job. In those days common sense played a big part in being a police officer. My, how I wish that was the case now. While I was waiting for the next course to start at the Police Training Centre for Wales, I was sent to my local station to work. Maindee was a sub division of Newport, a very busy little station, and I did everything there from tea-making and cooking breakfast, to going out on patrol in a panda. I was allowed to wear uniform but I could not get involved in anything. I learned so much in those four weeks, possibly more about the real world than I should have. It was to come back and haunt me a little bit when I dealt with my first incident at the school. I will expand more on this embarrassing incident in a later chapter.

I did not really realise at that time, but I certainly know now, that I was joining a police force that was exceptional and gave the public a service to be proud of. The officers who served in the force were hard but very fair. People respected the police and you could find yourself arresting a man one week and then that same man would come to help you if you were having trouble with someone the next. Rules and discipline were very hard and tight, and senior officers were 'gods' who you very rarely saw. But the force was very good at doing the job. Now we pay lip service to politicians who run this country like scared rabbits who are afraid to stand up for the public. The situation at this time (2007) is getting to a desperate stage. In London, they are averaging one killing involving firearms or a knife almost every week. I really fear for this country: the next ten years will make or break it a far as law and order is concerned.

The beginning

In March 1977, eight male and four female officers from Gwent police, all brand new and straight out of 'the box' arrived at Gwent police HQ for training. In those days, the training programme consisted of a one-week induction course at headquarters and this was followed by ten weeks at the Police Training Centre for Wales in Cwmbran. Immediately following that, it was back to HQ for a two-week local procedure course. Then, during the next eighteen months, we were to attend police HQ for three one-week courses. Finally, just before the end of the two-year probation period, we were to return to the Police Training Centre for a final two-week course. This was the start of life as a police officer and I could not wait to get going.

The twelve of us all got on really well and worked closely together in that first week. We also socialised as a group at night. I made some wonderful friends on the course, one in particular Martyn Prewett who, to this day, is as close to me as a brother. Martyn went on to have a successful 30-year career and became an outstanding detective completing his entire service with Gwent.

In that week we learned basic police-related matters, some little pieces of law and an awful lot of drill practice to get us marching to some sort of standard. On the Thursday we were all attested on oath and finally received our warrant cards. Where was my big shiny *Kojak*-style badge? This was not what I expected. It was just a piece of card with a photo on it and heat-sealed in plastic. But still, I had it now and it felt great. I was off to the Police Training Centre of Wales.

You're Nicked My Son

The Police Training Centre of Wales was only eight miles from home for me. It was almost brand new and very comfortable with each officer getting his or her own room.

All twelve of us arrived on the Monday and separated into several classes and our ten weeks' initial training commenced. I really enjoyed the next ten weeks; I found the whole course really enjoyable. The only problem I had was with the role-play scenarios. This was where the instructors would play acting parts while recruits dealt with things that developed in front of them. In the very first incident I got involved with, I found myself in trouble! This was all due to what I had seen take place while at Maindee police station, in the four weeks I spent there before going to training school.

The incident I saw while at Maindee occurred when a very nasty drunk had come into the counter at 'the nick'. I was there making tea and WPC Cath Bamford was doing her best to help the man. He became very aggressive and suddenly lunged across the front desk at her. She stepped back away from him but unfortunately for the drunk, a male officer was coming into the station right behind him as he lunged at Cath. The male officer immediately put him into an arm lock and he was dragged off to the cells fighting but losing the battle. *Brilliant,* I thought. *No messing about. I like that!*

The role-play incident I was about to take part in concerned an abusive and aggressive drunk in the front office; a WPC would be playing the part of a station officer. I was assisting her in the office. I really thought my luck was in as I had seen first-hand how to deal with such a person....

The drunk was Police Sergeant Ernie Robbins; he was actually a sergeant from my own force. He was also my class sergeant along with Police Sergeant Davies. As Sergeant Robbins got more and more into the role he got progressively louder and more aggressive. The WPC suddenly wilted and started to back away from him. With that, he leaned over the counter at her; I knew exactly what to do and went into action.

I leaped behind him and yanked his arm up behind his back and I heard him yell out in agony. *Great acting, Sarge* I thought. I had him face down on the desk in an armlock and said, 'You're nicked my son, for being drunk and disorderly in a police station.' This was exactly what

I had heard the officer say in the real incident. However, I then realised he was yelling in pain and it was for real! Sergeant Davies pulled me off him and I realised by the look on his face I was in real trouble.

Sergeant Davies was yelling at me: 'What the XXXX are you playing at? What are you doing?'

I then realised that Sgt Robbins was really hurt and in great pain.

Sergeant Davies was bright red in the face with rage. He was yelling at me and I said: 'Well Sergeant, that's how they dealt with it at Maindee.'

He stopped shouting and looked at me for some sort of explanation, and I told him about my four weeks at Maindee before starting my training. This set him off again and he tore into me once more. The rest of the class was in fits of laughter.

The whole matter ended up with me being torn up for arse paper by the commandant of the school and threatened with being sent back to my force if any further incidents happen like that again. Sergeant Robbins suffered torn tendons/ligaments in his shoulder but he forgave me after I spent several nights buying his drinks. Sergeant Davies was also fine after he had given me a few words of Welsh wisdom about what does and does not happen in the 'real world'.

I managed to survive the rest of the course without too much trouble. I had a great time and made some very good friends. The social life was excellent and the ten weeks went by very quickly. The highlight of the course was the passing out parade for all our families.

If I have one lasting memory of my ten weeks at the school, it related to this parade, and even now makes me smile when I think about it. All through the course we practised hard at drill marching. The drill sergeant was Sergeant Michael from North Wales Constabulary. He was a huge ex-military man with a great booming voice.

In my class was a boy also from North Wales Constabulary by the name of Norman Rigsby. Norman was a really nice bloke who would go out of his way to help anyone. He was well over six feet tall, thin, and had these huge feet on which he wore the biggest boots I have ever seen! Norman had one major problem: he could not march to save his life! He looked just like spotty dog when he marched and Sergeant Michael used to go berserk at him every time we practised, but he just could not get it right!

We got to our final week and we spent quite a bit of time perfecting the marching for the pass-out parade. One day, after about an hour of practice, Sergeant Michael suddenly lost his patience with Norman. He ordered all of us to attention and rushed over to stand in front on Norman. Sergeant Michael stuck his marching stick into Norman's chest and prodded him hard with it.

He then shouted at the top of his voice: 'Rigsby, there is a great big useless XXXX on the end of this stick.'

Quick as a flash Norman answered: 'Well he's not on my end, sergeant.'

With that Norman legged it across the parade ground closely followed by Sergeant Michael who was screaming at him. It was like a sketch from *The Benny Hill Show*. The whole class collapsed in hysterics. This event was folklore at the school for many years and I have heard similar stories and accounts many times. But I guarantee, this actually happened and is my favourite story from my training school days.

I passed out of the training school in May 1977. We all returned to police HQ for a two-week course called 'a local procedure course' where we learned everything relevant to Gwent, and I also found out then I was to be posted to 'B' Division and stationed at Chepstow. I was not pleased with this posting as I thought it would be a quiet little place. I was proved to be very wrong! Chepstow, for such a small place, had an abundance of public houses that were frequented by soldiers from the nearby Beachley Army Camp. They were a frequent source of annoyance to the local youths because they had money to splash out on the local girls. This meant the local boys did not get a look in and they would go out looking for army boys to fight with.

There was also a very large drug and burglary problem, which made Chepstow a busy station. I was posted there with another lad from my course called Johnny Wilce. We shared a room in the only bed and breakfast place available to the police in the town. A very nice couple who looked after us really well along with all the other single officers staying there, ran it. It was situated on the main hill down into Chepstow and was only a two-minute walk to the station.

The station was run by a Chief Inspector. He was called Jarvis and ruled with a rod of iron. He lived in a big police house about a mile from the station and expected to be saluted whenever you saw him either on or off duty. If you failed to salute him you were in big trouble! There were a couple of Inspectors and several Sergeants. The PCs made up four shifts, with three or four on each shift. The shift pattern was early turn, late turn and nights. Some officers would also drop off their shift and do 5 p.m. to 1 a.m. shifts to help out the night duty with some extra men.

I was given PC Chris Rann as my tutor constable to see me through the first few weeks. Chris was to teach me the beats etc and I owe a lot to him for the grounding he gave me. He was a great 'thief-taker' and taught me the art of diplomacy, which got me out of a lot of trouble throughout my service. Because it was such a small station, everybody got on well and worked for each other. You needed to because you relied totally on them, as the nearest help from anyone was fifteen miles away in Newport.

I settled in well and within a couple of weeks was finally allowed out on my own. It felt really strange; it seemed that everyone was looking at me as I walked through the main street. I must admit though, I thought I was the Billy Bollocks! *Look out you baddies: I'm here now!*

How not to impress the boss

ONE OF MY FIRST DAYS out on my own resulted in a telling-off from the sergeant for not saluting the Chief Inspector in the street. I tried to explain that I had not seen him to salute him. The sergeant told me that the Chief Inspector had apparently passed me in plain clothes while I was dealing with a motorist. I was obviously expected to have eyes in the back of my head! This made me determined to salute him no matter what.

Thursday was his day off and someone had to take the *Evening Argus* newspaper up to his police house. A few days after the non-saluting incident I was appointed the job of paper boy. All the way there I was thinking to myself, *don't forget to salute, don't forget to salute*. I walked up the big drive way to the house and rang the bell. No reply. I rang again: still no reply. I was about to just push the paper through the letterbox, when through the glass I could see a figure coming down the stairs. I was all ready to throw up a big salute when he opened the door.

When he did open the front door, there he was in a short quilted dressing gown, slippers and Eric Morecambe-type suspenders holding his socks up. I just lost it at the sight of this very tall military type man in those sock suspenders. I saluted him by throwing up the hand with the paper in it. The paper hit my helmet and knocked it off my head and I offered him an empty hand instead of the paper. I quickly gave him the paper from my other hand and tried to leave. As I picked up my helmet from the floor, I saw his socks again and went into the giggles. He slammed the door shut and off I went crying with laughter. I went straight back to the nick and as soon as

Andy Vick

I walked in the Sergeant ripped into me. The Chief Inspector had telephoned him and told him how disrespectful I had been to him. I told him my side of the story and he found it hilarious as well and let me off.

Reality strikes

On my first 5.00 p.m. to 1.00 a.m. shift, I was walking beats until about 10.00 p.m. Chris Rann then picked me up in his panda and we went off to the outer edges of Chepstow for him to show me around places that needed to be checked on a regular basis during night shifts.

Just outside Chepstow, in Caerwent, was a Ministry of Defence establishment. At around midnight we received a call from the security there, who was worried about a VW beetle they had found abandoned near the property. We arrived and checked the vehicle and discovered it belonged to a man who was reported as missing. He was depressed and may have been suicidal. This meant we had to search the woodland and I suddenly felt real fear.

I did my best to stick as close to Chris as I could. My new police torch was next to useless and the battery was running out. I started switching it off a little bit at a time hoping it would not run out, as it was pitch black. After about thirty minutes of searching I had started to relax a little. Suddenly, I fell over what I thought was a tree trunk. I stood up and shone my torch only to be met by the sight of a male lying on his back. My torch suddenly lit up his stomach area and there was a great big hole of blood and gore, along with a shotgun lying across him.

Before I could shout for Chris, I threw up all over the body. Once I started I could not stop and did not do so until the whole of the contents of my stomach were lying on or next to the body. When I had finished, the body on the floor had more colour in it than I did. Chris eventually came over and, as calm as you like, dealt with what had to be done. This was reality and the first of many horrendous situations I was to

Andy Vick

deal with in my service; some things you never really can get used to but some things you do learn to cope with. One thing it did teach me though, was to always buy the biggest and best torch you can. Thank God for Mag-Lite torches!

No Longer the New Boy

Five weeks behind me from training school was an ex-merchant seaman whose first name was Dave. He was a really nice bloke but he was very quiet and a bit of a loner, and soon things occurred which made me realise he was in the wrong job.

He came to Chepstow towards the end of June 1977. We eventually worked together on an 8.00 a.m. to 4.00 p.m. shift a short time later. The patrol sergeant instructed me to take him out and show him the correct way to do a vehicle stop check. I had been taught a very good stop routine by Chris Rann and intended to pass this onto Dave.

I took him out to the main road that ran at the back of the nick that was also the bypass away from the town centre. I did the first few stops. These were routine and I showed Dave how to do the checks and complete a HORT1 form for the production of the driver's documents.

Chepstow was, and still is, a very affluent area. It was not uncommon to come across the gentry from around the area with Sir such-and-such or Dame So-and-so in the vehicle. It was therefore important to deal with the people we stopped, with the manners you would expect of a police officer. Unfortunately, Dave had serious problems with this.

The next vehicle to come up the hill towards us was a Triumph Vitesse soft-top, with the roof down. The driver was a very classy lady in her thirties. She was dressed very expensively and her make up was immaculate. Dave stepped out into the middle of the road and signalled her to stop and she did so. As he approached her I suddenly heard him say: 'Alright love, there's nothing to worry about, just want to check you over.'

I saw her face turn sour as Dave walked around the car, kicking the tyres and knocking the rear lights with his fists.

I managed to apologise to the lady and explained he was nervous and it was his first proper vehicle stop. She seemed to accept this and Dave came back and asked for her documents. He then proceeded to write out a HORT1 for her to produce the documents at the station. The woman gave her name as Lady somebody or other and her address was a very posh place in Tintern. Dave was very blunt in his manner and I was very uncomfortable with the way he was behaving. Having been given her ticket, off the lady went, very unhappy.

Dave stood next to me and proudly displayed his copy. I said: 'Great Dave, except you have not put down the index number.'

Dave suddenly threw his helmet on the floor and set off running about the hill shouting at the top of his voice: 'Oi, you silly cow, I need your registration number. Stop."

She didn't.

A short time later on his first night shift, Dave discovered he was scared of the dark!

He could go no further than the arch in the main street without panicking and shaking. But the final nail in his coffin was the evening he upset Chief Inspector Jervis.

Dave was confined to the station office at the time. On the switchboard was a direct line to the chief inspector's house. One evening we were having a cup of tea when the line from the chief inspector's house rang. Dave answered it.

'Good afternoon, Gwent Police Chepstow. Can I help you?'

We all heard Chief Inspector Jervis bellow: 'Let me speak to the station sergeant.'

Dave said: 'Who is calling please?'

Under normal circumstances Dave was acting correctly, but this was not the right thing to say to your chief inspector.

Mr Jervis got louder and shouted: 'you know who I am, get me the station sergeant.'

Dave replied: 'No I don't know who you are.'

Mr. Jervis screamed: 'Get me the Sergeant.'

Dave replied with: 'I am sorry; unless you tell me who you are I am not able to get the sergeant for you.' Then before anyone could help him he put the phone down on the chief inspector.

When we tried to tell him what he had done, he would not believe us. Within minutes there was a screech of tyres outside the front door and in stormed the chief inspector. He grabbed Dave by the scruff of the neck and dragged him into his office. That was the last we saw of Dave.

The skills of a police driver

The village of Tintern is a very lovely place set on the banks of the River Wye between Chepstow and Monmouth which has always been very popular with tourists because of the famous Tintern Abbey ruins. It is policed via Chepstow and had its own small police station that was manned by Bob Jones, who lived there at the station with his family.

I had always thought that Tintern was an idyllic place to live and work. But I was to realise that no matter where you live, the life of a police officer and his family is never really safe. Bob was a very experienced police officer. He had spent quite some time in the traffic department and was a first-class, highly skilled advanced driver. He was also qualified as a sergeant and was awaiting promotion. Bob occasionally would come to Chepstow to assist when we were short of officers, especially drivers. One of my first full night-duty shifts was spent with Bob, and this particular night was to set me off on a road that was to be the main feature for the rest of my service.

I spent the first half of the night walking the beat and was due to join Bob in the panda for the rest of the night. We were sitting in the station at about 1.30 a.m. when the switchboard rang. Bob answered it and all I could hear was a female voice screaming and the sound of glass smashing. Unknown to me, it was Bob's wife calling from Tintern nick saying that someone was trying to smash their way in. Bob shouted for me to follow him and we jumped into the panda car as Bob explained what was going on and we raced off.

Tintern is about seven miles from Chepstow. The route there is very dangerous with narrow winding country roads. There are steep cliffs on your left and steep banks down to the River Wye on your right. There are no lights on the roads and it is pitch black in places. The panda car was a 1300cc Ford Escort fitted with a blue light but no horns. Bob drove this car at what seemed like Formula 1 speeds. We went through those lanes with tyres screeching, on the wrong side of the road cutting bends like they were straight lines. His driving was unbelievable and I was in total awe at the way he drove at speed and handled the car like a rally driver on a country stage of a rally event. Not once did I feel in danger or scared during the drive. This, apart from our car lights, was done in complete darkness.

We arrived at the station house in what seemed like minutes. The male was still trying to kick his way in. There was not a window left intact. He was completely oblivious to us arriving and we jumped on him and pinned him down. The man was raving mad, and out of his head on drink or drugs, most likely both. As we struggled with him a traffic car arrived to help. In those days handcuffs were only kept in vehicles and were not personal issue. They were very big and heavy which when you managed to get them on the wrists, you then had to screw them up with the key to tighten them. This we eventually managed to do and secured the man. Bob and I remained with his family and the traffic officers took the man to divisional headquarters to deal with him.

This was the first of several occasions I was to be involved in situations where the wife and family of police officers were put in danger from others just because their husbands were police officers. The first occasion concerned me a great deal and I learned a lot about being a police officer that night.

Something else that I discovered that night was the fantastic buzz of driving a police vehicle at speed, and with great skill. I decided that my career in the force was going to be guided in one direction: that was to becoming an advanced driver. I wanted the skill to drive the way Bob drove that car. That was what I wanted and I was determined I would get it. But that was all for the future. The next night I was back on the beat and normal service resumed. Fortunately Bob's family were not injured in the incident, but not long after, Bob received his promotion and they moved out of the station. There is no longer a station at Tintern; it was sold off quite a few years ago. The village has to rely on officers from Chepstow to deal with its matters now.

IT WAS WHILE ON NIGHTS I discovered the best piece of equipment I have ever been issued with: my thick woollen cape. It had a high collar on which your shoulder number went, with a black chain that held the cape closed across your chest. It was fantastic and kept you so warm on nights.

One night duty, in the early hours, I was absolutely shattered and could not keep my eyes open. We had no one to drive the panda that night and so I had been on the beat all night. Around 4.00 a.m. I reached the library and had checked it all to make sure it was secure and thought it might be nice to sit on the back steps for a rest. I sat there lovely and warm in my cape and fell asleep! I was woken an hour and a half later by the milkman leaving the milk on the doorstep. He frightened the life out of me and laughed his head off. I made it back to the nick just in time. The sad part was no one had missed me!

So, CHEPSTOW: ALTHOUGH A SMALL town did have its moments, I also had my moments for sure. My very first burglar: caught red-handed as he came out of the rear of a very expensive clothes shop in the town. It was 3.00 a.m. when the alarm went off at the station. There were only two of us on duty. I ran from the station, down the main street and over a wall that I knew was a short cut. As I got to the rear, there he was coming out the back. He had a great big pile of leather jackets in his arms. He stopped dead as I got in front of him. He dropped the jackets and went for the wall. But I was too quick for him, got him down on the ground and gave him my favourite saying – **'you're nicked my son'** – in my best *Sweeney* style. I then managed to keep him there until Chris arrived. I was chuffed to bits and woke up John, my room-mate to tell him all about it when I got in a 6.30 a.m. He was not too happy with me waking him up that early. Still, it felt great!

Another time there was just three of us on duty one evening to control about thirty young soldiers from the army camp who were threatening to fight with local youths. We three lined up between them and bravely said:

'You will have to get past us to get involved in any fighting.'

Wrong! They descended on us, picked us up and threw us over the hedges onto the riverbank. Well, it sort of worked because they were all too busy laughing at the three of us covered in mud to fight. Both groups left each other alone.

Then there was the time a body was found in the river near Chepstow Bridge. We were convinced the Gloucester police had pushed it over to our side of the river. The body had obviously been in the river some time as it was all bloated and discoloured. So, with the help of a local boatman we got the body to the bank. Four of us then waded through the mud to try and bring the body out onto firmer ground. I was at the front and supporting the right arm. Suddenly it became very light and as I looked back at the others, I realised the arm had come away from the torso. The others were just staring at me. The whole arm had come away from the shoulder because it was so badly decomposed. This time I managed not to be sick, but only just!

Six months into my service at Chepstow we lost the accommodation at the bed and breakfast. Due to illness, the owners were selling up to someone who was going to keep the place as just a home. No other single accommodation was available and all four single officers were told we were being moved to other divisions. We were asked where we would like to go. Rather tongue-in-cheek, I requested to go to Newport. This was my home town, but I asked for Newport Central, which was the busiest place in Gwent. It meant I could then live at home until I got myself sorted out. I never expected to get it – no one ever worked his or her hometown in those days – but I tried it on and to my surprise I was posted to Newport. Then, even more of a surprise, I was to go back to Maindee and on the relief I had been with before I went to training school. I was amazed! The only problem was that it was only two miles from my home and I would be working the area I had lived in all my life.

This was a really unusual decision by the force to let this happen but I was really very happy about it and knew I could make it work. As it worked out the next four years were to be fantastic for me.

'A' Division Maindee

Maindee police station was a great little nick on the main A48, which ran through from junction 24 of the M4. This was a completely different working environment to Chepstow. It was an extremely busy place and Maindee was split up into three major working areas of north, central and south. There was a dedicated panda car for each area. These cars were always single-crewed and the car would deal with all calls that came in. There were also eight foot-beats which were always manned every shift. The whole place was buzzing and it felt fantastic to be there.

The start of every shift began with a full parade. There were around twenty officers per shift at Maindee at this time and the normal parade strength was about fifteen officers.

The patrol sergeant would call us to attention and the relief inspector would enter and ask us to produce our appointments. These were pocket book, whistle and chain, stick and torch and, of course, your warrant card. Everyone was checked and parade would begin.

Your pocket book was your bible: everything went in there. Each new shift would be started with an entry in your pocket book as follows.

Day—Date-- Times of shift
Duty Inspector ....
Patrol Sergeant ....
Station Sergeant ....
Duty posted to ....
Meal breaks times. ....
Weather ....
Variations to duty ....

Then all the information from the briefing would be entered in your pocket book; for example, the entire list of stolen vehicles reported since the last time you were on duty. During parade someone always got asked: 'What was the index of the last stolen vehicle from yesterday.' God help you if you did not know it!

Then it was off to your beat. During the shift you did not go back to the station unless called back or you had permission to do so. The patrol sergeant would visit you daily on your beat and sign your pocket book. Things were very strict but I loved it. It was so busy and I could not get enough of it.

The hardest thing of all was getting used to the shift pattern. They were called continental shifts and rotated around a four-week rota.

This is a sample of how the shift pattern worked.

Early turn: 6 a.m. to 2 p.m. Nights duty: 10 p.m. to 6 a.m. Late turn: 2 p.m. to 10 p.m.

Week	Monday	Tuesday	Wednesday	Thursday	Friday	Saturday	Sunday
1	EARLY	EARLY	NIGHTS	NIGHTS	LATES	LATES	LATES
2	OFF	OFF	EARLY	EARLY	NIGHTS	NIGHTS	NIGHTS
3	LATES	LATES	OFF	OFF	EARLY	EARLY	EARLY
4	NIGHTS	NIGHTS	LATES	LATES	OFF	OFF	**OFF**

I found the quick changeover from nights to late turn always killed me off and I was always like a zombie for the whole shift. But life, apart from that, was fantastic.

I settled in very quickly. At the same time I joined 'B' relief, so did another man who set me on the course of being the type of police officer that I have been all my service. His name was John Caplin. He was a scouser from Birkenhead who had served time in the RAF before becoming a police officer. Prior to coming to Gwent he had been in the Metropolitan force, and had served his two years probation at Kings Cross division. He had met a Newport girl who worked in London; they married and she had persuaded him to transfer to Gwent, as she wanted to return home.

John was a complete one-off. He was always scruffy, loved a drink and did not take too kindly to the disciplined style of Gwent. The man, however, was a natural copper and the best thief-taker I have ever had the pleasure of serving with. Many others have come close but John just had that special something.

He was as hard as nails and feared no one. John was, and still is, a real hero of mine. He taught me the old-style police skills that I have, rightly or wrongly, stuck with for my entire service. John died tragically on duty in 1983.

So there I was on 'B' relief and raring to go. The relief was made up of officers who worked hard, played even harder and most of them were excellent coppers. I was to learn such a lot over the next four years, and that would set me on course for a very interesting career.

WALKING THE BEAT

I WAS FORTUNATE THAT I never had to be taught beats because I was working the area I had spent all my life growing up in. What I was taught was the best way to patrol your beat for each different shift.

The night shift in particular was real Dixon of Dock Green policing. I loved walking out of the station at night wearing my high neck thick woollen cape. On leaving the nick you would walk your entire beat, checking the doors and windows of all shop premises on your patch.

One of the tricks I was taught for nights was to always carry a reel of black cotton, then choose premises you felt were vulnerable. I would then stretch a length of cotton across a rear gate, or maybe an alley leading to it. Then during the night I would check the cotton on a regular basis to see if the cotton had been broken. This would give me an idea if anyone was about. This was a tried and tested trick that produced good results. All shop premises were checked when you went out, before you went in for meal break, as soon as you came back out and finally before you finished the shift. God help you if a burglary occurred on your beat and you did not discover it. You would get woken up at home and called back into work to explain why you had not spotted it.

Alarm calls were treated very seriously. They used to go directly to the divisional control room with a delayed audible alarm at the premises, so you had a great chance of catching burglars in the act. There were very few false alarms in those days. The panda car driver or the beat officer responsible for the beat where the alarm had been activated would take charge. As he knew the area best, he would direct officers to certain locations around the alarm scene to act as containment. He would go directly to the premises and if there were signs of a burglary, the whole place was kept secure until the dog section arrived and a search would take place. The whole thing was very professional, not like today's poor attempts at it.

As a beat officer I got myself into the habit of walking past shops close to the windows. I would tap the windows as I passed to make sure all was well. I would then rattle all doors to check them to ensure they were also secure. One night duty, I came out onto the main beat from the nick after finishing my meal break. I walked towards Maindee Square tapping the windows and checking the doors as usual. I reached Boots the Chemist in the square and tapped the window as I walked.

Before I could reach the doorway I heard a strange noise. I turned around in time to see the whole large pane of glass falling out of the window frame. It smashed onto the floor. You can imagine the noise it made; it was about 2.30 in the morning and I was dumbstruck for a moment.

Suddenly, I heard a very shaky voice say: 'I suppose you'll nick me for that as well.'

I looked and there stood in the shop was one of our local druggies. He had removed all the putty from around the window frame and gone into the store to break into the drug cabinet. He had not set any alarm off for some reason and had managed to put the glass back in the frame after going in. He had two rubber suction pads used by glaziers to do this. He had thought his luck was in until I had passed tapping the window. This was obviously enough to tip the window and out it fell. That's one in the bin for burglary, sarge.

Murder. Chepstow Road

Very shortly after joining the division, I was involved in my first major incident. About a quarter of a mile east of the nick situated on the main road was a long row of very large houses. Most of these once-lovely premises had been converted into flats. They were now home to a lot of the local drunks, drug users and general villains. The accommodation was basically paid for by social security and was awful.

Surprisingly, one of the houses had a cleaner who went there every morning and made an attempt to clean the place. One morning she turned up and found a lot of blood on the doorstep. This in itself was not unusual. What was odd was the fact that the trail led down the hall to a room on the ground floor at the back of the house.

The cleaner knocked on the door, got no reply and opened it to be met with the most horrendous sight of a heavily blood-spattered room and a very dead body on the floor. Police were called. I arrived on foot after the panda car. I followed the driver into the hall and stayed at the door of the room. He entered, let out a few expletives and I popped my head around the door. I will try to describe the scene.

The room was an absolute tip, with a mattress on the floor under the window. There was also a settee of sorts there. There were empty beer cans and bottles everywhere and so much blood that every wall, window, and even the ceiling, had blood on it. The only other thing in the room was a cupboard built into an alcove on one of the walls.

Lying on the floor, next to the mattress was the body of a male. The body was topless and the whole of his chest, neck and face were badly cut up. At this point I was despatched to the front door to secure the premises and await the arrival of CID.

They duly arrived and the investigation commenced.

The occupant of the room (who was not the deceased) was identified as a local drunk/vagrant male who was known as Ginger. He was Scottish with a large mop of ginger hair. CID officers began to follow the blood trail from the house. It led them to a pub just outside the town centre. They found Ginger and another male in the pub. Both had blood on their clothes and were arrested.

The story emerged that the victim was drinking with Ginger and the other male the day before. They all went back to Ginger's room and carried on drinking. During the night the deceased had started saying something to Ginger, who took exception and a fight had started. Ginger smashed a bottle and used it on the deceased, slashing him all over his body, face and neck. The man fell dying on the floor next to the mattress. Ginger and the other male carried on drinking until they fell asleep on the mattress next to the victim.

When they awoke they realised the male was dead. At Ginger's suggestion they tried to hide the body in the cupboard that was built into an alcove. However, by then rigour mortis had set into the body so they could not bend him into the cupboard.

At one point they stood the deceased up, facing flat against a wall and had swung a sweeping brush at the body hoping to break his back with the head of the brush so they could bend it into the cupboard. This also failed despite numerous attempts.

They eventually gave up and left the body on the floor and went out to get some black bin bags so they could cut up the body and dispose of it that way. Once they left the house, the lure of the early opening of a local pub for market day got the better of them and they started drinking instead.

Ginger got life for the murder and the other male imprisoned for trying to assist in disposal of the body.

Close to home

When I was posted to my hometown, there was some concern from supervisory officers that it might cause me a few problems. However, with a few exceptions I found quite the opposite. When I became a panda driver, and was given the Maindee south car to drive, I found it a great advantage. This was because I was working the area I had grown up in. I knew people who were strangers in the area; I knew when things did not look right. I believe it gave me a head start on criminals because it was a place I was very familiar with and I took great advantage of that fact.

This proved itself, particularly on night duty when strangers really stood out. This gave me three years of being one step ahead of things and, coupled with my young enthusiastic want to be a copper, led me to some great arrests which at times just seemed to come along in front of me. Just leaving the station, things would happen in front of me: I could not go wrong! I was soon given the nickname 'Golden Balls' because everything I did turned into an arrest. (At least that's the explanation they gave me to my face!) This also meant I did not have to get involved with silly little motoring offences or plague the motorist with vehicle stops. I managed to keep good work records using arrests instead of traffic offences.

While walking beats, good stops in the street would bring in all sorts of arrests for crime. Along with public order offences, these were the beat officer's best way to patrol. By getting off the main streets and roaming the back streets, especially at night, you would always get good arrests. I would even take out the station cycle on nights. This would allow me to get around the trading estates and branch out a bit from the streets. I always felt a bit of a dickhead, but then again it worked!

Now retired, the days of walking the beat in Newport still brings back great memories. It was real old-fashioned policing that I loved and I dearly wish it was still the way today. Being in my hometown working did have its pros and cons. Boys I grew up with did become involved in crime, and on many occasions I had cause to arrest them. They and I found it easy and no matter what they had done I dealt with them fairly and always kept my word to them. I even got to a stage where if they were wanted by police for anything they would phone me up to make arrangements to give themselves up to me. We would arrange a time and place and they gave themselves up.

They would tell me things they would not tell any other officer; more often than not it would be information about another villain who was committing a crime they did not agree with. I think this was because we had grown up together, and they did not see it as informing or grassing to the police. I may have been a copper, but I was Andy who they knew from school or from the football team. It was great for me and I loved it. It stood me in great stead at work and also earned me a little bit of overtime.

Only once did it get a little bit personal and close to home. My parents owned their own home. We had lived there from the time I was thirteen years of age. The house was situated in the Somerton area of Newport. My parents had grown up in the area and had bought a house that was next door to my aunt's home and the house was next to a very large council estate. This estate used to be a very nice area to live when my parents were growing up. Now, though, it was a dumping ground for the council to put their problem families.

Elderly people, who had lived there many years, occupied the majority of the estate, but there were also a few real problems. One such family were a large family whose children ran riot on the estate and eventually through the whole town.

The two eldest boys, Derek and Christopher, were out-and-out criminals and capable of anything. I had arrested them on a couple occasions for stealing cars; they would always try to fight their way out of being arrested and were a nightmare to deal with. Their mother always fought tooth and nail for them. I was always concerned they might take revenge on my parents' house but thankfully they never did. I think this was down to the fact my grandmother, who lived next door to us, was friendly with their grandmother, and she had warned them off.

The two boys did feel they were beyond the law and decided they had a better way to have a go at me. I have a brother three years younger than me. He was about the same age as the younger of the two boys. One evening as he cycled home, they jumped out in front of him and knocked him off his bike. The eldest, Derek who was about sixteen years old at the time, gave my brother a bit of a hiding. He told my brother to give me the message that from now on, every time I arrested one of them, my brother would get the same treatment. I was not too sure of the best way to deal with this and after a family discussion I decided to ask John Caplin for his advice.

His advice was: 'We do it our own way.'

What happened next was totally illegal but turned out to be exactly the right thing to do.

A couple of days later I was crewed on the car with John on late turn. We stayed as much as possible around the Somerton area looking for either of the two eldest brothers. Eventually Derek appeared on the small motorbike that he used to get around when committing crime. At the time our panda cars were Minis, small but very nippy. Derek made a run for the playing fields near the quarry where he thought we could not follow. Wrong! John found a gap in the hedge and through we went. The playing fields were set over a large area; it was called the quarry because of a very large man-made lake on one side. This runs alongside the main Swansea to Paddington train line. The fields were flat until you got near the quarry when the grass sloped quite steeply down to the lake.

We very quickly caught up and got alongside Derek. John wound down his window and told him to stop. You can imagine his reply. We were by this time running alongside the edge of the grass with Derek nearest to the lake. John suddenly had his truncheon in his right hand and I could not work out what he was going to do. He moved closer to Derek and poked the end of the truncheon straight into his ribs. This obviously winded him, and suddenly the bike veered right and hurtled down the bank. He went up and over a small wooden plank used by fisherman to fish from, and took off out over the water. He landed several feet out in the lake, which I knew to be very deep.

I went to jump in to try to help him out. John stopped me and said to let him sort himself out then we would have words with him. We then realised he was in trouble in the water and was shouting that he could not swim. Fortunately for us there was no one else around to witness this, or at least there were none that we could see. I have to admit, for a split second my thought was to let him drown as it would make the life of many elderly people on the estate a great deal better. But I realised I could not do that and I grabbed one of the life rings dotted around the lake and threw it to him and we both dragged him out of the water.

He started shouting and swearing. John took hold of him tightly by the chin, looked him straight in the eyes and said to him:

'I am going to tell you this once and this is your only chance. Let's look at this like a game: you do what you do to make a living and we do what we do. Sometimes you get away with it, sometimes you don't. You made it personal with his brother. If you have problems then take him on, not his brother. The uniform is in play but his brother is not. Every time you make it personal, we no longer play by the rules. The next time you or your brothers do not get rescued. Is that fair?'

Derek looked at us for a minute and said: 'OK, I get the message; you're in play but no one else.'

I said: 'Yes, I expect trouble from you – that's part of my job – but anything else changes the rules.'

He walked off after having the cheek to ask for a lift. Naturally, we refused as he was soaking wet. Although I arrested him and other members of his family many times after that and we fought every time, my family were never troubled again. A couple of years later I was involved in the arrest of Derek for rape. It put him away for a long time.

My driving career finally takes off

Just after I finished my probation I was given a driving course. I was really looking forward to this course and my wish to be able to drive the way I had seen Bob Jones drive that night in Chepstow was about to start.

I had a great time on the four-week course and came back with a recommendation for higher training. I was really pleased by this. I found the police style of driving very easy to adapt to and I knew even then that driving was going to play a major part in my career. During the course I was with two others in the car with the instructor. One of the others I knew well and had gone to school with him. His name was Simon 'no-neck' Harris. He was so called because his head just seemed to sit on top of his massive rugby prop shoulders. To look left or right he had to swing the whole top half of his body, as he had no neck to turn. He was a born comedian and used to have us in stitches laughing at his antics. However, the funniest memory of the whole course came one sunny day as we were on a country. Simon was driving and the sergeant was giving the usual advice and instructions as we went along.

As we drove along this stretch of road, that had some lovely big posh houses on both side, the sergeant said to Simon, 'I want you to take the next available turning on your left please.'

Almost straight away we began to turn left and I saw that we were in fact pulling into the driveway of a very large house. The turning we should have been taking was a little further along the road. Picture this: three very big ugly policemen and a pretty police woman in a marked panda car driving up a very large gravel driveway to a very nice large house. There is a large ornamental roundabout at the top near the front door. There in the middle of the roundabout is an elderly lady tending to a beautiful display of flowers with a very puzzled look on her face.

The instructor looked at Simon and said, 'I meant the next road turning you buffoon.'

In the back we were in tears laughing. The sergeant got out and apologised to the lady. She was not bothered a bit and said: 'Well as you are here would you like some tea and cake officer?' We all politely refused although the offer was very tempting. We left a very happy member of the public to carry on with her gardening and an invitation to drop in for tea any time we were passing!

I returned to my station from my course feeling very pleased with myself having got a good course write-up with the promise of a van and Land Rover course fairly quickly. The next thing was to get myself a permanent panda posting. There were three panda cars stationed at Maindee. Each relief had a permanent driver for each car along with a nominated reserve driver. The reserve driver took over the vehicle during the driver's meal break and at any other time he was not at work. Drivers normally got a permanent driving job as a reward for their hard work and good arrests, etc.

I was very lucky to be given the reserve post for the Maindee south car. The car covered a huge area that was rural and town-orientated. The area covered out as far as Penhow; this was in the countryside and was halfway to Chepstow. It was a very busy car and John Caplin was the permanent driver. It was from this time on that I really began to learn the unique art of being a police officer. On night duty after meal break or if we were very flush with officers, I would spend the shift with John double-crewing the car. I learnt so much from John that it is really hard to put into words what he did for me in respect of my career.

In my introduction, I mentioned the problems I had originally with my father not being happy about me joining the police. I will try to explain why. My father's family worked as dockers at Newport docks. It was only possible to get a job at the docks if your father worked there before you. I always remember from an early age lots of fruits, especially bananas, appearing at home. It was the done thing to bring home samples of what was being unloaded from the ships coming into the port. I remember a whole pig once being brought home and split between my father and uncle who lived next door to us. As a result the thought of having a policeman in the family did ruffle a few feathers, to say the least.

A lad I went through training school with was from the British Transport Police; his name was Lyn Webber. When we left training school he was posted to work at Newport docks. I saw this as a great chance to wind my father up.

I arranged for Lyn to stop my father in his car as he drove out of the dock gates at the end of an early-turn shift. A mate and I were hiding in the police office where we could see everything. My dad had met Lyn at the training school pass-out parade but did not recognise him in uniform as he pulled him over. In my dad's car boot was a box full of oranges. Lyn played the part of the serious copper very well and scared the living daylights out of him. He really wound my dad up for quite a while before letting my dad know who he was. When I popped out of the office in hysterics my dad did not see the funny side at first. I think the relief on his face told it all though.

The flow of fruit to the house stopped, but my dad started to mellow towards the police. Years later my father went to work for Gwent police as a civilian driver and he became my biggest supporter, which really pleased me.

Why do I always pick the big one?

In June 1979 I was working nights and covering the Maindee north car single-crewed. At around 1.00 a.m. I had parked my car in Heather Road on the St Julians estate in order to take a walk around the very large school grounds. This was my old school and it had suffered several burglaries over the previous few weeks and I decided to walk around quietly to see who might be about.

The estate, as a whole, was normally very quiet but the entire area had been suffering from a large increase in residential and commercial burglary offences.

The grounds to the school are huge with a sports field at the front of it. I entered the school via the west gate and walked right through and around the entire school before coming back out onto Heather Road from the east entrance.

As I came out of the gate, I walked up the hill to check a house that was empty, as I knew the owners away on holiday. As I did so, I saw two men coming out of the side entrance of a large semi-detached house on the other side of the road. I crossed over the road and was completely unprepared for what was about to happen over the next few minutes.

Normally, when people have something to hide you sense that something is not right. They show nerves and their body language gives something away. These two were completely calm, and gave no indication at all that they were up to no good. They were both in their early twenties and I recognised one of them as being local. I asked what they were doing and one of them, who was well over six feet tall, answered. He stated that he lived in the house with his elderly parents who were asleep in bed. He introduced the other male as his cousin and told me they were sneaking out to go to El Seiko's nightclub down in Clarence Place; he stated he did not want his parents to know he was going there because it had a bad reputation.

Neither of them had any identification and I told them I would need to confirm the story with their parents. They tried to dissuade me but eventually agreed. I was completely off my guard and fairly happy with them as I went up to the front door with one of them on either side of me. I had noticed the garden to my right was very large and well kept with a wide round ornamental pond in the middle of it, and was admiring it as I knocked the door.

Eventually, someone came to the door. An elderly male voice asked: 'Who is it?'

The boy to my right (the bigger of the two) replied: 'Open the door Dad, it's Martin, the police need to speak to you.'

The door started to open and stopped as a security chain locked in place. Suddenly, both men bolted in opposite directions. I jumped on the taller one in the front garden. What I can only describe as a real stand-up fight began with both of us throwing punches and I got lucky with a kick in his private parts and he went down like a sack of potatoes. He was face down and groaning and I got on his back and put him in the tried-and-tested police 'hammer lock and bar hold' and held him down on the floor with my weight on top of him. I then went for my radio and was about to call for urgent assistance and from that point the only other thing I can remember is a rather strange swishing sound... and then nothing.

I woke up in hospital the following day not really knowing what was going on. I found out what had happened to me from colleagues. The owner of the house was an eighty-year-old man who lived alone and he had been scared to death by the whole chain of events. He had answered the door not really knowing what was what happening, to be faced by me fighting with the big guy. He did not realise that I was a police officer and had shut his door and watched from the window of his lounge. In his statement he said as we were fighting on the ground then another male appeared from the house next door. (This was the other one who had run off to my left.) The male returned with a large piece of four-by-two piece of wood and he swung at me from behind and hit me straight around the head with it. The elderly male then saw them both kick me all over my head and body before they threw me into the ornamental pond. Then they both then ran off. The old man thought we were drunks fighting and decided to go to bed and leave it.

I was very fortunate that when they threw me in the pond my head landed on a large rock. This had kept my head above water otherwise I would have been in real serious trouble! It then seems that I regained consciousness for a short time because the control room at Newport central received a radio message from a strange-sounding voice saying '10-9-Heather' and nothing else. As county officers will know 10-9 is the code for urgent assistance. The control room checked around all the officers on duty and when they could not get a reply realised it must be me in Heather Road.

The relief then descended on the road and started looking for me. They quickly found my panda car but not me. Heather Road is a very long road running through the estate and there were blue lights going up and down it trying to find me. The old man in the house decided it would be a good opportunity to get the drunk taken out of his pond and called the police. PC Leighton 'Leggsy' Reid discovered it was me in the pond and pulled me out. I was unconscious.

Before I got carted off to hospital I managed to give Leighton a description of the two men. The relief also discovered the old man's house had been burgled and I had obviously come across them on their way out. The two who attacked me had been stopped outside El Seiko's nightclub two hours before they had assaulted me. They were caught urinating in the main road and cautioned by officers. These officers recognised the description given on the radio after my incident and by the end of the night shift both men were in custody. Unfortunately, the taller one fell out the back of a moving police van while trying to escape as it travelled to the nick! He received some hospital treatment but was not seriously hurt.

They both appeared in court the next day and were dealt with before I knew what day it was. They pleaded guilty to the wrongly charged offence of a section 47 assault. They received a year in prison for the assault and burglary after pleading guilty. It transpired later that an incompetent and corrupt CID officer had dealt with the matter and I have no doubt it was done in conjunction with that officer and the defence solicitor. There were repercussions, and a year or so later the same CID officer received a long term in prison on serious corruption charges.

After a short stay in hospital with a very sore head, a couple of broken ribs and partial memory loss, I spent several weeks recovering. To this day I still have no real memory of what happened after hearing the swishing noise, which must have been the piece of wood coming towards my head. Just as well really!

The whole incident did leave a very lasting impression on me though. Prior to this I had the confidence to take anybody on. I was a police officer and people respected that. I was of the opinion that I always treated people with respect until they showed they did not deserve it. I tried to deal with people as I would expect an officer to deal with my parents if they had dealings with the police.

The attack on me totally changed my style, I policed in a completely different way to the way I had been before the incident. When I returned to duty after the incident I had lost all my confidence. To put it bluntly, I had lost my bottle. I desperately tried to cover it up at work but people started to notice. No longer was I the first into any situation, taking the lead or being first up to answer a call. I did my best to avoid calls that involved any possible violence or confrontation. If I turned up at an incident, or even got involved in a stop of a vehicle, I would start to shake uncontrollably. This was pure fear and I was beginning to think I was never going to get over it. It took over my life. In those days there was no such thing as stress counselling and I tried to deal with it on my own.

It all came to a head one night duty. On the first night I let two colleagues down badly. They were young probationers who I should have been looking after. Because I was scared, I did not make the right decisions. This resulted in two burglars nearly getting away. It was only because the two youngsters were excellent officers and did it their way that I was saved from embarrassment. I was at rock bottom at this point and did not know which way to turn....

The following night was a Saturday night and in the early hours of the morning a near-riot occurred in the town centre as two rival groups of club-goers spilt out of their respective clubs. The fight erupted and a dog-handler was caught right in the middle of it. His dog was kicked and hurt badly and the handler thrown through the window of a large jeweller's shop. As I arrived I had no time to be scared. It was bedlam with the whole street just a mass of people fighting with fists, feet and any weapon they could find.

We tried to fight our way to the dog-handler in the window of the shop. I had drawn my truncheon and was attempting to fight my way through the large crowd. There were just too many of them to fight our way through and we realised we just had to hold them and wait for more officers. Suddenly, to my right, I saw a white male holding a lump of wood lashing out at a WPC who was being forced backwards. For some strange reason I put my truncheon back in my trouser pocket and forced my way over towards them just pulling people out of the way. I got in between the man and the WPC and faced him. He was screaming and swearing like a man possessed. He was also winding the stick around and around at me. I felt the shakes coming on and thought I was about to bottle it.

Before I realised what I was doing I had taken one step forward and slightly to the side. I grabbed the stick and at the same time punched the bloke straight between the eyes. He went down instantly. Straight away another man confronted me. I looked at him and realised I was no longer scared.

I shouted at him, 'Carry on and you will get some of the same mate.'

He thought better of it and as he did so the cavalry arrived from all over the place. Arrests were made by the dozen and the dog-handler and his dog rescued. Back at the station, one of the boys I had let down the night before leaned over me and said: 'Good to see you're back on side.' I realised I had sorted myself out and knew I would be fine from then on.

Don't get me wrong. There have been many occasions over the years when I have felt fear of all kinds. But I can control it and use it to my advantage. Unfortunately for certain people I deal with, controlling it means an early strike on my part. If I think I am going to get hit, I hit first. In the current climate, 'pre-emptive strikes' are considered an option that an officer can take if necessary. In those early days of my career it just meant I dealt with things the way I read them at the time. It has served me well throughout the rest of my service.

You're Nicked My Son

THE LATTER END OF THE 1970s was the start of some troubled times in this country and during those years I experienced a national steel strike and also a strike by the fire brigade. These times brought me two lasting memories.

The fire brigade strike in 1977. At first this just meant the police standing around outside fire stations on the picket line to ensure there was no trouble. This was quite a friendly time and the firemen went about doing what the felt they had to do.

However, the government then brought in the armed forces with the fire engines that were commonly known as green goddesses. They were to act as cover for the fire brigade and this of course stirred matters up.

The police were then used to assist the army. Officers were posted with them to lead the way to calls as the armed forces did not have knowledge of the area and needed to respond to fires as quickly as possible. This resulted in a great deal of animosity between police and the firemen. As far as I remember we all were in full agreement with their arguments for better pay and conditions. However, people's lives were being put at risk and the army stepped in and did a good job.

During this time I was posted to help out at the local TA centre where the army was based. As a local boy I knew my way around well. One night duty, there was a call to a large timber yard on fire. By the time we arrived it was well ablaze and spreading out to the yard. The yard was in Turner Street and residential property was close by. It was important to get the fire under control to stop it reaching the houses. The yard was full of timber stacked very high on top of each other. Someone came up with an idea to get a large fork-lift truck from Newport docks to the scene to move the large loads of timber. I volunteered to take the army to the docks and bring one back. There we quickly got hold of a truck and sped back to the fire. All went well until we turned off Caerleon Road and into Turner Street. I was in the cab of the forklift with the soldier driving. I was perched on top of the engine compartment as there was only one seat. We were moving quite fast and to do so safely the driver had the forks quite high off the ground. Unfortunately, I had forgotten about the railway bridge halfway down Turner Street. Suddenly there was an almighty bang as the top of the forks hit the bridge. The truck stopped on a sixpence and I flew forward.

I was knocked unconscious as I hit the windscreen and took no further part in the saving of the timber yard. I ended up with black eyes and a terrible headache!

Also around 1979 to 1980 we found ourselves pulled into a situation with regard to the steel strike. This started off as a great chance to earn some overtime, which was very scarce at the time. However, it very quickly turned into a major problem.

All forces at this time had what was known as PSUs. These were police support units and officers trained to be able to go to other forces to assist if required for major events relating to public order. I was trained, along with many other officers, for this role. We were all recently trained in the new-style public order method of trudging and wedging. This was a new technique designed to give us an advantage against large crowds; the technique basically meant two long lines of officers walking into the crowd linked to each other by means of holding the uniform belt of the man in front of you. Having got into the crowd both lines of officers would then link arms and fan out into a V shape that pushed the crowds away to clear what ever they were doing.

Then along came the steel strike. At 3.00 a.m. my PSU was sent every morning to the valleys and normally we would end up at the Crown Cork bottle factory in New Tredegar. Our task there was to assist the lorries getting in and out of the factory. There were some really venomous verbal attacks on the drivers each day. Those who dared to cross the picket line were verbally abused.

The road up to the factory gate was only just as wide as a big lorry. It was a slight incline up to the gates and the lorries had to go slowly to make the tight turn through the gates to the factory. At the start the situation was all very friendly between police and pickets. We used to stand around their braziers getting warm. They would share their tea with us. We would share our frozen sandwiches and pork pies with them.

However, things started to happen and daily it was getting more difficult to control the pickets. One morning very early, a lorry arrived and all the pickets got into the road and refused to move. People blocked the whole road.

Here was our chance to test our trudging and wedging, as it was famously called.

Into the crowd we went. All linked together, fanned out and wedged into them and they were all pushed to both sides of the road. The lorry entered with no further problems. That was one-nil to the old bill. We really thought we were the business. However, the next day was a different story!

As the first lorry arrived, the strikers got into the road again, we thought this was going to be easy, and lined up again to trudge and wedge into them. Suddenly from nowhere a large group of males appeared. (I still swear to this day that they must have had the pack from every local rugby club they could find.) They were enormous. All these men went to the front of the crowd and took up the first four or five rows.

Well, in we went, trudging and wedging. It was like walking into a brick wall. Then the fun started. One by one we were being picked up in the air and we were thrown over a hedge. This sent us down a grass bank. We kept trying but each time the same thing happened and we ended up over the hedge. It was going on for well over thirty minutes before more PSUs arrived to help out. We eventually got the lorries through purely by sheer force of numbers. We all thought that the situation would now change and the strikers would start to turn nasty and aggressive towards us. But no, they continued being friendly and we continued to get on well, except when the next lorry would arrive and battle would commence again.

It remained this way right through the strike.

The petrol shortage

One of the other strange things I had to contend with in my early years of service was the time in the late 1970s; early 1980s when there was a petrol shortage. This put a lot of difficulties on the way we policed the town. Every vehicle was limited to only thirty-six miles each shift and when you consider the size of the area each vehicle covered, that could mean going out on the first call of the shift and returning with all the mileage allowance gone. We were expected to just park up somewhere between calls and not patrol at all. Thirty-six miles was a totally unrealistic figure but it was strictly adhered to: you had some serious explaining to do if you went over the limit. If it was possible to walk to your next call that was what you were supposed to do. Still, somehow we managed to carry on doing the job although I can confess now that in order to do the job on nights it meant an awful lot of driving backwards to keep the milometer showing a low mileage!

Later in the petrol shortage we also discovered that it was very easy to disconnect the speedo cable from the back of the clock on our mini panda cars, so the first job on a night shift was to open the bonnet on one of the cars, disconnect the speedo and double-crew for the night, and then that car took all the calls. We also got away with that one and continued to do so until the end of the petrol shortage. Where there's a will there's a way!

The Old Barn arsonist

In the latter months of 1979 a very disturbing crime started on an estate in Newport. The estate was called the Old Barn estate and was quite modern at the time. It was made up of many houses and every so often there was a set of flats, which were designed for the elderly. The flats were on three floors with two flats on each floor. A series of arson attacks began to take place on these flats. Someone, in the middle of the night, was pouring paint and lighter fuel over clothing or paper that was placed at the bottom of the door to the OAPs' flats. Fortunately, the doors were fire-resistant for some time, which allowed the fire brigade to arrive in time on every occasion and rescue the occupants.

After the first couple of offences, I volunteered to work permanent nights to try and catch the person responsible. CID carried out the investigation and I spent every night carrying out observations with the help of a couple of officers from the relief who were also on nights. The estate was spread over a very large area and even with me there the suspect was still out and trying to start more fires. It was very frustrating and so I worked permanent nights for eight weeks.

There were some things we knew about the suspect, in particular the pattern on the sole of his training shoes. This had been left in paint at one of the offences. Then one Saturday morning our luck changed. At 2.00 a.m. I left the observation point with a colleague, Mark Wheatstone. There had not been an attack for two weeks and we were wondering if the arsonist had been scared off. I decided to have a drive around the estate see if anyone was about.

Suddenly as Mark and I drove down the side of the estate I caught sight of what looked like a hat dropping down behind a car. I turned around and stopped alongside the car but there was no one there. We then started to walk along the road. The side of the road was the back of some large houses and then suddenly, as we got to a garage entrance, I saw a man stood in the shadows of the brickwork. I called for him to come out into the open and as he did so I immediately I knew I had the arsonist. So did Mark – I could tell by his excitement that he also realised that this was our man.

Mark was a new probationer at the time and he was like a bottle of pop. He was always on the go and worked non-stop. He was now to the side of this man, almost hovering off the ground and with a great big grin on his face. He was also pointing at the man's trainers. The trainers were covered in paint and the toes had the ends of the sole coming up over them. They were the same pattern as had been left at one of our offences.

This man was huge. He was well over six foot four, and built like a rugby player. At this time I did not know how well Mark would react in a punch-up if this man kicked off. So I tried to play it calm until I could get other units there. The man claimed he lived locally and was just out for a walk. He almost seemed as if he was on another planet and was getting very agitated and I could tell by his body language that he was not far from breaking point.

Mark was getting more and more excited and I thought it was better to get hold of him sooner rather than later. I then told the man he was being arrested. He did not seem to understand a word I was saying but seemed to accept it and just calmed down and was very passive, much to my delight. Then the problem arrived. At the time, the force used Austin Mini's as panda cars. Along came help and I walked the prisoners to the vehicle.

He said: 'I am not getting into that car, it is too small.'

I tried to talk him into it but he refused. I tried to get a van but that was busy elsewhere. I again tried to get him in the car but he still adamantly refused. Mark suggested we forced him in, but that was not an option as he was far too big to be forced. I tried to be tactful and again tried to talk him into getting in by him self.

Suddenly he snapped and kicked off. He grabbed hold of the car from the underside of the roof at the open driver's door. He lifted the panda car up onto its side and then let it drop back onto its four wheels.

He said: 'I am not getting in that xxxxxxx little car.' Fair enough, sir; we will just wait then until a van is free. This is exactly what we did!

He subsequently pleaded guilty to the offences. He actually lived on the estate and was depressed after being made redundant. He said he was drinking heavily and committed the offences unknowingly while under the influence of drink and anti-depressant tablets. He subsequently received a long term of imprisonment. That was also a start to a great career for Mark Wheatstone. He never calmed down and still has to keep going at 100 miles an hour. Mark is currently an inspector in Gwent.

A scary horse box story!

One of the funniest but scariest moments that I can recall from my Gwent days relates to a man called Dilwyn Hayden Prior. He lived in a road called Constable Drive. Yes, that is the real address.

Dilwyn was a jack-of-all-trades and a bit of an Arthur Daley. He was known all over Newport and although he had committed some very minor offences in his younger days, he was quite a decent bloke and was liked by police who knew him.

A colleague who knew him fairly well was Dixie Dean. One day I was with Dixie having a cup of tea at the police office in St. Julian's, when we received a call to Constable Drive. We were told that a man had committed suicide with a shotgun. The man was in a horsebox in the street. Dixie knew this was going to be Dilwyn Prior as his wife had thrown him out of the house after a row and he was living in the horsebox in the street!

I drove Dixie there. When we arrived there were a few people in the street who told us they had heard the sound of a shot go off in the horsebox. The gate of the box was closed so I climbed up and looked inside. Sure enough, there was Dilwyn on his back, shotgun laying on his chest and his face a mess.

I said to Dixie, 'it looks awful mate, sorry.'

'What do you mean, sorry?' he said.

'Well it's your beat, get in there and see if he is dead.'

'Well of course he's bloody dead, he shot himself with a shotgun,' Dixie moaned.

Dixie pulled the back gate down and climbed in. I stayed outside and watched. Dixie gingerly approached the body; the back of the box was covered in blood and bits of body tissue. The scene looked dreadful. Dixie knelt down beside the body and went to try for a pulse on the side of his neck (the side that was still in one piece). As he did so, Dilwyn said 'Alright Dix, sorry mate!' Well Dixie jumped so high he hit his head on the roof of the box. I was outside the box and he scared the life out of me, so god knows how Dixie felt.

Dixie was now ranting, 'You stupid bastard what do you think your doing scaring the shit out of me like that.' The sight of Dixie hopping up and down in full uniform, ranting and raving at Dilwyn who was lying there with half his face blown off was unreal. I fell in to hysterics. Dixie shouted,

'You can fxxxing laugh; get in here and sort him out.'

I was finished and just collapsed laughing.

It ended with Dilwyn being rushed to hospital. He lost his right eye and had to have a lot of surgery to his face, but he survived. We discovered he had decided he was going to commit suicide and lay down in the horsebox to do it. As he pulled the trigger he changed his mind. It was a bit too late and managed to turn his face to one side, which saved him. Dixie eventually saw the funny side of it and forgave me for my outburst of hysterics.

Lost in Translation

Another funny story occurred at Newport magistrate's court. I was there listening to a case, waiting for my case to be called. The defendant in the case was of African origin and was having trouble understanding what was going on. The magistrates stopped the case and instructed the sergeant of the court to get an interpreter for the defendant.

At the back of the court was a real old-style PC whose name, I believe, was George. He was not far off retiring, and was known as a straight and very strict old-style copper. He was helping the court sergeant out that day.

George stood up and said: 'Your worships, I may be able to help you. I spent a lot of time in Africa in the army and used to converse with the native's quite well. Would you like me to assist this man?'

The magistrates appeared very impressed as were all of the officers sat in court.

'Very well they said please explain to the defendant what is going to happen.'

Well, George got up, stood in front of the defendant and took a deep breath and what happened next was a classic.

George said in English: 'Me policeman', and he put his helmet on his head. He then pointed at the buttons on his tunic and said, 'With big shiny buttons.' He then held his wrists together and said, 'You arrested for stealing and running away.' George then made actions with his arms and legs as if running. He then said, 'You understand Joe?'

The defendant actually nodded at him.

Well, if you can imagine the whole thing happening in the space of about twenty seconds, it was just so bemusing. The whole court fell about; even the magistrates were laughing. The best bit of all was the defendant nodding as if he had understood everything George had said. George genuinely thought he was doing the right thing. He said later that he used to communicate like that when he was in the army and it always got through to them in the end. Fortunately, the court saw the funny side of it and nothing was made of it. The defendant did eventually get a real interpreter.

It's not big and it's not clever!

Following the activation of a burglar alarm one night duty, I attended the Windsor Club in Conway Road, Newport to find the steward and stewardess had been attacked and tied up and the club had been robbed. It was a very nasty robbery. As a result of this incident I became friends with Tony and Elaine, the steward and his wife, and I have remained close friends with them to this day.

They were both shaken very badly by the incident and from then on if I was on night duty and able to get there, I would try to be in the club after closing time whilst Tony counted the money. This led one night to one of the funniest moments ever in my career and I hope the person it involves forgives me for repeating it in print.

The Windsor club was just one of many that were robbed by a team from London. They were nick named THE HOLE IN THE WALL GANG because they normally took out bricks from an outside wall to gain entry. They were very good and could get passed most alarm systems. As a result on night duty all big clubs were checked as regularly as possible.

If we were short of cars, sometimes two cars were joined to cover two areas with one car. This particular night I joined Gary Probert for the night and we were using a blue escort 1300cc van. It happened to be Gary's birthday and at midnight I stopped into the Windsor Club to check on Tony. It was very risky to have a pint whilst on duty as the section Sergeant would visit you during the night and if you smelt of drink god help you. Whilst there Gary mentioned it was his birthday, Tony insisted he had a drink to celebrate and off it went. Gary was normally a very strict officer and although he liked a drink, he would normally temper it whilst working. However, this night he was suddenly 'on it' and before I knew it he was well on the way to being the worse for wear. I left him there on a couple of occasions and went to deal with a call. Each time I came back he was in a worse state that before I left.

Eventually in the early hours I managed to drag him out of there. He was in a hell of a state. I now had the problem of keeping him away from the station and the Sergeant for a while. I put the back seat of the van down flat and sent him off to sleep. I drove around for several hours too scared to go near the nick. Fortunately it was a very quite night with very few calls for a change. By 4:00 am I could hardly keep my eyes open, I was knackered but I realised I had to get around the entire two areas we were covering and check all the clubs to make sure they were secure.

At this time Newport County Football Club was still in being and doing well. I was a big supporter of the club and I always checked the grounds and the club within it with an extra special look around. The club was situated on the Cromwell Road side of the ground. It had a long concrete drive that led to a car park near the railway lines. The club ran for some distance down this drive and at about 4:15am I drove down towards the main entrance.

As I passed the large fire escape doors I saw they were wide open but because I was so tired it just did not register. Then as I reached the car park at the end, it suddenly dawned on me. I shouted out 'Shit' very loudly as I made a quick spin around and sped up to the doors. I had forgotten all about Gary asleep in the back and I was shouting and ranting and raving at myself.

As I got out of the van I suddenly heard the rear doors burst open and Gary went racing off back down the drive. He was running like hell, a bit like Tom Hanks in the film Forrest Gump. He disappeared into the darkness and I did not have a clue what was going on. I made my way through the fire escape doors and up to the club. Sure enough the Hole in the Wall gang had struck again. The place had been cleaned out completely. Now I was really in trouble. No sign of a drunken colleague and a burglary at the club. I had no choice but to call in the troops and hope for the best. I made out Gary was already off having a look around.

Andy Vick

Whilst the rest of the relief, aided by a couple of dog handlers began searching for any possible suspects, I started searching for Gary. His radio was in the van and I was starting to get a bit worried. I found him after about 20 minutes fast asleep in the main stand. He did not have a clue what was going on but managed to sort himself out before we had any contact with the Sergeant and thankfully we got away with it. I found out later that the Sergeant knew all along something was going on when I kept away from the station all night as well as avoiding him. But the Sergeant, Ken Carey was one of the best supervisors I have ever come across and he let it ride. If we had been caught by him he would have slaughtered us and rightly so. But he was old school and played the management of his relief very well.... Thank God

Complaints against the police

Being complained about by members of the public and people you have arrested was an occupational hazard. I have had quite a few complaints made over the years. None of them have had any foundation whatsoever and most have been just attempts to help suspects get off with what I have arrested them for.

However, the one that caused me the most trouble was in relation to a sudden death, which for a period of time did cause me a lot of concern. This was because I had done nothing wrong, but it still could possibly get me in a lot of trouble.

One late turn I received a call to attend an address in Victoria Avenue; the control room told me that they had received a call from a lady who was concerned about her sister, as she could not get a reply on the telephone. Her sister had been unwell and she was concerned for her safety.

I arrived at the address; it was a very imposing large detached house. It was set in its own grounds and even thought it was only about 3.00 p.m., the place looked a bit strange and dark. I must admit it was quite eerie. It felt a bit like the Munsters' house.

I went and knocked at the front door and rang the bell but got no reply. I started to walk around the outside of the building and when I got to the first window and tried to look in I suddenly saw a huge wolf-like dog come charging at the window. It scared the living daylights out of me; I thought it was going to come straight through the window. It hit the glass and bounced off and was going ballistic at me. The same thing happened at every window I went too. It obviously had a free roam of the whole house. I thought I had no chance of getting into the address. I even climbed a large tree which put me near an upstairs window but the bloody thing was there waiting for me!

As I got down from the tree, a lady was calling to me from the front gate. She asked me if everything was all right. She was a neighbour and I explained to her why I was there. The lady told me that the woman lived there with her husband and she had seen the husband leave about half an hour before I arrived. She also said he was carrying books and was probably at the library changing them. If that was the case, he was not likely to be very long. I was in the process of calling the control room to let them know the situation when my inspector and patrol sergeant arrived.

I explained everything to them and they themselves went to the house and had the same problem with the dog. We were still concerned because there was no reply and I called for a dog-handler to come down to the address in case we had no choice but to gain entry. However, the fact that the husband was around and due back helped a little and we decided to wait for him to return. He arrived within five minutes of my inspector and sergeant. He walked up to us at the gate. The gentleman was quite elderly himself; I explained to him why we were there.

He said, 'No it is quite alright, my wife is fine, she has been unwell but I left her in bed.' He also explained she could not get out of bed to answer the door.

I asked him if we could come in and make sure she was OK. He refused at first and appeared to be getting upset by our presence. However, we eventually persuaded him to let us in. He went inside first to lock the raving mad dog away. He apologised for the dog who was now locked in a room and desperately trying to tear his way through the door. I was praying it did not get out or we would be in big trouble.

The man tried to assure us his wife was all right and still did not want us to speak with her. We persuaded him we had to ensure ourselves she was fine and we would then leave. He went upstairs and said, 'Let me make sure she is decent first.'

He went upstairs calling his wife's name. Behind us all hell was breaking loose in the room where the dog was and I was sure it was going to escape. The man suddenly appeared at the top of the stairs and said, 'Do you think you could come up please I think my wife is ill.'

You're Nicked My Son

We went up and entered the bedroom and were met with a rather strange sight. The lady was lying, with her legs on the bed and the top half of her body hanging off the bottom of the bed. A dining room-type chair was lying across her head that was resting on the floor. We picked her up and lay her flat on the bed and it was obvious she was dead. I also noticed that the telephone handset was off the hook and lying on the floor nearby. We assumed she had been trying to get to the phone to call someone as she was feeling ill and had collapsed as she did so.

The husband must have gone into shock as he was behaving rather strangely. I explained to him his wife had passed away but it did not register with him at all. We obtained details of the lady's doctor and called him. He arrived fairly quickly and pronounced life extinct. He explained that she had a chronic heart condition and had been ill for quite some time. He also stated the lady had only been dead for no more than an hour. I felt so guilty that the lady could well have been alive whilst I was attempting to get in, but I had been prevented from doing so by the raving mad guard dog. The husband was suddenly there with a cup of tea and before we realised it he had hold of his wife and was trying to feed her the cup of tea; no matter what we tried we just could not get him to understand she was dead.

I had to sit down with him to take the coroner's statement and I just could not get through to him at all what had happened. He continued as if she was still alive, calling to her when I asked him some information about his wife. It was very strange and I have to admit I found it very difficult trying to deal with him. Eventually, the undertakers arrived and dealt with his wife. He would not let them put her in a body bag to remove her and got very distressed and upset when she was eventually removed from the house. However, within a very short time he was back to behaving as if she was still around and continued calling upstairs to her asking if she wanted a cup of tea.

Eventually another member of the family arrived and I left still with the dog going mad in the room he was locked in. I have to say I was very glad to get out of there. I returned to the nick and completed the full report. A death certificate had been issued so there would be no need for a post mortem, so I thought that was to be the end of it. Boy was I wrong!

I may have been still a little naïve at this time but I never believed for one minute that I had done anything wrong in dealing with the matter. However about two weeks later I got called into my inspector's office to see him. Colin Durham was a real gentleman and even if he was giving you a roasting for doing something wrong, he did it nicely.

Andy he said, 'We have a problem. You know the sudden death the other day? Well, a member of the family has made a complaint against you.'

I was shocked. 'For what?' I asked.

Mr Durham explained that the complaint was for neglect of my duty by failing to deal with the incident properly and as a result the lady had died.

I just did not know what to say. As far as I was concerned there was nothing more I could have done. The call only said that the caller was concerned for her sister, I did not even know if she was in the house or not. The fact that the dog would have prevented me from entering was a factor, but it was only a concerned call not a call to say the lady was ill inside.

Mr Durham said, 'Well, there is a slight problem there.'

The call was recorded and as the lady was on the phone talking to her sister, she heard a groan and the line went dead, she tried ringing it back but it was permanently engaged. Then she called the police.

I remembered the phone in the bedroom being off the hook and the lady lying there and suddenly realised I was in big trouble here. I explained that I was only told by the control room that the caller could not raise her sister on the phone, I was never told that she had been in conversation with her and the phone went dead. Had I received that information then my actions would have warranted a more urgent response (although I still do not know how we would have got past the dog to get in to help her). Mr Durham was fully on my side and had heard the original message I had received him self and assured me he would help me with this matter.

I was still served with official complaint forms and interviewed regarding the incident as if I was responsible for some crime. It was an awful time and I had three or four weeks wondering what was going to happen to me over the incident. At the worst I could be sacked!

Then one day, I was in Victoria Avenue dealing with a burglary, only a few doors away from the sudden death address. I dealt with the matter and was having a cup of tea with the occupier. There was a knock at the door, the lady answered it and came back in with another lady. I recognised her as the lady I had spoken to on the day of the sudden death and who had told me the husband was at the library. She recognised me as well. She told her friend how she knew me.

Her friend said, 'Are you the officer the family are complaining about.'

I explained that I was. She then told me that she speaks with the sister-in-law of the lady who died. She had told her of the complaint and how the husband was hoping to get a lot of compensation from the police. She then said that the whole family are strange and that had I been trying to gain entry into the house two weeks prior to the incident, I would not only have had a dog to contend with but also a half-grown alligator that the man was keeping there! He had only got rid of it after neighbours complained to the RSPCA.

I went back to the nick and explained to Mr Durham what I had been told. He went and visited the two ladies and got statements from them. The lady I had spoken to at the gate said in her statement that she had watched me try every window downstairs and had even seen me climb a tree trying to get in upstairs. Eventually, after six weeks of worry, the complaint against me was dropped as an unfounded allegation. I was so relieved and it was all down to the two ladies who spoke up for me. But for them I might not have had a job much longer, and would not have been able to write this book.

Taxi, gentlemen

If we were sometimes flush with staff on night duty, it became quite a normal thing for a couple of us to go out for the second half of the shift in a spare CID car. We would use it to have a nose around in areas where we might be getting regular burglary or theft from motorcar offences. It also made a nice change to be able to go out and do your own thing in plain clothes and gave you some freedom.

Someone had managed to get a battery-run 'Taxi' sign and we used to stick this in the window on the dash and an old stick on aerial on the boot and off we would go.

It is amazing because we would be able to go onto estates and into areas where no one took any notice at all. One of us would drive and the other would sit in the back playing the passenger. It worked really and brought in some very good arrests.

The funniest thing happened one night when I was out with a new probationer on the relief. It was about 3.00 a.m. and we were out in the Ringland area. There had been a lot of burglaries where the electric meters were being broken into on an almost nightly basis. We had gone to the area after a call from a local resident who had heard some strange noises in her back garden in Howard's Close. I dropped Bob Webber off to walk through the area and had gone around the other side of what was basically a very large cul de sac. I was parked at the junction with Howard's Close and Hawkins Crescent with just my sidelights on and engine running, waiting Bob's return.

Suddenly, from down the side of two houses came two lads, one who I recognised as one of our local toe rags. He had until recently lived in Howard's Close. He knew me and I thought he would just walk on.

You're Nicked My Son

No, he stopped across the road from me and said, 'Hey cabbie, you free for a fare?'

I said, 'No, not really mate.'

He replied, 'I'm going to call one, do you want the fare or not?'

I said, 'Where to?'

He replied, 'Bettws mate.'

I said: 'OK get in.'

He came across the road carrying something quite heavy in a canvas bag. As he got closer I realised from the noise it was making it was a bag full of loose change. The car I was driving was a two-door Escort, I switched off the interior light so it would not come on when they opened the door and I had pulled the seat back forward so that they could climb in the back. They got in without even looking at me.

As they did so, there was suddenly a lot of shouting of a female's voice in Howard's Close. The youth I knew said, 'That's my Mam, she'll be after me. Can we go mate?'

I switched the internal light on and looked around at him. It suddenly dawned on him he was in the back of a police car.

I said, 'Been at the electric meters again then have we?'

All he could do was stare back at me in disbelief! I took the bag from him and found it was full of 50p pieces. I turned my radio back on and called Bob. He had been trying to call me to tell me he had at least three burglaries in the close and all the meters had been broken into. He had the pleasure of telling the victims we had the persons responsible under arrest.

When Bob got in the car we started laughing when I told him what had happened. The youth did not find it funny. He begged us not to tell anyone about him walking straight into a police car and getting arrested. Of course we wouldn't tell anyone would we? Not!

What good is a piece of wood?

The good old police truncheon was there supposedly for the protection of the officer. In all the time I had a 'stick' as we called them, I only remember using it on two occasions to protect myself. It was very good to smash windows to gain entry into houses on searches and things, but as a defence weapon it was absolutely useless.

One occasion in particular was pretty scary. It was a late turn on quite a warm day. I received a call to a domestic incident in a road that was situated just off a main road known as Corporation Road. I was given the family name as Bell. This was mistake number one: I had no one with me or any other car backing me up. I was not too worried as most of the time these calls could be sorted quite easily on your own. As I travelled along Corporation Road, I suddenly saw what appeared to be a nasty fight taking place; this was about half a mile from my call. I slowed down and right away realised it was Ginger Bale and one of his sons. Suddenly, Ginger broke free from his son and jumped into the middle of the road in front of a lorry that screeched to a halt without running over him.

The Bale family were a very well-known family. The father, 'Ginger' Bale was in his day an ace safe-cracker from the old school of villains. The Bale family had three boys. Two of them were villains like their father and another, Anthony, was the black sheep of the family. He was a huge man, fast approaching twenty stone in weight and he was a real nice guy. So much so he led a scout group and was well-known locally for the help he gave to the elderly.

The two people fighting were Ginger and Anthony. I got to them as Anthony pulled his father out of the road. They were now exchanging punches with each other.

Anthony saw me and shouted, 'He is trying to kill himself.'

I found out later that he had drunk at least a bottle of whisky and taken a load of tablets. It all then kicked into place: it was not the Bell family I had been sent to, it was the Bale family. I went to help Anthony just as his father hit him with a haymaker punch and down he went. Before I had chance to do anything Ginger had hold of me and pushed me back against a wall. His strength was amazing and the look in his eyes made me realise I was in trouble; I went to go for my radio to call for help. Suddenly Ginger had his hands around my throat and was squeezing tight. He was also lifting me up so my feet were off the floor. I thought my time had come.

Then I saw Anthony had got up behind his dad and was now carrying a large plank of wood. He thumped his father around the shoulders with it. All it did was make him squeeze me tighter. The next hit was over the head and this time it was enough to annoy him and he let me fall to the floor. His attention was now back to Anthony.

I immediately called for urgent assistance and then drew my stick. Ginger was now punching the living daylights out of his son. I went behind Ginger and hit him straight over the back of his neck/shoulders with all the force I could muster. Ginger just turned and looked at me. It was like coming face to face with 'the Hulk' and before I knew it he had me by the throat again. I swung my left hand full force and brought my stick down across his head I looked in disbelief! It had snapped in half and did not affect him one single bit. Now I really was in trouble.

Then I was hit from behind with what I thought was a ten-tonne truck and ended up on the floor. It was Anthony saving me again. Ginger was now face down on the floor and appeared exhausted. Anthony and I were sat on him trying to keep him there. Then I could hear the cavalry arriving in convoy along Corporation Road. Several vans, cars and support group carriers arrived almost at the same time.

We were still sitting on him. Suddenly from out of a CID car burst DC Brian Lloyd; he raced towards us and thinking Anthony was fighting against us he dived straight on top of him with a rugby tackle and pulled Anthony from his dad's top half. That was it; Ginger did a press-up with me on his back and off it went again. Fortunately, there were enough officers now to subdue him and he was handcuffed and taken to direct to the Royal Gwent hospital for treatment.

At the hospital I was sat in a cubicle with him. Even though he was handcuffed I felt at any time he might go for me. He looked at me calmly and said, 'You have one minute to remove these handcuffs or I am going to break them.'

He repeated this several times. I was praying the doctor would come soon. Ginger just stared at me then suddenly I heard the loud crack and realise he had actually broken open the handcuffs. I made an attempt to stop him but the next thing I knew was waking up on the bed in the cubicle with a nurse looking at me.

It seems he head-butted me and tried to run off but fortunately, the support group were still outside and detained him again after a big fight. He was then taken to a specialist hospital and it was there they discovered that Ginger had a tumour on the brain and it was this causing his bouts of trying to kill himself and others, and also his great strength. I know he recovered after a successful operation.

I always remembered after that day that the truncheon was a complete and utter waste of time and offered me little or no protection. We might as well have been using peashooters than our sticks.

The boss is always right!

There have been many times over the years when I have come across senior officers where it appeared to me that they would never be good police officers for as long as they had holes in their backsides. If they were ever any good at their jobs, they must have had some sort of lobotomy when they reached the higher ranks of the service. They seemed to lose all track of the real world and became obnoxious and arrogant.

My first such senior officer was a detective chief superintendent whose name escapes me (he left that much of an impression on me). He was in charge of Newport CID at the time, and someone like me would not normally have any contact with such a high-and-mighty rank. However, one early turn just as we were briefing, a call came out to a sudden death.

The call was to a lovely Roman village just outside Newport, called Caerleon. Within the town was a large walled area with a couple of very large houses. A call had been received from one of these houses which was occupied by a Sir Somebody-or-Other. The call stated he had found his daughter dead in the bath.

I attended with my patrol sergeant, Ken Carey. We arrived at the big imposing detached house and were met at the door by a very distressed elderly gentleman. He identified himself as the man who called us and stated he had got up to go to the bathroom and found his daughter dead in the bath. He showed us upstairs to the bathroom and we were met with the sight of a female of about twenty-one years of age hanging half in and half out of the bath. The bath was full of water and the water was dark red in colour. It looked like blood and it was obviously suspicious,

Ken Carey immediately ordered us out of the bathroom and preserved the scene for forensics.

We learnt from the father that the night before he had retired to bed fairly early, as he was in poor health. Some time later he heard his wife and daughter arguing. This was happening quite regular at the time. His wife eventually retired to her own bedroom. He then awoke in the morning and found his daughter. When asked where his wife was now he replied that he could not find her.

While Ken Carey called in CID, he despatched me to search the house to see if the wife could be found. The place was very big and eventually I could hear a female voice talking behind a door. I knocked but got no reply. I opened the door and found the wife sitting on the edge of a bath in what was another bathroom. She was rambling to herself. I asked her if she was all right, and she nodded. Then completely out of the blue she said, 'I did it: I wanted her to die. I wanted to put her out of her misery. I did not want her to suffer any more.'

I realised what she was saying and told her she was under arrest on suspicion of murder. She just kept repeating the same thing over and over again. I did not want her to suffer: I had to kill her for her sake. I wrote down everything I could in my pocket book verbatim. By now other officers had arrived and I was joined by a WPC. I could see the mother had cuts to both her wrists and that her clothes were slightly damp.

I asked her to tell me what had happened to her daughter.

She said: 'I was in the bathroom as my daughter was bathing. She suffers with rheumatoid arthritis and I was making sure she was all right. I could not see her suffer any more and I went behind her, put my hands on her shoulders and pushed her down under the water. I held her there until she stopped struggling. I then climbed in the bath with her and cut my wrists with a razor blade. I wanted to be with her, with her where she was not suffering any more.'

She was crying but I felt the tears were forced and not genuine.

She carried on: 'I woke up a while ago in the bath with her, I realised she was dead but I was not. I have taken a lot of pills; I just want to be with her. I came here to die before anyone found me.'

An ambulance arrived and I let the mother go to the ambulance, she was still repeating the same things over and over. I left her in the ambulance with the WPC still writing things down. I went to fill the sergeant in on everything. As I got to the bathroom I saw several senior CID officers arguing with Ken Carey. They wanted to go into the bathroom and he was refusing saying it was a crime scene and he was letting no one in until scenes of crimes arrived.

Suddenly, the detective chief superintendent came in behind me and his men explained they were not being allowed past Ken Carey. Instead of backing Ken up for doing the right things he went mad at him. He was ranting and saying his men should be allowed access and they were experienced officers who knew what they were doing. With that at least four of them, including the Detective Chief Superintendent went in.

Ken Carey was furious. It was against all the rules of securing a crime scene. I started to tell him what had gone on with regards to the mother when there was a noise of water running. We both looked in the bathroom and one of the so-called senior officers from the CID had put his hand in the bath and pulled the plug out so they could examine the bottom of the bath. Even I, so young in service, knew that vital evidence might well know have gone down the plughole. Ken was about to explode and sent me off to the hospital with the woman.

In the ambulance and at hospital the mother repeated the same things over and over. I always believed and still do, that it was a complete act. I was relieved there by CID and returned to the station several hours later. I went and saw Ken Carey, filled him in and showed him all my notes in my pocket book. He was still annoyed at what had occurred at the house but he had been overruled on everything by the Detective Chief Superintendent, who assured him that he knew exactly what he was doing. Ken told me to make a full statement regarding the arrest of the woman and her admissions and take it around to CID as soon as possible.

I made my statement explaining in detail how I had discovered the mother, her initial admissions and my arresting her. I then detailed all her admissions from then on. There were several pages and when I finished I walked around to the CID office.

I opened the door and could see the detective chief superintendent stood in front of a large gathering of detectives. He was calling them all the useless wankers and other abusive names in a torrid rage. He was ranting that the mother had been at hospital for several hours and all her talking and admitting that she had done was inadmissible in evidence because she had not been arrested. He was going berserk at them. I could not believe what I was seeing and hearing.

Detective Sergeant Lindsey Bennett was an ace detective (he later became detective chief superintendent himself and was one of the few who remained a human being and a top-class detective). He noticed me and crept across and said, 'Andy if I was you I would disappear this man is after blood, the last person he wants here is a uniformed officer.'

I said, 'But sarge, the woman has been under arrest since before she left the house, I arrested her after I found her and she started admitting what she had done.'

His face lit up and he said to the detective chief superintendent, 'Sir, it is all right; the mother has been under arrest all the time, this officer found her and arrested her.'

The detective chief superintendent looked at me and his face went even redder. I thought he was going to hit me.

I held out my statement and he snatched it from me, he read it and turned to me and said: 'who the fu** do you think you are? You're a uniformed officer, what gives you the right to go arresting a suspect for murder? That is a job for a senior detective. I will speak to your inspector about this. Now get out of this office.'

I remember his words to this day. I was stunned: one minute he was going mad because no one had arrested her, then he went mad because someone from uniform had had the sense to do the right thing. I almost said something back but the look on Lindsey Bennett's face made my think otherwise. I walked back into the station and explained all to Ken Carey who in turn went to my inspector, Colin Durham. He called me into his office and congratulated me on doing the right thing. He told me he would ensure the matter was resolved correctly.

Well the story came out that the daughter was in fact a sufferer from rheumatoid arthritis and had one time been very ill with it. Her father had over the years paid for expensive treatment abroad that had allowed her to live a fairly normal life. She had in fact just passed all her exams to become a barrister. No one except her main employer knew she suffered with it. The mother was believed to be very jealous of her daughter and had killed her in a fit of temper, during the row the father had heard taking place.

The mother was sent for trial but continued with what I personally believe was a complete act on her behalf. She was found guilty of manslaughter but sent to a secure mental hospital and not prison. She was released only a few years later after a miraculous recovery, literally getting away with murder.

The petty-mindedness of so-called senior officers was to continue to bemuse me for the whole of my career. They are either very good or very bad, never in between.

The final thing that made me laugh over this incident was that several days later I discovered the custody record for the arrest of the mother had been altered to show the detective chief superintendent as the arresting officer and not myself. The local papers were full of his quotes for several days. What they didn't say though was **'what a complete and utter knob head he was'** and how he and his senior CID officers had nearly ruined the entire crime scene. God help us.

How do you cope with this?

I THINK ONE OF THE hardest things for any police officer to deal with is death involving children. The most upsetting experience of my five years in Gwent was a cot death of a very tiny baby who was only several months old. I was on early turn and had gone out doing my usual drive around on the Maindee south car. I was driving around the Ringland area when I received a call to a baby not breathing at an address in Ringland Circle. I was only about a minute away and rushed there as quickly as I could.

The house was a three-storey council house. I rushed up to the front door, which was wide open, and called out as I entered. There was a man who turned out to be the father in the hall looking up stairs crying. At the top of the stairs was the baby's mother who was in total shock. I started to make my way up the stairs and had only taken a couple of steps when, the mother screamed and jumped down the stairs right on top of me. We fell to the bottom and she was hysterical, she was punching and screaming at me. Her husband pulled her off me and held her so I could get upstairs.

I found the baby laying face down in his cot. He was very blue but his body was still warm. There was no pulse but I started mouth-to-mouth and gentle heart massage and did this until the ambulance arrived very shortly after. Unfortunately, the baby had died before I arrived. I found this – my first dealing with a cot death – very hard to cope with. Sadly, I dealt with several cot deaths in my time in Gwent and I never ever got used to it. It is a terrible experience to go through; God knows what it must be like for the parents. What I experienced as a result of it was bad enough. Nothing you can say can help the parents in any way at all. All I can hope is that in some way I helped the families to get through one of the most difficult times they are ever likely to face.

Nearly a watery grave

ONE LATE TURN SHIFT IN April 1982, I was driving the south car and my good friend, Gary Probert, was driving the North car. I heard a call on the radio to Gary regarding a 999 call to the effect that a female was in difficulties on the banks of the River Usk near the Glebelands sports ground in the St Julian's area of Newport. Gary accepted the call and I offered to back him up.

The Glebelands sports ground is a very large area situated just off junction 23 of the M4. The M4 in fact runs over the top of the playing fields and the River Usk. The river itself is a dangerous river, very fast-flowing in places and known for it's quickly rising tides. The banks are very deep when the tide is out and they are made up of deep thick brown mud.

Gary and I arrived at the same time and began trying to find where the female was. After a while of checking the area we saw two young boys running towards us and they directed us to where they had seen the woman. When we eventually got to her I was shocked to find that the woman was embedded in the mud so deeply that only her head and shoulders were visible. I knew straight away we were in big trouble as I could also see that the tide had turned and was on its way back in.

The woman who was in her late twenties or early thirties, was six or seven feet down the bank and had obviously jumped into the mud as there were no signs of her sliding down to the position we found her in. Gary tried talking to the lady who was completely calm and seemed totally unaware that we were there with her. Gary then tried sliding down on his stomach across the mud to her with me holding his legs. He was quite a bit taller than me and just about reached her but soon started to sink into the mud and I had to pull him back quite quickly. We then asked for the local fire brigade to be called in the hope that they would have some ropes or harness type of equipment that might help to get the woman out. In the time we had been there she did not appear to be sinking any further but it was obvious that the tide was starting to rise and we began to get very concerned that this woman may drown before we could get her out. This was now a race against time and tide.

Then we were aware of a tractor coming towards us; it was being driven by a local farmer, George Pintches. He had been the person who had spotted the lady jump in and had gone to call the police from his farm. It had taken a while for him to get there as he was on foot and he then decided to come back to see if he could help.

We were hoping Mr Pintches would have some rope with him on his tractor but all he had were several long lengths of cable/wire-type stuff. It was quite thick and appeared strong, and Gary had the idea of getting it around her somehow and trying to pull her out with it. So with some cable tied around each of us as a safety measure, Gary slid back down the mud to her right side and I slid down to her left. The mud was horrible. It smelt disgusting and stuck to you like glue. I was very glad Mr Pintches was there holding onto the end of the cable attached to Gary and I and I remember thinking, *what the hell am I doing this for? If we start sinking who will rescue the rescuers?*

Well, we reached the woman and we both ended up on our backs alongside her and she still appeared calm and unaware of us being there. At this time my boots were getting wet from the water as the tide was slowly rising. This had to work or she was in deep trouble, and if we did not hurry up, so were we!

We managed to get the cable around her chest and up under her arms by dragging mud away with our hands. We then both struggled to get back up the mud and onto the bank. I do not think we would have been able to do so if Mr Pintches had not been there to help pull us back up. I was knackered from the exertion and it took a few minutes for us to get our breath back. All three of us then tried to pull the woman free from the mud. We were concerned that the cable may hurt her but we knew we really had no choice. The location was so out of the way that it may take some time for any other help to get here and find us so it was down to Gary and me and, of course, Mr Pintches.

We tried pulling, all three of us together. The top half of the woman went rigid and taut, but she did not move an inch. She was still calm and made no sound at all. After several attempts to pull her out manually it was obvious it was not going to work. We then took a big risk and tied the cable to the back of the tractor. Mr Pintches then started the tractor and as slowly as was possible he inched the tractor forward until the cable was tight. We knew this might cause the woman some serious injuries if he pulled too quickly, but the way things were, we felt it was the only option we had to stop this lady from drowning right in front of our eyes. Under Gary's direction Mr Pintches crawled forward. At last we had movement, suddenly there was this great sucking noise as the mud gave up the grip it had on the lady and out she came. Once she was out of the hole, Mr Pitches stopped the tractor and Gary and I slid back onto the mud and between us we managed to get her and ourselves up onto the bank. At this point the water was only a foot or so away from where the woman had been trapped.

We lay her on her back on the grass and covered her with our tunics. She just lay there, calm, and with her eyes wide open staring at the sky, still not replying to either of us when we spoke to her. The ambulance eventually arrived and by the time they took her off from the scene, the hole where she had been stuck in the mud was covered by the tide. When we eventually left about twenty minutes later, the tide was at its highest.

After expressing our gratitude to Mr Pintches we then had to think about getting ourselves sorted out. We were both covered head to toe in stinking River Usk mud. We both looked a bit like that famous rugby photograph of the England player, Fran Cotton when he was called the mud monster. We looked the same and were also soaking wet from the mud. We could not get into our cars in that state so we got some other officers to drive the cars and Gary and I stood up in the back of the station van.

First stop was the nick for Gary to collect a change of clothes which fortunately he kept there just in case of emergencies such as this. Then it was off to my parents' home, just a couple of miles from the station, for a shower. My mother's face was a picture when we arrived. After a long hot shower and a couple of hot coffees to warm us through (with a little something else for medicinal purposes) we headed back to the nick to fill out the necessary reports.

We then discovered that the lady was in fact a missing person from St Cadocs nursing home in Caerleon. She had suffered a nervous breakdown and had tried to commit suicide; she was being treated for this at the hospital and had gone missing that morning. Unfortunately, several weeks later she again escaped from the home and this time, at her third attempt, managed to throw herself in another part of the river at full tide and her body was found two weeks later.

Time to move on

In 1981, my mentor John Caplin decided he had seen enough of the Gwent police and he transferred back to the Met. It was a decision that was also to change my life. After a couple of visits to London to see John, I also decided to apply to transfer to the Met.

This decision caused a great deal of consternation within my family life at the time. I had been married to my first wife in July 1979 and things were not going that well for various reasons. I used that as my excuse for moving away. In reality, I now know I was just looking out for myself and wanted to do what I wanted to do. I had visions that the Met was the place for a proper policeman to be and I was lured to it. I was selfish in doing what I did.

I dragged my wife and six-month-old daughter away from the rest of their family for my own reasons and did not give a thought to how they really felt. There was a period of time that I was not sure if I had done the right thing. However, I knew several years later that I had done exactly the right thing. I have some regrets over some things I did to my family and to some close friends in particular. But I do believe strongly that what I did was right for me, that fate took a hand and I was meant to do what I did. With the exception of not having precious time with my daughter, Natalie when she was growing up, I have no regrets whatsoever.

I applied to transfer in the summer of 1981. I was called to London in the October and travelled up by train and was put up overnight in a hotel in Paddington. The next day along with many others I turned up at the recruitment centre attached to Paddington police station. As

I was already a serving officer I did not have to do the entrance exam. I had a medical and then was told to wait for the interview.

I went into the interview very nervous and sat in front of a panel of three senior officers. After the experience of my interview to join Gwent I was expecting a bit of a hard time. I was told to take a seat and the three of them were heads down reading something. The senior officer in the middle looked at me and said, 'Well, PC Vick, do you have any questions to ask us?'

I replied, 'No thank you, sir.'

He replied, 'Well, we have nothing to say either; your file from Gwent is very complimentary and tells us everything we want to know. Welcome to the Metropolitan Police.' And that was that.

My departure from Gwent was delayed for six months due a complaint from a raving mad woman who was in custody for shoplifting. She alleged that I had stolen £1.00 from her whilst she was in custody. Despite her custody record showing that she did not possess a penny when she came into the station, it still held me up for six months due to the stupid complaints system that still has got no better to this day.

Before I left, my inspector, Colin Durham called me in his office to say goodbye to me.

The last thing he said to me was, 'Andy you have become a big fish in a small sea here in Gwent. You will now become a very small fish in a very big sea in the Met. Do not let them change your ideals or your professional principles.' I have always remembered those words because Mr Durham was spot on in what he said.

Off to the Met

On Sunday 23 April 1982 I travelled by train from Newport to Paddington and then by tube train to Hendon. I arrived there late in the evening and was allocated a room for the night in the infamous tower blocks in the Met Police Training School.

I clearly remember getting into my room and suddenly having this real feeling of loneliness and thinking *my god what have I done?* I had left my wife and daughter living with her parents, as there were no married quarters available for me. This had caused a few problems and, along with other matters that had arisen prior to my leaving for London, had caused a massive rift between my wife and I.

I then realised it was my daughter, Natalie I was missing; she was only six months old and I hated leaving her back in Newport. I took comfort in the thought I was doing this for her to have a better future and that is how I got through the time I spent in London without her.

That night in the bar, I met another officer who was also transferring into the Met the next day. His name was Andy Murphy and it was the start of a great friendship that still continues today. Andy is a Welshman born in Cardiff. He had moved to Durham when he was thirteen years old and was transferring from the Durham police force. We clicked straight away and became firm friends. The next day after all the paperwork and formalities we discovered we were being posted to the same division. So off to 'F' District together we went via the tube. We left Hendon in the mid-afternoon with instructions to report to the chief superintendent at Hammersmith police station.

Now, I think this is where I had a premonition of what was going to happen in the future and I helped Andy carry his very heavy suitcases. I must have known then that he was destined to become a high-ranking officer and he did. Andy was and still is one of the hardest-working officers I have ever known. He has been responsible for several very high-profile cases and is one of the most honest and trustful people I have ever met. However, at one point, his career was nearly ruined by the incompetence of a senior officer in the force. Thankfully, after a very long year it was put right and Andy went on to become a very high-ranking CID officer in charge of the whole of the Metropolitan police murder squad.

So, later that afternoon we arrived at Hammersmith but the chief superintendent had gone home. We were shown to a police section house close by, allocated rooms and told to report back at 8 a.m. the following morning. The section houses were large blocks of accommodation meant for single men to live in. Again, after living in a house with a family it was a bit of a shock, but it was fine for a short-term solution. The next day we return to Hammersmith and see the chief superintendent. After a severe bollocking for not arriving before he left the day before, Andy was sent off to Shepherds Bush station and I remained at Hammersmith.

After a day of normal duties getting all the admin done, I was due to start with my relief for late turn the next day. I duly turned up nice and early, I was introduced to the sergeant and told to find my way into the basement just before 2.00 p.m. The parade room was in the basement and I walked through the doors, very nervous.

The room was quite large with a table tennis table in the middle. There were chairs across a back wall and some to the sides. I noticed right away there was an obvious divide. To my left all the officers appeared fairly young and to the right they seemed older. I did not really think about it but went to sit in the next empty seat on the right side. I looked across at the left side and I noticed a few of them looking a bit embarrassed and not really wanting to acknowledge me. I was thinking *what on earth was going on here?* when a lad from my side of the room stood in front of me and said: 'You are not allowed to sit there mate.'

I was a bit unsure and said 'pardon?'

He repeated what he had said.

I then said, 'Why? Is it someone's seat?'

The lad said, 'No, but this side is for the senior members of the relief; new probationers sit over that side.'

I looked to the left and the youngsters did not know where to look.

Now, I stated at the start of this book that I have a habit of speaking out and this was to be no exception. I really took the hump over this and said to the lad, 'Oh, I am sorry, do you normally sit on this side then?'

He looked chuffed with himself and sat down. He said, 'Yes I have earned my seat here.'

I said, 'How much service do you have then?' sounding interested and in awe of him.

He replied 'Three-and-a-half years.'

I looked over at the youngsters and then turned and stood in front of the lad. I took him by the arm and pulled him out of his seat and said to him.

'Well, I have five years' service and I think I'll have your seat.' And I sat down.

The room went completely silent, I could see the younger ones giggling and some of the older ones unsure what to do. I was ready for a confrontation but nothing happened. The inspector and sergeants then came in and immediately introduced me and the situation calmed down. I will never forget my introduction to uniform life in the Met. It was the start of many changes for the relief and I am pleased to say they were all changes for the better.

Something I was really looking forward to was night duty. In the Met they worked a full week of night duty, where in Gwent the most I worked was three over a weekend.

It was a chance to get around Hammersmith and the surrounding divisions very quickly as there was a vast difference in the traffic compared to the daytime when Hammersmith Broadway and the adjoining roads were permanently at a standstill.

I remember my first set of nights. It was really busy and I was put in the back of the area car to get to see my way about. The area car was a Rover SD1 and it was kitted out with blue light and two tones. Each division had at least one area car and advanced drivers to drive them. Operators then had one-month postings on the car as RT operator for the main set radio and the car was the first to receive all 999 calls via the radio from Scotland Yard. The car would receive it before the station

You're Nicked My Son

and it was its main priority to attend the call as quickly as possible. I loved it; real boys' own stuff and I knew it was for me. It was what I had always wanted to do and set my plan out to get myself an RT advanced driving, course as it was called then.

My lasting memory from my first set of night duty was the infamous Hammersmith Palais. The Palais was at this time a very busy place most nights of the week. It was a great source of entertainment on night duty, especially on Thursday, which was famously known as grab-a-granny night and, my God, did we see some sights! My first experience of trouble at the club was the Thursday night of that first week. We were sitting outside watching the crowd preparing to leave about 2.00 a.m. and suddenly a female came across and told us there was a huge fight going on around the dance floor.

I stepped in through the foyer with three other officers and entered World War Three. There were two rival gangs stood at each end of the dance floor. Pint glasses were being hurled at each other like hand grenades. As soon as there was a lull they would charge each other and fight it out hand to hand. We just withdrew to the safety of the foyer and waited for them to tire themselves out and then, with half the Met from central and west London having arrived, we just went in and arrested them en masse. It was like the Wild West and I thought that nights were obviously going to be interesting here. I was certainly not wrong about that.

That very same set of night duty towards the end of the week I was passenger in a vehicle travelling from Shepherds Bush nick, having just dropped someone off there. It was about 2.00 a.m. and as we drove down Shepherds Bush Road I noticed a bit of a fight at the junction with Blythe Road. As we stopped one of the men bolted across the road and my driver was out of his door and after him like a whippet. I got out and started to make my way towards two other males. As I did so one of them pointed something at me and I realised it was a rifle of some sort. Suddenly, there was a little pop and something flew past me and the man with the gun had turned and was off, running like hell, as did the second male who for some reason tried to run past me. I tackled him to the floor and detained him, but this allowed the man with the rifle to get away and he was never found.

Well help arrived; the man I had caught hold of was arrested after I found a stash of drugs on him and I then went to help search for the first male who had ran off. My driver was convinced he had the man trapped in the road. He had to be either in a house or hiding as he could have not made it to the end of the street.

He had been waiting for a dog van but they were all tied up at an incident elsewhere. So we started to search one side of the street each. About halfway down the row of houses I could not get the front gate to the house open. The other side of the gate was in complete darkness and as usual I did not have my torch with me. I decided to jump over the wall of the house next door so I could check to see that the suspect had not gained entry to the house. As I landed in the garden I landed right on top of the suspect who was hiding against the wall in complete darkness. I grabbed him and called for my driver; as I did the suspect decided he wanted to fight and, as usual, he was bigger then me. We traded punches until a few seconds later my driver arrived and jumped in as well. There were dustbins and bottles going all over the place but in the end it took four of us to control and arrest him.

A couple of hours later in a garden a few door away a police dog recovered an imitation firearm that had obviously been dropped by our suspect. The interesting thing about this guy was he was Irish and when we made some checks he was of some interest to Special Branch. That was the last I saw of him. My assumption is that he had some sort of IRA connection and I was never able to find out what happened to him. At the end of my first ever week of night duty I did not know what day of the week it was, but I had enjoyed it, despite being shot at. I knew then I had made the right decision to transfer.

Shortly after starting at Hammersmith I went to Hendon for a check test for my driving. After a day of tests I was authorised to drive vehicles up to a transit van standard. While there I saw an advanced driving course practising on the skid pan and again my desire to become an advanced driver came to my mind and made me more determined to get an advanced course. This proved harder than I expected. However, I then got my first posting as van driver. Two things happened on that month's posting that I will never forget.

THE FIRST WAS ON 20ST July. I had been dispatched to deliver a couple of officers to New Scotland Yard in the van. Having dropped them off, I made my way back from via Knightsbridge and then through Kensington. As I was driving along Kensington High Street, there was an almighty noise. The side of the van seemed to be sucked inwards and my ears popped like they do on an aeroplane. I did not have a clue what had happened. Suddenly, all hell let loose on the main set radio and I then realised a bomb had gone off in Hyde Park. I was less than a mile away and was in the process of turning around to go there when I was called on my personal radio and told to get back urgently to Hammersmith. I did so and was then engaged in running every available officer around to various parts of Hammersmith, designated as potential places for attacks by the IRA. I suddenly realised I had come fairly close to being at or near the scene of the bomb. Several minutes previous to the blast going off, I had driven within 100 yards of the scene.

When I saw the news coverage of the incident I realised how lucky I had been that day. A few minutes earlier I had driven right past the scene of devastation where a car bomb had detonated killing eight members of the Household Cavalry and seven of their horses. This was to be a truly horrendous day because less than two hours later a bomb was detonated at the bandstand in Regents Park where the band of the Royal Green Jackets were playing to 120 spectators. Six soldiers were killed in this attack and twenty-four other people seriously injured. The Met's response to major incidents was and still is absolutely astounding, and it made me realise that I was part of an amazing police force where the possibilities were endless as far as my career was concerned.

I was to be involved in several major incidents at times during the rest of my service and knew that no other police force in the world were capable of doing the big things as well as the Met.

THE SUNDAY NIGHT DUTY OF that week was also a time which amazed me. At this particular time in the Met's history, manpower was very low and officers were working all hours of the day and night. Overtime was unlimited. Unknown to me there was a little ritual that took place on Sunday night into Monday morning, which was a stress release after the week of nights. It was totally against all the rules and regulations and at first I was shocked by it. I did however quickly realise it was very necessary.

At about 1.00 am I was called back to the station. I reversed into the yard as usual and when I got to the back a couple of lads came out carrying a barrel of beer. Everybody climbed into the van and I was directed to the rear of Wormwood Scrubs prison and onto the scrubs itself. There I was greeted by the sight of a barbecue, and officers from Notting Hill, Hammersmith and Shepherds Bush basically having food and a drink.

I was absolutely amazed. I was not sure what the hell to do. The rear doors of my van were opened. The barrel was pulled to the edge and then tapped. The most amazing thing of all was an area car (a Rover SD1) with the hatchback up. This was supported by two pieces of wood and attached to the parcel shelf were three pub optics. each with a bottle of spirits attached.

I soon learnt that this was a regular occurrence in summer to aid stress after a hard week of nights. Officers from each station took it in turns not to join in and they were responsible for dealing with any calls that might come in during the night. It took some getting used to but I soon found myself following suit. Although this was completely out of order and just would never happen now, I can honestly say that at the time, with the chronic manpower shortages and with the amount of work that officers had to put up with, this without a doubt prevented many officers from going mad under stress.

My first transvestite!

Towards the end of 1982, Flying Squad officers attended an address in Paddington, West London to arrest a man who was to become infamous for a while, His name was David Martin, and he was wanted for numerous serious offences including armed robbery. When officers tried to arrest him he produced a gun and one officer got shot in the neck. Martin escaped and this triggered off a massive manhunt throughout the MET. It also brought about the infamous shooting of Stephen Waldorf in January 1983. He was shot about eight times in a mini car on the Cromwell Road, near Earls Court. He had been mistaken for MARTIN and was travelling in the car with a female believed to be Martins girlfriend and although it is still strongly believed that Waldorf was in collaboration with Martin and had dressed to look like him, he was lucky to survive with his life.

Waldorf survived the shooting and the two officers who had shot him stood trial but were cleared of all charges. Mr Waldorf subsequently received £150,000 compensation. The wanted man Martin was arrested about a month later. He was spotted and chased down into a tube station where he jumped down onto the tracks and made off into a tunnel. After the power was switched off officers eventually arrested him in the tunnel after a bit of a struggle. He was eventually sent to prison but hung himself in his cell before he stood trial.

A funny story came out of this one night duty, during the height of the manhunt for Martin. In the early hours of the morning, a chase came up on the main set radio; it was coming from central London towards Hammersmith on the A4. Officers believed that the driver of the vehicle was David Martin. I was observer in Foxtrot 2 our area car.

We joined the chase from Hammersmith Broadway and it went down Fulham Palace Road. Also in the chasing convoy were armed officers from the Diplomatic Protection Group.

The chase suddenly came to a stop just short of Putney Bridge and a bit of a stand-off took place. The driver of the vehicle refused to get out of the car and negotiations continued for quite a while. The driver was dressed as a woman and bore a striking resemblance to Martin who was well-known for dressing as a woman as a means of disguise. The driver at one point jumped in the back seat of the car so he was well out of sight and refused to do anything he was told to do. However, after quite some time he gave himself up and was arrested and taken to Fulham police station.

There it was discovered he was not David Martin, but he refused flatly to give any details of himself. This chap was all dressed up to the nines and even had stockings and suspenders on. While he was being booked, his identity was discovered when a senior CID officer came into the charge room. The man was recognised by the senior officer as someone he'd had dealings with at the Old Bailey central criminal court. The surprise was that he had not had dealings with him as a prisoner, but the man had in fact been the prosecuting barrister for the crown in one of the officer's cases. No wonder he did not want to stop for police or give his details; here he was dressed up as a woman. How embarrassing. Attempts were made to keep the matter quiet, that failed and it made it onto the pages of several police magazines as well as some of the daily papers…

THE FOOTBALL YOB

THE LOCAL COURT FOR HAMMERSMITH was a very old court known as west London magistrates situated in Vernon Street. The court was renowned for being strict, especially on football hooligans. The court had two old-style stipendiary magistrates who were excellent, Mr Cook and Mr Crowther. They sat on their own in court and were very swift in dealing with cases and gave yobs and career criminals a very hard time.

One Monday morning I was sitting in Mr. Crowther's court waiting for my case to be called on. As usual, the overnight custody cases were dealt with first. They were the usual round of beggars, drunks, etc, followed by several for offences that had occurred at a Chelsea football match on the Saturday. Suddenly, up in the dock was a thick Chelsea skinhead. He was standing there looking hard and waving to some friends who were at the back of the court. He had a big smile on his face as the court officer read out the facts of the case.

The arresting officer gave his evidence: he had seen the youth throw a full beer can at visiting supporters. It had hit one of them and cut his head and the youth was arrested. He was kept in custody, as there was a warrant for him for a similar offence for which he had failed to turn up at court for. He was found guilty and was sentenced to six months in prison. The youth mumbled something that Mr Crowther did not quite hear.

He said to the court officer stood in the dock next to the youth, 'Officer, did you hear what the defendant just said?'

The officer said, 'Yes sir, I did; he said six months? Is that all, you wanker? I can do that standing on my head.'

Andy Vick

The youth looked horrified and screamed 'No, I didn't.'

Mr Crowther looked at him over his glasses and said, 'Young man, if you can do six months standing on your head, then I will give you another six months for contempt of court just to get you standing back on your feet. Officers, take him away.'

The youth just collapsed in a heap and bawled his eyes out; he had to be carried out of court. It was great to see justice in action.

Another lucky escape

One summer night in 1982, I was out driving an unmarked police car around the back streets of Askew Road, Shepherds Bush, just having a quite nose around. With me was a new probationer, Peter Kirkham. Peter was a very keen officer and we were hoping to pick up a burglar or stolen car.

As it was quite warm we had the windows open and Peter said, 'Can you smell burning?'

It was getting stronger and we drove around and suddenly saw smoke pouring out of the front living room window of a terraced house in Askew Road. We called for the fire brigade and more officers and ran to the door and started banging on it and trying to kick it in.

Suddenly, a male and a female came out of the front. They were gasping for air and told us there were two people upstairs and the house was alight right through the ground floor. They were asleep on the ground floor and had been woken by our knocking and banging on the front door. There was no way in through the front as the fire was so intense.

Peter and I went through the next-door house and into the back garden to see if there was any way to get access from there. The back had a huge set of aluminium-framed patio doors and all you could see through them was flames. I peered through and then moved towards the back door, and as I did so there was this huge explosion and blast of hot air. Peter and I ended up being blown back over the fence into the neighbour's garden. When we looked, the whole of the patio window had been blown out and was lying in bits in the garden. Fifteen seconds before, we had been standing by that window. How lucky were we?

We looked at each other as several firemen came out from the neighbour's house and looked at us as if we were mad. They helped us out to the front of the house and when we saw the state of the house from the front, I realised that if I had gone into the house from the rear I would most likely not have got back out again.

The fire was so intense, that firemen were unable to get in and rescue the two other people inside. Their bodies were not recovered until the next morning. I was a bit charred and stinking of smoke but suffered no injury at all, nether did Peter. The smell stayed with us for days but I realised we had a very lucky escape that morning.

The fire had started as a result of a cigarette not being put out completely. It had then fallen down the back of a settee in the living room, smouldered away and then caught fire. It was a very tragic accident.

Definitely the wrong move

I decided after about a year at Hammersmith that I needed to do something about buying my own house. I was living in married accommodation in Shepperton in a very nice house and I wanted to be in with a chance of buying it. However, my financial situation was not very good. I had become aware of a specialist department in the Met that looked after all the embassies and the embassy staff of foreign countries who were present in this country. I had been told that it was a fantastic money-earner and that also after six months' probation I would get an advanced driving course. That sold it for me and I applied. I sat a board for the job and I was accepted on the proviso that I passed a firearms course. This was another new matter for me. I had never fired a real gun before and found the thought quite daunting. Nevertheless, in July 1983 I found myself at Lippetts Hill, the Met's firearms training camp for a two-week course.

I really enjoyed the course and passed as a marksman. I then transferred to the Diplomatic Protection Group and was based at Kensington. Now, I have to say at this point that this was, without a doubt, the worse career move I made in my entire thirty years. You were expected to forget about being a police officer. Your only concern was to stand outside the embassy you were posted to, and do nothing else.

You did two hours on and two off, then another two on and two off. Sometimes you got two hours in one of the cars or vans if you were lucky. What you were not meant to do was anything like police work, because if you did, it meant that someone who was on their two hours off had to cover your post and that just caused trouble. It was like working for a bunch of old grannies. If someone did not get their full two hours off it really ruined their day and you were not allowed to forget it for days.

I CAN HONESTLY SAY I hated the first six months. I did my usual thing of challenging things I did not think were right. For instance, I was with another officer nicknamed Mary as he was such a moaner; he was driving and refused to stop to help a local officer who was fighting with a suspect.

'We must not get involved; you have a gun,' he said.

'Bollocks,' I said, and jumped out of the car and ran to help, just as the suspect tried to drop a breeze block on the head of the officer. By the time I got back to the base the driver had reported me to the sergeant and the duty officer. He then tore me up.

'If you want to do police work, go back to relief,' was his advice.

Things like this happened all the time I hated it. However, the money was fantastic. I could work as many rest days that I wanted, too. I also enjoyed the firearms training we used to do as well as learning all about explosives and bombs; this kept me going and eventually my six months' probation ended. I was not sure if they would keep me after all the problems I caused by refusing not to get involved with police work. How can you not deal with something if it happens in front of you, which it frequently did?

One incident that nearly did cost me my job there occurred one morning when I was standing covering the Russian visa section on the Bayswater Road. About 100 yards up the road from me was a double zebra crossing. It was just out of my sight but it was to my knowledge a very busy crossing. A taxi driver pulled up and reported a bad accident on the crossing. A driver on the wrong side of the road had hit a woman on the crossing and had crashed the car into a wall. I called up on my radio and reported the accident and offered to go and take a look until the local officers arrived. I was told I was not to go.

Several minutes later, another driver stopped and told me things looked serious and that members of the public were now fighting with the driver of the car. I again called up but was told to stay where I was. However, things got the better of me and I ran up there.

There was a young woman lying on the crossing with a massive hole in her head. Several members of the public were trying to hold down

You're Nicked My Son

the driver who had tried to run away. I helped them and handcuffed the man to a road sign and a couple of men remained with him. I went to the young woman. As I did so the first local officer finally arrived and I told him to deal with the driver. I knew the woman was in a very bad way and did what I could to help her. Without thinking, I took off my tunic to fold up and gently place under her head to protect the large hole in her skull from getting dirt from the road into the injury. I gave no thought about having a gun on my waist and as far as I was aware, no members of the public seemed bothered. In this area most people were fully aware that officers from the DPG all carried guns and it was no big deal to them.

As the ambulance arrived and started treating her, a local inspector arrived on scene and launched into me for having my gun on show; I tried to explain but he was having none of it. He reported me to my duty officer and I was in trouble again for leaving my post outside the embassy and for having my gun on show to the public.

BY NOW, I REALLY DID not give a damn. I was fed up with being a security guard and with the exception of a few people on my relief, I was working with the biggest bunch of tossers I had ever met. They would never be the good 'old bill' as long as they had holes in their backsides. I was ready to fight them on this one even if it meant I lost my chance of an advanced driving course.

So the next day I was up in front of the chief superintendent. He ripped me up hill and down dale and told me I was finished on the DPG. Amazingly, I kept calm.

Where I got the next sentence from, I will never know but I suddenly said to him: 'Sir, when I joined the police, I swore an oath to protect life and property. In my book the protection of life is way ahead in priority against property, especially that of another country. As far as I am concerned I have done right and I may have just helped to save that girl's life. I do not care what you or the Metropolitan police think: I know I did the right thing. I am more than happy to leave the DPG if that is your decision. Thank you, sir.'

I then just walked out.

I was then office-bound while they sorted out where I was going to be moved to. However, three days later I was called into the chief inspector's office. He told me they had decided to let me stay on the DPG. I told him I did not want to stay and it was then that he told me that they had received a letter from a surgeon at St Mary's Hospital in Paddington, thanking me for my prompt actions with the lady in the accident. It also said that it was highly likely that had I not done what I had for her, she would more than likely have died. They had no choice but to change their minds about moving me. I asked for time to think about what I wanted to do. I eventually decided to stay for the money and, hopefully, my advanced driving course. As an aside to the incident, it also turned out the driver of the car was an escaped prisoner and the car was stolen.

Almost a deadly mistake

After a very short time you get used to having a gun with you; it was very alien to my policing style at first but you just had to treat it as another part of your appointments, just like a truncheon. Although there was the possibility that something might happen, you thought it would never happen to you.

One of the static embassy posts I actually enjoyed doing was the Royal Jordanian in Upper Phillimore Gardens, just off Kensington High Street. This was a very nice road with massive houses, and people such as the Rothschild's banking family lived there. All the houses seemed to have maids and butlers and they used to keep the officer on duty supplied with tea and cakes – all very pleasant.

During the summer of 1983 the house directly opposite the embassy was undergoing a massive refurbishment and was always full of workmen. There were always piles of bricks and equipment in the front garden; this was an excellent place to stand out of view. At the time there was a very high threat to the Jordanians due to things happening in the world and the premises was a likely terrorist target.

One late turn in July 1983, I was standing in the garden of the house under renovation. I knew that there was shortly likely to be members of the embassy arriving because of the activity around the front door. The premises were fairly easy to control as it was a one-way street and you could see vehicles approaching from the right for quite a distance. I saw a green Volvo, which I knew was an embassy car, come around the corner into view. A black Bentley that came from premises next to the embassy closely followed this. Immediately behind that was a Granada estate at speed, full of people, and also a motorcycle. The rider was dressed head-to-toe in black leathers and black full-faced crash helmet. I could see he had something large and pointed under the front of his leathers. I immediately thought *Oh shit, this is it: the embassy car is about to be hit.*

The embassy car obviously thought the same. It screeched to a halt directly outside the main door and at least three people jumped out of the car and dived into the embassy. I quickly put up a call for assistance and drew my gun. I was behind a pile of breeze blocks in the front garden. The black Bentley was not able to get past the abandoned Volvo. The Granada screeched to a halt and about six males were running towards the Volvo and Bentley. The motorbike flew past and stopped sharply.

I had already made up my mind that the large item under his leathers was a gun and I thought by the size of it that it was most likely a machine gun. I knew I would have had no chance against it and decided that as soon as I could see the gun, I was going to shoot the motorcyclist straight away. I was banking on the fact that my little wall of breeze blocks had given me enough cover and I would surprise him.

It was me that got the surprise; I concentrated on the motorcyclist as he ran towards the cars, undoing his leathers. I took aim at his chest and thought to myself, *you have got to hit him with your first two shots.* Suddenly, in his hands was a camera with a large round lens on it. That really threw me into confusion. I turned to look at the men who had got out of the Granada and realised they all had cameras too. What the hell was going on? Well, instead of going near the embassy car they all flocked around the Bentley. By now the troops had started arriving and very quickly all was brought under control.

I suddenly realised I was in a bath of sweat. What the hell had happened? I was convinced the embassy car was about to be attacked; the embassy staff obviously had thought the same. Well, after a short while all became clear and I was so glad I had not fired any shots.

The house to the left of the embassy as you look at it was a very large house which was rented out at an extortionate cost per month. The likes of Mick Jagger and Paul Hogan had rented it in the period of time I had been working on the DPG. The current people renting it were Portuguese. The head of the family was, unknown to us, a very prominent figure in the country and was leader of the main union in

Portugal. He had left the country with what was believed to be millions of pounds-worth of union money. He believed he was in danger of being kidnapped as a result of this. He had just been back to Portugal in an attempt to sort things out with the government. He apparently was claiming the money was all his and did not belong to the government. Unknown to him he had been followed from Portugal by a hard-core band of journalist determined to track him down for the unions.

They had done so and been met at Heathrow by photographers and had followed him from the airport. Their intentions were to find where he was living and to expose him there. They were not aware of how close some of them came to being shot. I realised then how close I had come to actually shooting someone by mistake. It did get me noticed by the embassy staff though. They looked after me really well every time I did duty at their post after that event.

Advanced course here I come

Towards the end of January 1984, I finally got on my advanced driving course. This was to be one of the best six weeks of my service. I loved every minute of the course. After passing a written exam on road craft, the course began. My instructor was a lovely man called Roger. Once we had settled into the course we spent most days driving around the country at great speed learning the skills of high-speed driving. I absolutely loved it and was totally in my element.

We used to go out on long runs where we travelled with another course car and were away from the driving school all day. The instructors on the advanced wing all carried Home Office dispensation cards. These cards gave authority for them to take us on high- speed training runs. As soon as we hit any de-restriction signs off we went.

Each car had three students and the instructor. When you were driving he would be constantly pushing you harder and harder into bends and overtakes to improve your skills and vision. Each drive lasted about forty minutes and all the time you were driving you would be giving a running commentary to show how much you were actually taking in and considering dangers, etc, as you sped along. That was the hardest thing to learn and probably the best aid to high-speed driving as it really concentrates your mind. We had some very hairy times during the course and you always knew when it was getting a bit tight when the smoke from Roger's pipe would start coming out in large puffs.

One day I was driving on the first leg of the drive towards RAF Lakenheath where we would be stopping for lunch. I was driving a Rover SD1 and the following car was a Ford Granada. Having cleared London and entered to Hertfordshire countryside we had begun my fast drive and I had started my commentary. In country lanes, a trick taught is to watch the tops of the hedges or the line of telegraph poles to give you a good idea where the road goes ahead of you when you have no vision. As we hurtled down this country lane I was looking ahead for my vision and it looked for the entire world that it all just went straight on. I was aware however that there was some serious smoke coming out of Rogers's pipe and I knew he was getting worried about something.

Suddenly, I realised that what I thought was the road going straight on was in fact a track and the road itself went left and turned back on itself. I knew I could not brake because, at the speed we were going, we would have just overturned in the bend. I decided the best thing to do was try to power around. I keep the speed on and we literally crabbed around the bend and clattered along with my side very close to going down the ditch.

I looked at Roger and he was still puffing on his pipe and nearly crying with laughter. I was mad and said, 'You could have given me a little warning.'

He could not speak but pointed over my shoulder, I looked just in time to see the Granada travelling behind us about to land about sixty feet inside a farmer's field. They had not spotted the turn and had gone straight through a farmers wooden gate and taken off over a small hump and landed undamaged in the field. Their speed had meant they landed so far in the field the farmer had to tow them out with his tractor. He was fine about it, as it seemed it was a regular occurrence – so much so that he did not bother replacing the gate after our follow car had been through it. We all laughed about it afterwards but, my god, it scared the living daylights out of me at the time.

There were numerous times through the course things got a bit hair-raising, and I know this may sound stupid, but it just added to the enjoyment of the course. We went through the skid pan training and onto lorries and coaches and everything was going well. In the latter part of the course we moved onto learning the art of 'bandit-chasing'; this was the method of safely chasing a vehicle to a correct conclusion. The instructors played the bandit cars and they made it as real as possible for us to really test our driving skills.

Then on 1st March 1984 came the moment we were all dreading, the day we sat our final drives. We would be going out for about an hour each with the chief instructor.

The test consisted of about half an hour of high-speed driving and safe driving following his instructions. The second half of the test was the bandit chase. The intention of this part was for you to try to force the bandit car into a position where he had no choice but to give up. This did not happen very often.

We all pulled straws to see which order we went off in. I pulled the shortest and was delighted because it meant I was due out first, and I would not have to sit around getting nervous. It was also St David's day and, being Welsh, I thought the gods were on my side.

I went out to the car at 9.00 a.m. and got in to carry out all my pre drive checks. The car for my final drive was a Ford Granada. I adjusted everything to my liking and waited for the chief instructor. I waited and waited, and forty minutes later I had adjusted everything a thousand times and was a bag of nerves. He apologised and said he had been dealing with an urgent matter. He then told me what he expected from me and off we went. At the driving school gates we turned left and he told me to turn right at the roundabout. I went to indicate and switched on the windscreen wipers instead. At the next roundabout I did exactly the same and I just fell apart as I knew I was in trouble here.

The next half hour was a blur; I did not have a clue what I was doing. Then suddenly I heard the chief instructor start to give me details of a vehicle, and I knew my bandit test was coming up very shortly. Then in front of me was a Ford Capri, identified to me as the bandit car. I switched on the blue lights and two tones and off I went, launching into my chase commentary. The chase had only seemed to go about five minutes through the Hertfordshire countryside when I saw the bandit swing left onto a small village green area (it had in fact been about twenty minutes).

The green formed a triangle off the main road and it suddenly hit me that we had been here before practising. On that occasion the bandit had used the triangle to get behind the driver of the pursuit car and actually chase him. I realised that if I stayed on the main road I only had to move forward or backwards to cover each exit back onto the road. It was only about 20 yards to each exit and I covered them both very easily.

The bandit had obviously expected me to follow him into the triangle and I am sure his intention was to end up behind me so he was actually chasing me. I stood my ground just mirroring his actions. After several moves back and forth the driver (another instructor) got out and waved. The chief instructor then told me this part of the test was complete and he then instructed me to drive to the police sports ground at Bushey where the next person was waiting to take over for his test.

I was absolutely distraught; I knew I had driven badly and that I had more than likely failed. The pass at the time was set in two standards. Eighty per cent plus was a class 1 pass, 70 per cent to 79 per cent a class 2 pass. Anything less was a failure. I was certain I had failed and did not think I had done enough to even get a retest. It looked to me that I would have to try to get another course. I then had to wait all day for everyone else on the course to complete their drives. At 4.00 p.m. we all ended up back at the driving school and one by one we were called into the chief instructor's office for our result. Roger, my instructor, was there looking very worried. I feared the worst.

The chief instructor said: 'PC Vick I am not really sure where to start. Just before I came to the car, your instructor told me to sit back and enjoy the ride as you had not had any problems all through the course and that you were on course for being awarded top student. I know I was late and you had got nervous but after about five minutes I very nearly called a stop to your test. You were bloody awful. I even checked your shoulder number to make sure I had the right person in the car. I decided to give you a little longer as I had been the one to get you all nervous and you did pick up. I was still debating about stopping the test and bringing you back to do it again next week when we came across the bandit. Suddenly, it was like I had a different driver in the car and I congratulate you on an excellent chase and for forcing the driver to give up. You saved yourself with that last drive and I realised the first half of the test was just purely nerves on your behalf.

'I am going to give you a choice. You are well capable of getting a very high-grade class 1 pass. On your overall performance I can only give you a high-class 2 pass.

'Your choice is that if you wish you can come back on Monday for a retest and try for a one or you can leave today with a pass of a class 2 advanced.'

I was totally amazed and I could have quite easily leaned over and kissed him. I could not bear the thought of going through it again and accepted the class 2 pass. Thank God. I had finally reached my main ambition. I was now an advanced driver in the Metropolitan Police.

In December that year, I returned to the driving school for a check test prior to returning to a division and actually driving an area car as part of a relief. At that check test I obtained a pass as a class 1.

Terrorism

I mentioned earlier in this book how close I had come to being caught up in the Hyde Park bombing. Joining the DPG had been a real eye-opener for me in respect of the various terrorist groups that affected this country. During my induction course into the DPG, I had learnt a lot about terrorism and had been fascinated by a lecturer from PC Trevor Lock. He was the officer on the door at the Iranian embassy siege in 1980 and he gave us his side of the story. We were also shown confidential videos taken of the siege that were quite shocking at the time. None of us at the time believed anything like that was ever likely to happen again. We trained hard for it but hoped it would never happen.

Then in April 1984 we were hit again by terrorism. Over the Easter period, I was to be posted as driver of Ranger 500. This was a transit mini-bus that contained four officers and a sergeant. Our role was that of an initial armed response to any armed incident in central London and certain other sites outside the Met area. This was a two-week posting made up of an officer from each of the four DPG bases plus a sergeant.

I loved this posting; it was like real police work again. The blokes on the department who had forgotten how to be real PCs did not want to do it, and I used to regularly take their places.

On 17 April a demonstration in St James's Square went horribly wrong for the Met. The target of the demonstration was the Libyan Embassy. Suddenly automatic gunfire was heard and people dived for cover. In the large bursts of gunfire WPC Yvonne Fletcher was hit by a high-velocity round. It came from a machine gun. The bullet spiralled through her causing a fatal injury. Ten other people were injured by the automatic gunfire that came from an upper floor window of the embassy.

All hell let loose and all available DPG officers arrived within minutes and after only a very short space of time the square was sealed off and the Libyan siege commenced. A command post was later set up in a bank at the corner of St James's Square and Charles II Street. I later found myself on a roof at the rear of the embassy with other officers, guns drawn, in order to cut off a possible escape from the rear from the embassy. Everyone learnt that Yvonne Fletcher had died from her injuries and the sense of loss spread across the square.

I was on this roof for hours. Eventually, a relieving system was put in place and I was relieved for an hour to get some food and drink from the command post. I stood in Charles II Street, just around the corner from the embassy. As I stood there, drinking my tea, I was suddenly aware of WPC Fletcher's police hat lying in the middle of the square where she had fallen. The urge to retrieve it was unbearable. I was told that several officers had tried to do so but had been warned off by senior officers due to the danger. It remained there for a very long time into the siege. I returned to my post on the roof. It was now dark and I was there with another DPG officer and also a D11 officer.

This was the force firearms unit now known as SO19. The D11 officer had a rifle and I felt somewhat safer with him there as I did not think our model 10 revolvers would be any match for what the Libyans obviously had inside the building. I remember lying on the roof thinking to myself *what the hell are you doing here? You are absolutely mad. You are in the middle of a full-blown terrorist incident expected to stop heavily armed terrorists from leaving a building and all you have is a little revolver.* But on the other hand I was completely in awe of the way the Met had responded to the incident. It all went like clockwork and everything seemed like we knew exactly what we were all doing. All the training had worked and here I was taking on these terrorists who had killed one of our own. I do not mind admitting I was initially terrified.

As THE DAYS WENT BY we got into a routine. If I remember correctly, there were eight armed posts to cover. On each post were two DPG and two D11 officers. The main post was at a set of doors to the bank that allowed you with the use of cameras to see the front door of the embassy. The whole square was surrounded and cut off by armed police and the negotiating had commenced.

Now, I have to say at the time D11 was a source of humour to us on DPG, who came into contact with them more than the normal uniformed officer might. The source of amusement was certain officers on D11; they were real cowboys, and behaved like they were something out of the SAS. It became obvious very quickly who was ex-armed forces and who was just a gun nut. If you went on post and you were posted with a cowboy, he would spent all his time polishing his guns, putting the rifle or machine gun up to his eyes and making shooting noises with it. They could not settle and leave them alone. Some had weapons vests on and carried so much equipment, knives, stun grenades and spare magazines they could hardly stand up.

On the other hand, there were the ex-army guys who as soon as you were on post with them would instruct you how to fire all their weapons.

They used to say, 'If we get shot, you might as well know how to use the big guns to fire back with.'

The jokes used to fly around the canteen that had been set up in the bank, and it did get a bit touchy at times. On one occasion there were several D11 boys in having a drink. They were all wearing the equipment vests overflowing with gear. One of the DPG lads who was a bit of a comedian thought he would have a laugh and went up to the plastic cutlery grabbed a handful and went out of the room.

He came back in carrying a sweeping brush like a rifle and with plastic knives, forks and spoons coming out of every possible space of his tunic. He came in singing some song he had made up about D11 and their equipment. It was meant as a little light relief and people fell about laughing, including some D11 officers (ex-army ones, anyway). However, the cowboys took exception and one of them lost it and went for the comedian, and had to be pulled off him. Tempers were getting a little frayed at this point and instructions were issued by senior officers to calm things down.

Also around the building, there were some very unusual-looking men. I first saw them coming over roofs at the rear. They were examining the roof and chimneys of the embassy. They did everything so quietly it was eerie. I realised these were SAS men and they looked as hard as nails. I was very glad they were on my side. I wondered what the hell was going to happen next.

Eventually, after days and days of negotiating the people in the embassy were going to come out. I was posted with a lot of DPG and D11 officers in Duke of York Street behind large blue screens. Our job was to receive the Libyans as they came out six at a time, and turned from the square to behind the screens. We were only allowed to give then a quick search for firearms and then lead them onto a bus to be taken away. This was so hard.

We were instructed not to upset them in anyway. I for one was livid and just wanted to punch every one I came in contact with. They were all smug and smiling. I just could not believe we were letting them go; it made me so angry and was just hoping one of them would do something that would give me the chance to respond with some gratuitous violence towards him.

The atmosphere after was one of sheer disbelief. They had been allowed to leave as easy as if they were just leaving to go on a day trip. What on earth was going on? The Home Secretary let us down very badly on this one. It was a two-week period in my career that caused me great concern. I did not know WPC Fletcher, but she was one of us. How on earth could we let everyone from the embassy walk away without someone being arrested for her murder? It is something that is still being debated to this day.

It was not long after this event that I decided I wanted to go back to normal policing. I felt as if I was just a complete and utter waste of time doing the job, or rather not being allowed to do it. Due to circumstances at home, and other things that were occurring in my life at the time, I just wanted to get back to what I did best: uniformed policing. However, my request to return to division was met with a complete no-chance as the DPG was short of men as it was.

However, I was experiencing some domestic problems at the time and after a fight I was allowed to transfer. But they had the last laugh and instead of letting me go to a division where I could use my advanced driving skills they posted me to Heathrow Airport, which did not have an area car for me to drive. Despite a fight, I lost and went to Heathrow in June 1984.

Oh no, not Heathrow

This was a particular hard time for me. By choice, I had separated from my wife and I had returned her to Wales with my two-and-a-half-year-old daughter. The split was my decision and I missed my daughter an awful lot. I used to go back to Wales on my days off and see my wife and daughter but I knew there was no way I wanted us to get back together and just threw myself into my new posting.

Heathrow Airport is a very strange place to work and I did not want to be there. There was lots of crime, and if you liked aeroplanes and pretty air stewardess it was great. But you did come into contact with some very unusual people, and I was not happy there at all. At the time Heathrow was a division with Staines and West Drayton. They were normal nicks, but I was on the normal duty side of the airport. There was also an armed security section that I was told I would have to go onto after about a month of getting to know the airport.

A week or so after being there, I was called to a male causing a disturbance at a South African Airways check-in desk. As I arrived, this very large black man was ranting and raving; he suddenly charged and tried to get through a crowd of people checking in.

I managed to catch hold of him and when he looked at me I saw the look in his eyes that all police officers dread, the look of a complete and utter madman. Suddenly, I was involved in a massive punch-up. It was a bit one-sided really, he was throwing me about like a rag doll and when I felt the most horrible pain in my right shoulder I knew I was in trouble.

My police radio had come off my belt clip and was dangling off my tunic just by the handset lead. As he came at me screaming again,

I swung at him with the business end of the radio and hit him straight on the forehead and down he went. I jumped on top of him just as help arrived in the figure of a little WPC. As the man tried to turn sideways to lift me off his back, she kicked him straight between the legs and he went flat again. More troops arrived and he was nicked.

It turned out he was an African male who had lived in this country for some time. He had lost his marbles and decided he was going to go home. That was, without paying for a ticket or without a passport. I ended up off work with torn ligaments in my shoulder and he ended up in a mental hospital, which is where I knew I would end up if I had to stay at Heathrow. I moved onto the security section shortly after returning to work. It meant looking after high-risk flights such as El-Al and Air Lingus. We used to carry out exercises on aeroplanes and deal with aircraft emergencies, so it was quite busy. However, I can honestly say that the best day's work I had there was the day I was tasked to look after a VIP.

Coming to the airport to fly out on Concorde was Maurice Gibb of the Bee Gees. Someone had made a threat on his life that had been taken seriously. Another officer and I were tasked to keep him safe while he was at the airport. There was, however, bad weather that day that was causing havoc with flights, and as a result we spent about six hours with Mr Gibb. The vast majority of that time was spent in the Concorde VIP lounge where he entertained us with food and drink while we waited. It was the easiest work I had ever done and very enjoyable. We eventually escorted him to the plane and on the way there he took my details and promised me tickets to the next show they did in London.

He kept his promise some months later. He was a very nice man; down to earth and not what you expect stars to be like. I was to meet a few over the rest of my service, but he without a doubt was the best of them.

HEATHROW IS MASSIVE AND TO drive airside you had to take a special driving course and learn how to cross live runways, etc. The hardest thing was at night; it was very easy in the dark to get disorientated when airside at night. I never really mastered the art and would always have to get the tower to light up a route with green lights to get me back to civilisation.

Political incident

I did find it extremely difficult to settle in at Heathrow; the people I was working with were great but I just did not want to be there. All I wanted was to move to a station with an area car so I could go and use my advanced driving ticket to its best use. I put in several requests to move to West Drayton without success. That all changed, however, after a particular incident.

It was quite common for VIPs to arrive in the country with protection officers who were armed, and it was quite a regular thing to attend a newly arrived flight and take possession of the protection officer's firearms, as they were not allowed to leave the plane with it. The gun would be kept secure at Heathrow police station and then returned to them on the aircraft just prior to flying.

In early December 1984, I went with another officer to meet a Portuguese airline flight that had the Portuguese prime minister on board. He always had armed protection with him and I had made the collection from his protection officer several times before. I went onto the aircraft and spoke with the officer who spoke broken English. He gave me his equipment and I then realised there was a second officer with him who was also armed. I waited for this officer to hand me his gun but he did not do so. When I tried to speak to him he appeared not to understand English. I tried to get the first officer to explain what was required but the second officer, who was slightly older, just kept shaking his head.

When I got a steward to explain in Portuguese exactly what it was I required, again the man just kept shaking his head. He also tried passing me to leave the aircraft but I stopped him from doing so and he got very angry. I contacted my duty inspector on the radio and explained the situation. He told me to let him leave and we would sort it out in the VIP lounge where the prime minister was waiting for his men. I was not happy with this as it was completely against everything we were instructed to do. There were strict regulations in place and I was being told to ignore them.

However, I let him go and followed him to the VIP lounge. There I again had it explained to the man. He still refused and tried pushing passed me. Before I knew it, I had him against the wall face first and his gun out of his holster. I passed it to my partner and as I restrained the protection officer in an arm-lock, I told him he was under arrest for possession of the firearm. This caused quite a stir in the VIP lounge I can tell you. I saw the look on the Portuguese prime minister's face and thought this will be interesting.

I took the man to Heathrow police station in a Land Rover; he was going mad. At the station the custody sergeant listened to the facts and booked him in. The man refused to give us any of his details and was placed in a cell. The sergeant was great and said, 'I think this is going to cause a few problems but as far as I am concerned you have acted correctly.'

I went off to make my arrest notes. About twenty minutes later I heard a tannoy for me to go to see the chief inspector. I went to his office and his face said it all.

He started ranting at me saying, 'You have started a major diplomatic incident; the man you have arrested is the chief inspector in charge of the Portuguese protection squad. This is really going to cause some shit.'

'Well, he should have known better then, sir,' I replied. 'He was totally out of order and should never have been allowed off the plane. I did so under the instruction of the duty officer.'

The chief inspector went off on one again and threw me out and I went back to my notes. A short while later he called me back.

'Look Andy,' he said, 'we need to sort this out quick. Are you prepared to forget the whole incident?'

I was not and told him so.

'What if we come to an agreement?' he said. 'Do you still want a move to West Drayton?' I knew what was coming: I was being bribed to let it all lie for a move out of the airport.

At first I declined; I felt that this could come back to haunt me in the future if I was not careful. He kept on offering me the move. I finally agreed on the understanding I had a letter from the chief inspector himself exonerating me from any blame and an assurance from him that there would be nothing on my personal record. He agreed and he did the letter there and then. Ten minutes later all traces of the Portuguese chief inspector had been erased from the custody records and he was whisked away. I moved to West Drayton a week later. Hooray.

There is, however, a sequel to this story. About two years later, after meeting my wife Paula, I decided to apply to return to the DPG as a way of earning extra money to buy a house. It was a course I did not really want to take but it was the only way I could see of being able to set up a home with Paula when we married. I applied and was given a date for the interview board.

On the day of the interview I arrived at the old Cannon Row Police Station and went into the interview.

The chief superintendent said to me: 'PC Vick, I have to tell you that you do not have a chance in hell of ever coming back to the DPG due to the diplomatic incident you caused while at Heathrow. Your record mentions it but it gives no details. I wanted you to have an interview so I could hear the story from you.'

I was stunned; they had put something on my record after all. It made me so mad. I blew my top at the chief superintendent and ended up throwing my warrant card at him and telling him to stick his job up his arse. I stormed out and it was not until I got to the tube station that I realised I did not have my warrant card (my money was in it) and I needed to get the tube back. I managed to just get on the tube in uniform.

By the time I got back to West Drayton, my chief superintendent was screaming for me. He had been telephoned by the DPG chief superintendent; luckily I had the letter from Heathrow in my locker and took it with me. After a torrid of verbal abuse he calmed down and I told him what had happened. I then showed him the letter and he went mad again, this time at the way I had been treated. He got on the phone

Andy Vick

to the DPG chief superintendent, had a go at him, and demanded my warrant card be returned immediately. My warrant card arrived within the hour by DPG motorcyclist and, as far as I know, the matter was removed from my file (well, the one I know about anyway).

And so to West Drayton

AND SO IT WAS THAT in December 1984 I found myself at West Drayton police station. Big changes were about to occur here as the station was about to leave the airport division of Heathrow and join up with Hayes police station as part of X division. This was to be the start of five years where I was to deal with every aspect of policing you could think of. The policing went right across the spectrum and I was about to start a part of my service I really loved.

Working at West Drayton and Hayes was very much like being back in Gwent; the main difference was that I was now an area car driver with a high-powered Rover SD1 to respond to emergency calls quicker, with the chance of getting in first to make an arrest. It gave me freedom to cover not only a greater part of the Met but also to wander into Thames Valley and Surrey areas and get involved in high-speed pursuits which were something of a very regular occurrence at this time. My time at West Drayton provided me with many great friends who I really enjoyed working with.

One of the very first people I met was PC Ian Chawner. Ian was half-German and half-Scottish and from an army family. Ian could be very abrupt in his manner and a bit of a chauvinist, but you would not find a more faithful or supportive friend who would back you to the hilt and be the first to help you out if you were in any sort of trouble.

We became very close friends and have remained so to this day. How, I do not know, because we have always played some outrageous practical jokes on each other; it is a wonder one of us had not killed the other one.

When I joined the relief, Ian was almost at the end of his two-year probation period. He had however been led astray by a couple of older PCs and Ian's reporting sergeant was not convinced that he was going to be suitable to be confirmed as a PC.

I persuaded the sergeant to give Ian to me for a month's posting on the area car and see what happened. Well, we then spent the next month dealing with everything that came our way and as much as possible, especially on night duty, we would race off to other divisions to help out and also to try and nick their prisoners. During that month we made a lot of arrests and dealt with a huge amount of incidents and Ian really did well; as a result of his hard work he was easily confirmed at the end of his probation

I really enjoyed working at Drayton but we also had time for a bit of fun in winding each other up. This was our way of relaxing and keeping a bit of sanity. Ian, I have to say, was quite often the target for my jokes.

One afternoon I was late turn driving the area car with another great friend, Chris Roberts We returned to the yard at Drayton to grab a quick cup of tea. As we drove in, there was Ian sitting in the station van having a cigarette. As we drove past him, we both got the usual verbal abuse and I decided a wind-up was in order. I tried to look mad and grumpy at Ian, and, thinking he had upset me, he came over to the car and asked what was wrong.

I told him I had just hit something very hard underneath the car and might have caused some serious damage and that. I would have to call out the garage sergeant and was bound to get suspended from driving.

Ian said, 'don't worry we will get it sorted without the garage sergeant.' He then went to the front of the car, got down on all fours and tried looking under the front of the car. As soon as he did so I flicked on the switch which activated the old-style two-tone air horns. All of a sudden, Ian was flying upwards like a cat on all floors with the most terrified look on his face. He landed face first on the floor and started ranting and raving. I had scared him so much he was like a raving lunatic. He started running around the yard yelling and screaming at me.

'You bastard you could have given me a heart attack. I'll kill you,' he said.

I had to lock myself in the car. Chris and I were crying with laughter just watching him. We had to stay locked in the car until he had calmed down and he swore revenge which came later.

This was the start of a friendly war of tricks that we played on each other for years. They were harmless bits of fun that help to keep stress levels down. In this day and age none of this is acceptable in the modern police force that is now so politically correct it has started to work its way up its own backside.

ON ANOTHER PARTICULAR NIGHT DUTY, when it had gone very quiet, we were sitting in the front office having our refreshment break. Ian was looking out of the front office window when he saw something climbing a big tree in the front driveway of the nick. Ian was quite good at spotting different types of animals and was positive he has just seen a rare squirrel climb into the tree. He decided he was going to go outside and see if he could see it.

At that time, surrounding the nick was a twelve-foot wall. Ian managed to climb up this wall which he started walking carefully along, towards the large tree where he had seen the squirrel disappear. He looked so ridiculous in uniform walking along this wall I just could not resist the chance.

I went and got the large crowd control megaphone out of the cupboard and sneaked to the front door with it. Just as Ian reached up and started looking through the branches of the trees, I yelled through the megaphone: 'Get off that bloody wall, you numpty.'

Ian jumped a mile in the air, grabbed a branch of the tree and was left hanging there, about 10 feet in the air. We all had to run outside despite our hysterics and help him down. I really thought I was going to get thumped that time but he was so jumpy he left me alone and did not speak to me for hours, and again vowed revenge.

The revenge came one night when I had taken a night duty off because I was due in court the next day. I stayed that night with my fiancée in her room at the Excelsior hotel where she worked at the time. I woke up the next morning a little late and desperate to get to court in Uxbridge on time for an important case to be committed to crown court, and I needed to spend time with the solicitors to make sure everything was in order.

I had a small 100cc Suzuki motorcycle at the time and I got dressed in all my gear and went down to the rear car park of the hotel where I had left my motorbike. When I got there my bike was missing and I went into a panic. How the hell was I going to get to court on time? I tried ringing the nick but everyone was busy and could not help me. Time was getting on and I thought *I know I will walk over the bridge to the police section house and wake up Ian to borrow his car.*

Well, that's what I did. In a blind panic now, I woke Ian up as he had not long gone to bed off nights. He told me his car was in the garage (a complete lie) but he had a pedal cycle I could borrow. I thought, *Well, I have no choice* and said OK.

How he kept a straight face I will never know. He walked me around to the back of the section house to get his bike and there was my motorcycle. He had come into the hotel during the night with the station van and put my bike in it and driven off with it. I was ranting and he just fell about laughing.

But then it all went wrong. I got on my bike and tried to start it, it just would not go at all. Then I saw Ian's face looking down at the engine. When he had been lifting it into the van he had knocked and snapped off the top of the spark plug and I had no spare for it. I was now in deep trouble and going to be very late. Ian rushed me in his car to court, but I still got slated by the magistrates for being late. Revenge at last for Ian.

Firearms incident

On 1 April 1987 I was at work on a late turn and called was urgently back to West Drayton due to a firearms incident. A woman had attended the station claiming her ex-boyfriend, who had just returned from America, had turned up at her home. He had learned that she had a new man in her life and had called around on the pretext of collecting some of his property that was still there. In reality, he had with him a .38 Magnum revolver that he had smuggled in from the USA and he intended shooting his ex-girlfriend with it.

The male, Eugene Murphy, had appeared quite friendly at first and as they sat in the house the lady was pleased that he seemed to want to stay friends. However his mood changed and suddenly he produced the gun and told her he was going to kill her as if he could not have her no one else could either.

The lady ran to the back of the room and out through the patio doors, as she did so two rounds flew through the glass just missing her and went flying off down the garden.

The lady made it to the safety of a neighbour's house and they watched Murphy drive away in her car after stealing the keys from her handbag. The neighbour took the lady straight to Hayes police station and the four authorised firearms officers on duty, including me, were called straight back to the station.

The matter was being dealt with by CID, with firearms advice from Inspector Colin Wooley from D11 (now SO19) our firearms department. It was decided that local firearms officers would deal with the situation, as D11 were very busy with other matters. Inspector Wooley came out to give us tactical advice.

The stolen car was found at first in the car park of the Adam and Eve public house. Intelligence gained from there showed that Murphy had been drinking heavily and had been openly showing the gun around in the bar stating that it was fully loaded. He had the gun in the waistband of his trousers. Somehow, the vehicle left without being seen before we arrived but was then found at the Wagon and Horses pub on the south side of Uxbridge Road just east of Southall Bridge.

A plan was put together to let Murphy get in the car and drive off. He had to go westbound because of a fenced central reservation and we planned that there would be a car in front with two armed officers and the same at the rear. A hard stop would then be carried out in a safe area. When Murphy came out he was hardly able to stand. He got into the car and the plan changed so as not to let him drive and take him in the car park. A van full of officers went straight into the pub to prevent people coming out and we drove onto the car park and trapped his vehicle there.

I got out, gun drawn and found I was nearest to him. I challenged him and gave him instructions to get out of the car with his hands up. He ignored me totally; I kept repeating it, but he took no notice. Suddenly, he got out of the car looked directly at me and laughed. He still ignored all my instructions but there was no sign of any gun. He then walked all the way around his car, he even picked up small stones and threw them at the police dogs we had with us.

When he got back to me after going full circle, he stood about 10 feet away, looked directly at me and began to smile. I had my gun up in the aim at him but he did not seem to care. He then deliberately took his right hand and moved it across his waist and under his jacket on the left side of his body. I thought, *Here it comes, get ready he is going for his gun.* He seemed full of confidence as he did it, then the smile went from his face and he looked puzzled.

Suddenly, from my left, a dog-handler followed by his dog (I thought it should have been the other way around) jumped on Murphy and he hit the floor face first. We all moved in and a search found there was no gun on him. However, I then searched his car and in the driver's door pocket I found the silver .38 revolver with four rounds of live ammunition and two spent cartridges in the chamber.

Murphy was completely intoxicated and was shouting: 'I would have shot you all you bastards.'

The next day he was interviewed by CID and fully admitted everything he had done. He also stated he was convinced that the gun had been in the waistband of his trousers (a place he had kept it all afternoon). His plan was to go out in a blaze of glory in a shoot-out with the police. I would have had no choice but to shoot him if he had produced it from his waistband. Fortunately, it did not come to that but, my God, it was close.

Fatal road crash, M4:
how money talks

THERE HAVE ONLY BEEN A few occasions in my service when I have come across someone who was so rich that he would try anything to get off with an offence at court. This is one such story.

In the early hours, on the morning of 25th June 1986, I was night duty driving the area car X-ray 7. Colin Hale was my operator and we were quietly driving around all the airport hotel car parks as car theft was a major problem at the time.

As we drove slowly without lights on, a figure suddenly appeared in front of our car. He was middle-aged, very well-dressed and appeared to be bleeding badly from his head. On seeing us, the male ran into the hotel, through the rear doors. We chased after him and Colin found him hiding in the kitchens. He refused to answer any questions and was obviously very drunk. We walked him out of the hotel and intended taking him to West Drayton to find out what was going on with him.

As we got to our car, a Vauxhall Cavalier came screeching into the car park and stopped. The driver got out and he was in a terrible state. He managed to tell us that there had been a serious accident up on the motorway right by junction 4. Realising the man we had caught must have had something to do with the accident; we immediately drove up onto the motorway at junction 4. I could not begin to describe the carnage that faced us as we got onto the carriageway.

East of the slip road about 100 yards away was a car that for all intent looked normal from the front? It was facing the right way. Leading from that vehicle was a mass of debris and marks across the three carriageways, and these marks led to a Range Rover which was on its roof about 30 yards from the junction. It appeared that the whole contents of the Range Rover were strewn all over the motorway.

We were immediately approached by two lorry drivers who had been travelling in the opposite direction, and had seen the accident occur, and stopped to help. On seeing the man sat in the back of our car they both pointed him out as the driver of the Range Rover and said he was driving like a madman and had run straight into the rear of the Honda which had been travelling at a normal speed in the nearside lane. They had seen the Range Rover career from the fast lane across three carriageways and smash into the Honda; it had then overturned and spun down the motorway on its roof, hitting the central reservation several times before coming to a halt. They had then seen the driver of the Range Rover kick out the rear window, climb out and run off. They also said they were pretty sure that the driver of the Honda was dead.

I ran up to the other car and was shocked by what I saw. The rear of the Honda did not exist. It had been smashed away by the impact. The front passenger seats were the first part of the car visible from the rear. The rest of the car was untouched. I could see the driver lying across the two front seats. I leaned in and thought I could feel a pulse.

I ran back to my car, handcuffed the other male to the two lorry drivers and sat them in the back of our car, and then I went with Colin to try and help the other driver. We got him out of the car and lay him on the road and tried resuscitation until the ambulance crew arrived and took over. He was, however, pronounced dead at the scene.

The traffic department and the duty inspector arrived and took charge of the scene. I went back to my car to see the other driver a bit worse for wear. One of the lorry drivers had been offered two hundred pounds by the driver to let him escape. He got a punch in the mouth for his trouble from one of the two men. Because of the cut on his head, received in the crash, the driver had to be taken to New Charing Cross hospital to be checked over. It was also the place for the police to undertake the drink/drive procedure.

In situations where a suspected drink driver has had to be taken to hospital, a breath or blood sample can only been taken with the consent of the doctor dealing with the driver. There we discovered the driver's name to be Melvin Harrington Griffin, a property tycoon.

In this case the Accident and Emergency doctor was a young South African. Harrington Griffin was complaining of all sorts, saying he could not breathe properly and that he was scared of injections, and we knew it was going to be a problem getting any sort of sample from him at all.

It took quite some time for the doctor to actually get to see Harrington Griffin, who had on two occasions got up from his bed and tried to sneak out of the hospital.

He just made complaint after complaint, trying his hardest to stall everything that was going on. The doctor had made a very early assessment that he would give his permission for a blood sample to be taken after he had finished his treatment with Harrington Griffin. He told us that the cut to his head was very minor and only needed a stitch or two, which was dealt with quite quickly.

The doctor then made several attempts to take a blood sample for the drink/drive procedure. Harrington Griffin was a real pain and tried every thing he could think of to stop the doctor taking the sample. He was pretending to faint, have chest pains and any other thing he could come up with. In the end, the doctor got very annoyed with him and told him he knew he was putting on an act, got hold of his arm with the help of a male nurse, and took the blood sample from him literally by force. The sample was eventually taken four-and-a-half hours after the accident had occurred.

The blood sample taken was sent off to be tested and because of the length of time between the accident and the actual taking of the sample, it was calculated by a backdating method to show what the blood/alcohol content in the body would have been at the time of the accident.

The reading from the blood sample showed 130 milligrams of alcohol; that is 50 milligrams over the limit. The back calculation put it to at least 200 milligrams of alcohol at the time of the accident. This showed him to be at least two and a half times over the legal limit.

Specialised police traffic officers reconstructed the accident and conservatively put the speed of the Range Rover at being 120 miles per hour when it hit the Honda which they calculated was travelling in the inside lane at a speed of between 30 and 50 miles per hour. The impact had shortened the length of the Honda by four feet and it was later determined that the driver of the Honda had died instantly when his spine was snapped in two by the impact. It was also discovered the driver of the Honda was on his way home to Windsor after finishing work in Chiswick.

Being a man of very substantial means, Harrington Griffin, who by coincidence also lived in Windsor, obtained the services of a highly respected barrister for his trial at Isleworth crown court. This trial took two years to actually get before the courts. Harrington Griffin managed to get the case put off on nine occasions, mainly because he was either away working in the USA or claimed he was ill. The inspector who dealt with the case was outstanding and chased the driver all over the place to keep track of him as he feared he would use his power and money to leave the country and avoid prosecution.

The one attempt he made at not attending court finally caught Harrington Griffin out. We all arrived at court expecting the case to commence. All of the victim's family were there as they had been on every other occasion. Harrington Griffin, however, was not

The reason giving by his barrister was that he had been playing in a celebrity tennis tournament for charity in America and had suffered a heart attack. He was allegedly in hospital there receiving treatment and no time had been given for his expected return. The barrister had faxed proof from the hospital and the trial was adjourned.

The inspector was very unhappy about this and using a contact in America via a British newspaper, a reporter went to check out this story. There was indeed a man in hospital with a heart attack called Harrington Griffin but he looked nothing like the photograph the reporter had been sent of him. It then was discovered that the man was in hospital with a real heart complaint and had been paid by Harrington Griffin to give his name in hospital and get himself admitted for treatment with Griffin paying all the medical bills for the man. The inspector went straight back to Isleworth crown court with this new evidence and a warrant was issued for his arrest. He returned to the country and was immediately arrested.

The trial eventually started in June 1988, two years on. The trial lasted seven days with some very dirty tricks played by the defence. The best one they tried was having a go at the young South African doctor who treated Harrington Griffin on the night and took his blood sample. They tried to say that the injury done to Harrington Griffin's head was very serious and permission to take blood for the drink/drive procedure should never have been given. The doctor denied this very strongly saying it was a minor cut that was the type that did bleed very badly but would have no ill effects on the injured person.

The defence then went into great lengths about how specialised head injury matters were and only an expert and experienced doctor could say how bad the injury was.

The barrister then went on to ask the doctor with a smile: 'How much experience does a young doctor like you have of head injuries? Minor, I would suggest – just things you see in accident and emergency.'

The barrister was looking very smug until the doctor replied, 'Actually I am very experienced in head injuries.'

The barrister replied, 'Come, come doctor do you expect this court to believe that a man of your young years had experience in this much specialised field.'

The doctor replied, 'Before coming to Britain to further my medical experience, I had been a qualified doctor for some time. I spent two years practising in townships in and around Johannesburg where daily I would treat injuries which were so severe most people would die from them. The favourite method in the townships was to attack each other with axes, knives, guns and anything they could get their hands on. The head was always the favourite place to attack. Please believe me when I tell you there is nothing in the way of a head injury that I have not seen or dealt with. Mr Harrington Griffin's injury was superficial and required no more than a stitch.'

The face on the barrister just went a funny colour and it completely took the wind out of his very blustery sails; you could see a big smile on each of the jurists' faces.

At the completion of the trial, Harrington Griffin was found guilty of causing death by dangerous driving and drink/drive offences. To everyone's utter amazement he received a prison sentence of a mere thirty months. He was banned from driving for seven years and fined a total of £3,180.

There was uproar in the papers the next day and to this day I still say it was the power and the wealth that Harrington Griffin possessed that keep his sentence so light. He never showed any remorse for what he had done. He had devastated the life of a very close family, did his best to hoodwink the court on many occasions and kept his trial at bay for two years, allowing him to carry on making his millions work for him. Justice was never seen to be done!

The Cosworth crowd

One of the biggest problems experienced at West Drayton persisted over a period of a couple of years, and started just after the Ford Motor Company brought out their infamous Ford Cosworth. This was an awesome car; the speed and road-handling was exceptional and it became *the* car to steal for thieves.

Down at Heathrow Airport are all the car hire rentals firms you can think of. Certain of them became targets for the car thieves, who would set out to steal all their high-performance cars almost on a daily basis. Favourites for them to steal were the Cosworths, Ford Scorpios and Golf GTi's. The people responsible were youngsters between fifteen and eighteen years of age. The cars were then used in what was to become termed as ram-raids on business premises throughout the Met, Surrey and Thames Valley areas, and became a massive problem.

The drivers of the stolen cars were complete maniacs, very often high on drugs and drove without any fear for their own lives or those of others. It was quite a normal occurrence at night to get behind one of the stolen cars and a high-speed pursuit would sometimes end up going through all three force areas, but they were very difficult to catch because of the dangerous things they did. A favourite trick if chased was to get on the A4 around Heathrow and then travel on the wrong carriageway against the traffic at speeds in excess of 100 mile per hour. Everything always ended up back at Colnbrook, Wraysbury or Iver where most of these toe rags came from.

It was very frustrating not being able to catch this lot most of the time; they would be so far ahead of us they would abandon the car and be long gone before we found it. They even got so cheeky that they would pull alongside a police car and take a photo of the officers inside before racing off. They would then deliver the picture by post to the police station with comments written all over it, taking the mickey out of the old bill. One night, a Ford Cosworth drove into the rear yard of Slough nick in the early hours of the morning. The driver then sounded the horn until someone came out of the nick and a chase started. They took picture as well, which made the local papers.

Most of the little team were eventually arrested, mainly due to forensic evidence recovered from the cars. To my knowledge there were only two occasions when anyone actually got caught in possession of one of the cars.

The first was after a long chase in the middle of the night from Surrey, after a Golf GTi had been involved in a ram-raid. I got behind it going west on the A4 from the A312, after it had been forced to leave the M4 motorway at junction 3. As we got to the major junction outside the Excelsior hotel, which was opposite Heathrow police station, the GTi went straight through red lights and onto the wrong side of the road – a dual carriageway at the time – and it hurtled off. Even though it was the early hours of the morning, traffic was still about, but the GTi just roared on.

I stayed on the right side of the road but then we reached the junction with Hatch Lane. Now the carriageways became divided by a wide central reservation, which at times was so wide you could not see the other side of the road. At the end of this dual carriageway was the Moor roundabout. Straight on took you over the M25 towards junction 5 of the M4. Left took you down the Stanwell Moor road towards Colnbrook and Staines.

Well, even at the speed I was travelling, by the time I reached the roundabout the GTi was nowhere to be seen, completely out of sight. However, a Surrey car came up the Stanwell Moor Road so it must have gone down the A4 and over the M25 bridge. There were police cars everywhere looking for it. A few minutes later a Thames Valley traffic car picked it up at junction 5 and it was heading into Colnbrook village.

Unknown to us, sat in a Ford Escort diesel panda car was a Thames Valley officer who I had met a few times before. He had made it is mission in life to put as many of the Cosworth crowd in prison. He was not far off retirement and was a real old-style bobby.

Over the linked main set radio came his voice: 'All chasing units ease off, this chase is about to come to an end.' That all he said.

The next thing we knew, the GTi was upside down in a ditch and the Ford Escort had severe frontal damage. This is what happened.

The TVP bobby had seen the GTi go past him earlier and he recognised the occupants as two brothers who lived in Colnbrook. He guessed they would go back that way to abandon the car. He went and reversed into the entrance of a set of park gates on the road that ran from the A4 into Colnbrook village. Then he heard the chase coming his way and called off the other police drivers. As the stolen GTi came hurtling down the road he just pulled out and broadsided the car, putting it into the small water-filled ditch upside-down.

When we all arrived the two occupants were screaming to be let out as water was getting in the car. The bobby was stood there looking at them just smoking his pipe. A couple of officers went to get them out of the car.

The bobby said: 'Do you mind? They are my prisoners; I'll say when they can get out. This might teach them a bit of a lesson.'

Eventually the brothers were rescued looking very sorry for themselves and for once were very cooperative and good-mannered. A good old-style lesson taught.

An arrest at last

THERE WAS ONLY EVER ONE other time where hands were physically laid on any of this gang whilst they were in a car. A friend of ours lived in Colnbrook high street and a colleague of mine, Barry O'Callaghan, and I had been invited to his house for dinner with our wives.

We had a lovely evening and Christine, Barry's wife, was driving so Barry and I had partaken of a few beverages, as you do. Well, past midnight as we started to get ready to leave, I went with Christine to get their car as it was parked off the high street as the road was so narrow.

As we did so, a Ford Scorpio roared through the village. I saw the driver and passenger, and I recognised them both. The driver was a very fat lad from Iver. In the back were two young girls. I ran back to the house and told André, our host, to phone the police and Barry and I went outside to see if we could see the car. Then suddenly we heard it coming at great speed, engine screaming

As it came around a right-hand bend towards us it went out of control and hit a corner house. Barry and I started to run towards the car. I told Barry to go for the driver and I would get the passenger. Both being a little worse for wear through alcohol, we both steamed towards the car. I saw the passenger door open and the lad get out and run towards me; I could not believe my luck: he was coming to me and I did not even have to chase after him.

He was quite tall, but very thin. *Ah, no problem,* I thought. *I'll hit him with my best rugby tackle, round the knees and slide down to his feet and take him over to the floor.*

He hit me at speed and nearly went straight through me, but I got him down and we started fighting. He was as strong as an ox. Without a doubt, he was on some sort of drug because his strength was immense. I was suddenly left holding his jacket and he was off like a long dog. I went after him just in time to see him leap over an eight-foot school gate like it was two feet high.

There was no way I was going over that so I ran back to help Barry. He did not need any. He had fat boy by the throat, restraining him. The two girls were still in the back of the car and immediately confirmed to me who I believed the escaped passenger was. He was nicked at his home nearby by local officers a short time afterwards.

So, after a lovely evening out we sent the girls home and spent the rest of the night at Slough police station dealing with two very unhappy members of the Cosworth crowd.

A return to Gwent

Just after starting night duty at West Drayton on a lovely summer's night, I got called back to the nick and the duty officer said to me, 'There is a prisoner to be picked up from Gwent at Chepstow nick. I know you are from that way so you will know the way to go. Do you want to go and collect him?'

I jumped at the chance and was told to take another Welsh lad with me, Phil Thomas. My old sergeant from Maindee, Ken Carey was now an Inspector at Chepstow. I have huge admiration for Ken he was a real old-style copper and I had loved working with him. I telephoned the nick to see if he was around. I was told that he was on duty until 1 a.m. I explained to the PC who I was and that I knew Ken well, and that I was just about to leave to come and collect the prisoner. I asked him to let KC, as I fondly called him, know that I was coming.

Off we set and duly arrived in the rear yard some two hours later, just before 1 a.m. As we arrived, there was a very young-looking traffic patrol sergeant also pulling into the yard in his posh patrol car. Now, bearing in mind in those days sergeants in the county forces were the men to be feared and inspectors were gods who you very rarely had anything to do with, I did not know this sergeant at all and said to him, 'Morning sarge, we are from the Met come to pick up a prisoner is it all right if we come in the back door with you.'

With a look that could kill he said, 'It is sergeant to you; don't think you can come here with your Met ideas.'

Although we were in uniform he still wanted to see our warrant cards and having done so he then said quite sharply to the both of us, 'If the inspector is still here make sure you show him some respect and salute him and call him sir; I know what you Met are like when it comes to respecting rank.'

I looked at Phil with a smile and I could feel some fun coming on.

We walked in through the rear of the nick past the cell area and towards the front office; as we did so I could hear KC's voice. As we entered the office he was sat at the reserve desk on the phone. There was also a very young PC sat drinking a mug of tea. The traffic sergeant stood in between me and KC, dying to speak with him. As KC finished his call I winked at him and nodded towards the sergeant.

The sergeant then said, 'Sir I found these two Met blokes in the rear yard, they are here to collect a prisoner.'

KC replied, 'Ah, you're the two I have been expecting then?'

I said, 'Yes that's right. Come on you grey-haired old fool, I've just driven 130 miles to this God-forsaken place. What about a cup of tea?'

The sergeant went several different shades of colour and was about to explode when KC said, 'I am sorry officer, you're right. Here, have my seat and I will get you both a cup of tea and would you like some biscuits too?'

I continued, 'But make sure they are chocolate ones, will you mate? And hurry up will you? We are in a rush.'

Off KC went into the kitchen and as soon as he did the sergeant went into hyperspace, ranting and raving, demanding my inspector's name and saying how he was going to have me disciplined. I could see KC peeping around the corner and I could not stop myself from laughing. Phil was in the same state. KC then came in with the tea, put then down in front of us.

'Leave these Met yobs to me, sergeant. I know how to deal with their sort,' he said.

He then took his truncheon out of his pocket and started hitting me across the arm with it (something he always used to do as a joke when I worked with him in Maindee, especially if he had to work on a Sunday late turn). The traffic sergeant thought he would have some of it as well and took out his stick. Before he could hit me I stood up and KC and I shook hands and started laughing hysterically.

Realising he had been part of a joke, the traffic sergeant stormed out of the nick. I then spent a very pleasant hour catching up with Ken before heading back to London with the prisoner. KC is now enjoying a very happy retirement.

The builder's skip

It was always the culture of the police force to play practical jokes on probationers at some time in their two-year probation period. They could be great fun and it used happen to everyone at some time or other. There was never any malice meant in the tricks played, although there were occasions when they were carried out on someone to try to get a point over to them. On the whole, they were just harmless bits of fun which normally brightened up a very dull night duty and it did wonders for the camaraderie on the relief. This was one of my favourites.

Dave Fletcher had been on relief for some time and was not far off finishing his probation. Dave was an excellent police officer, very keen and efficient, and had a great knack for crime arrests; he was very highly thought of by senior guys on the relief and, being a Yorkshire lad, always spoke his mind. One night duty Dave was operator on X-ray 7, being driven that night by Brian Houston. Things were really quiet, and people were restless for something to do. It was a bitterly cold night, it had been snowing on and off over the week and there was a lot of ice around.

One of the lads, Graham Prentice, came in with a foam leg off a dummy that someone had stopped and showed him in a bush thinking it was a really body. Graham saw a chance of a wind-up. Just off Yiewsley high street was a small trading estate and he had been there earlier in the night and noticed a couple of rubbish skips there. The estate was overlooked by the rear balconies of the flats above the high street shops. Graham got one of the girls to get him a pair of her police issue tights and they cut off one leg and put it onto the foam dummy leg. I have to say, it really did feel life-like.

Graham and a few others then went up to the trading estate to set up the plan. They put the leg into one of the skips, well covered with other rubbish. One of the other girls had got hold of some old underwear; bra, knickers etc and these items of clothing were strewn around the skips onto the snow and ice. A bottle of tomato ketchup was then liberally smeared around the area and rubbed into the snow and ice turning everything blood red. The scene was very convincing.

Most of the relief then went and hid on the balcony overlooking the estate and the joke was set in motion. In those days, all 999 calls went direct from information room and New Scotland Yard to the area car covering that particular station area. However, that night there had been trouble with information room and calls were coming direct to Hayes police station to be forwarded out. At about 3 a.m. X-Ray 7 was given a call by the sergeant from the control room at Hayes to the effect that a man walking his dog had discovered what appeared to be female clothing which was blood-stained on the trading estate. The member of the public was going to take his dog home and then meet X-ray 7 at the scene.

We were all in place when the car arrived. Brian the driver was in on the joke. The estate was quite dark and eerie in places although the skips were lit by security lights. Graham Prentice put on a great false voice and pretended he was from information room and now linked into our PR system. He passed over information that earlier in the night a female had been heard screaming loudly in the area and a local traffic car passing had checked the area with no result.

Brian then started pretending to liaise with the fictitious information room inspector saying, 'I have found blood-stained clothing and also there appears to be a lot of blood stains in the snow, can you call CID, etc.'

The pretend radio transmissions just made it even better. Suddenly, Dave yelled, 'Brian, quick, quick, look at this.'

He had just found a huge machete covered in red stuff by the side of the largest skip. Dave then got on the radio to say what he had found for the inspector's information. I will never forget the fear in his voice. The road was really icy and both Dave and Brian had trouble staying on their feet. We were all watching from above and it looked hilarious.

Brian then told Dave, 'You get in and check that skip, and I will do the other.'

Dave replied, 'Are you sure shouldn't we wait for CID?'

Brian said, 'She could still be alive somewhere; we have got to check everywhere correctly.'

Dave jumped into the skip and carefully started checking through all the boxes and rubbish. Suddenly, he let out a mighty scream and he came out of the skip at a great rate of knots, doing a backward somersault and landing on his backside.

He started screaming down the radio, 'I found a leg; it's all warm and there is nothing else attached to it. Get the CID, it's a murder – get the CID.' He must have repeated it half a dozen times.

Then he saw Brian lying across the bonnet of the car having a laughing fit and then he heard us all doing the same up on the balcony. He went mad at first but then realised what a great joke it had been and was proud to tell the story himself in the end.

A VERY STORMY NIGHT AHEAD

There are not many people who do not remember that night in October 1987 when the weatherman, Michael Fish, famously got his weather forecast wrong. I was night duty and experienced a night I will never forget.

I was posted on X-ray 7, a Rover SD1 with Chris Roberts as my operator. Some time around midnight everything suddenly changed and the winds started to pick up and were getting stronger and stronger. The next thing we knew were getting calls from people that there were trees coming down all over the place.

At about 1 a.m. we were driving south through Hayes town and had just come over Hayes railway station bridge where there in front of us was a massive tree that was completely blocking the road from one pavement to the other. We called for another unit to come down to help us block the other end of Hayes bridge as other trees looked like they were about to come down as well.

Phil Thomas and a fairly new probationer, Roland Boyland arrived and I asked Roland to go to the brow of the railway bridge and make sure no one else came over the bridge. Chris, Phil and I were just deciding the safest and best way to go about dealing with this massive tree when the wind suddenly increased to the most amazing gust. It was like trying to stand up in a wind tunnel going at full power.

I looked up to see if Roland was OK and I saw him just flip up in the air backwards and land on his backside. He was looking around convinced someone has just hit him from behind but it had just been the sheer power of the wind.

Suddenly, there was this almighty crack. Phil and I were standing by the five-foot wire fence of a nearby house. We looked up and saw this huge branch break from the top of a very high tree. It seemed like slow motion as the branch came floating down, hit the ground and slid right into us, knocking up both up in the air and over the fence. We both escaped uninjured but it was very close. The council came out and moved the tree and we then spent the whole night running around answering calls for help from the public. It was just getting worse and worse.

At one point we stopped to speak with PCs Ian Chawner and Ed Bird who were in the van at the junction of the A4 and the airport perimeter road by what was then the Aerial hotel. We suddenly saw this huge piece of corrugated roof sheeting come flying through the air from a building on the airport perimeter. The sheeting flew right into the top of the van, sliced off the blue light and disappeared off into the night. If it had hit one of us it would have killed us without a doubt.

The incidents carried on all night with the storm getting worse all the time. At about 4.30 a.m. Chris and I parked on the Bath Road A4 junction with Sipson Road to prevent cars using the road as the trees were falling all the time. Suddenly, out of the darkness came a male figure trying to ask a question. Chris opened his door to get out and speak with him when the wind got hold of it and completely took it off its hinges. It was just being held on by a bit of metal completely flattened against the front nearside wing. That was the end of that car and we limped back to West Drayton. The man was only asking what time the next bus was.

Because people were having trouble getting into work, most of us did not finish that morning until 9.00 a.m. We all decided to take in a big breakfast before going home as we all deserved it after surviving such an amazing night duty. At the time, the Post House hotel in Sipson Road used to do a breakfast special for the police with all you could eat for £5.00, so off we all went to stuff ourselves silly. Something happened that morning that was so silly but funny it just relived all our stress and we all later slept well.

WE HAD ALL ATTACKED THE cereals first and then went up to the buffet counter to help ourselves to a huge cooked breakfast. There were about ten of us on a big table. Next to us arrived six Japanese people. They seemed a little unsure about what they had to do. They seemed to be looking at what we had and I assumed they were deciding what to eat by seeing what we had ourselves.

Well the next thing we saw, the six of them were coming back with great big plates full of cereals each. The thing was they had them on dinner plates and not in cereal bowls.

Before we realised it they had started all to pour milk onto the cereal and the next thing they knew was it was all flowing over the sides of the dinner plates and into their laps. The sight of six Japanese men jumping up and down with the front of their clothes covered in milk and Rice Krispies was just too much and we all collapsed in hysterics and could not stop. It became contagious and the rest of the guests and even some staff started laughing with us.

We later apologised via the manager after explaining the night we had been through and how much of a tension release it had been. He was quite happy in the end, as were the six Japanese men

Harmondsworth immigration centre

On the A4 Bath Road, Harmondsworth, is situated a government immigration centre that services mainly people who come into the country via Heathrow airport. People are held there ready for deportation back to whence they came.

It was quite common to get called down there by the security staff that ran the centre when they had problems with the detainees. Mass break-outs were commonplace and security there was a joke. There is now a state-of-the-art building that was erected on almost the same site as the old one, the new one looks more like a prison

On 25 August 1988 I took a call to a riot taking place in the centre. I was the first there, and it was bedlam. The guards had lost control and the detainees were running amok. All our troops arrived and we brought the situation under control fairly quickly.

However, one male who was from Somalia had got hold of a knife and had climbed up onto the roof of an outbuilding to try and escape but found himself trapped. Anyone who tried to get anywhere near him would be threatened with the knife and he was saying he would kill anyone who got too close, and then he would kill himself.

I eventually got a ladder and went up onto the roof and built up a conversation with him. He kept the knife pointing at me all the time, insisting I came no closer or he would kill me. After about ten minutes, something distracted his attention away from me. As he looked away, I punched him hard in the head and as he went down I managed to grab the knife out of his hand and throw it over the edge of the roof. There was a bit of a roll-around, with punches exchanged, until I pinned him down as help arrived on the roof in the shape of Ian Chawner.

We had cuffed him with his hands behind his back and he calmed down. Now we had to get him back down off the roof. I sat there and said to Ian, 'Get him down if you don't mind mate; I'm knackered – I will be down in a minute.'

I saw Ian walk to the edge of the roof with the Somalian, who was beginning to struggle again. I got up and saw the man spit at Ian, before I knew what was happening Ian just pushed him straight over the edge of the roof and I heard a thud below.

I screamed at Ian: 'What the hell are you doing? You could have killed him.'

Ian replied, 'He was about to kick of again so I thought it best to get him of the roof as quick as I could and that was the quickest.'

I got down to the man and he had landed on his side and hurt his shoulder and cut his head. It had, however, changed his demeanour completely and he became completely co-operative with me.

I really expected to get into some sort of trouble as a result from the security staff, but far from it. They were chuffed to bits, and the man got taken straight to Heathrow and put on a plane for deportation after receiving treatment for his injuries.

The security senior management were so impressed with the way we dealt with the situation, in particular the man on the roof with the knife, that they wrote to my chief superintendent to express their views. As a result, I received a deputy assistant commissioner's commendation, which pleased me but seemed strange, as a man had been pushed of a roof while handcuffed. I had been fully expecting a complaint, not a commendation.

The traffic car

For some reason or other there has always seemed to have been an attitude of 'them and us,' between advanced drivers who are members of traffic patrol, and advanced drivers who drove the area cars at stations. Traffic seemed to think they were much better drivers and did things such as ambulance escorts and other things that we were never allowed to do on division.

Traffic also had an abundance of high-powered patrol cars which were kitted out with all sorts of video equipment and other things for catching people speeding.

There were occasions where X-ray 7, our area car, would be off the road for a while and there were no spares at workshops for us to use, so we were completely without an emergency car. There were always spare cars sitting at the traffic garage, immaculately looked after, but it was never possible to get a loan of them. Well, on this particular occasion my duty inspector talked the garage sergeant into letting us borrow one for the weekend.

What was picked up was a beautiful Rover SD1 three-litre that was absolutely immaculate. We were warned it has to be returned in exactly the same condition.

I was night duty all over the weekend and warned all the other drivers to look after it as well, because it meant if we needed to borrow a car on another occasion then they would be more trusting of us.

The car was lovely and exceptionally fast, and I really enjoyed driving it. Also in the car was a lot more kit, half of which I did not even know how to use. One of the things was a very large clock face-type of dial that was a calibrated speedometer for proving people were speeding. It was linked to the car's normal speedo and calibrated on a regular basis. The clock face was about ten inches in diameter.

I had no need for this speedo and left things alone. By the early hours of the Monday morning everything was fine with the car and I was pleased it would be going back undamaged. Chris Roberts, my operator that night, then said, 'Have you noticed that the calibrated speedo has stopped working?'

I looked, and he was right. I could not understand why. I tapped the glass a couple of times with the knuckle of one of my fingers and it did not move. I tried it again and to my horror, when I did, the whole of the glass shattered right across the face of it.

I looked at Chris, and my face must have been a picture; he started laughing, but all I could think was *what do I tell the traffic sergeant?* I stayed on late and drove it straight back to the traffic garage myself and I went to confess what I had done. Fortunately, he was as good as gold and was so pleased we had managed to bring it back without a scratch on it. He said not to worry; the calibrated speedo would be easy to sort out. He also said he would let us borrow at car another time when we were desperate.

While I was having a cup of coffee with him before heading back, a traffic officer took out the car I had just brought back. He got no further than the A40 dual carriageway when he was involved in an accident and the car was badly damaged. So much for traffic drivers being better than divisional drivers!

M4 MOTORWAY CRASH

ONE LATE TURN IN 1986, a Ford Luton van laden with cases of bottled beer was travelling west out of London on the M4 when, for some reason, the driver decided that he wanted to turn around and head back into London. Also in the van was a fifteen-year-old boy who was helping the driver to carry out his deliveries that day. The van pulled up on the hard shoulder just near the Heston services.

The driver then made a fatal decision: instead of driving another half a mile to junction 3 and coming back on to the motorway, he decided he was going to cut through the central reservation at a point where there were the collapsible cones that the motorways used to have every so often for the emergency services to use.

So the van tried to make a dash across the three lanes of the westbound carriageway to go through the cones. He made a fatal error of judgement, as there was a National Express coach in the middle lane heading towards the van. The coach driver tried to move over to the outside lane to avoid the van but they collided. The van was forced head on into the central reservation and the cab broke free in the impact and landed in the fast lane of the eastbound carriageway. Both the driver and passenger of the van were thrown out of the cab. The back of the van exploded in the collision and covered both sides of the motorway in bottles of beer.

The coach, having hit the van, then hit the central reservation at the point where the barrier sloped down to the gap with the cones. The coach went up the sloped area of the barrier and took off across to the other carriageway and hit another coach head on, which was travelling in the middle lane of the eastbound carriageway. This coach was full of American tourists returning to London after visiting Windsor.

I WAS DRIVING X-RAY 7 on this particular day with Chris Roberts as my operator. The call came via the main set and we were there within several minutes. X-ray 6 the area car from Hayes had arrived just before us. The scene on our arrival was utter devastation. The two coaches hitting each other head on had left both buses with their entire fronts as mangled wrecks and both of the coach drivers were trapped within the wreckage.

The front seats on both coaches were the first part you could recognise. After the impact, the coaches had bounced 10 feet apart from each other. There were bodies lying everywhere: on the carriageway, the hard shoulder, and also the grass embankment. It was difficult to know where to start first. As we considered where we were going to start the fire brigade and ambulance started arriving. Thank God, because they were brilliant.

Then we noticed that hanging from the wreckage of the coach carrying the American tourists was an arm. There was no body attached to it and to my knowledge, one was never found; it was the general opinion that the body had been thrown from the van and it landed between the front of the two coaches at the moment they collided, and the body quite literally disintegrated on the impact between the two coaches. The arm of the driver of the van was all that was left of him. The body of the fifteen-year-old boy was found in the fast lane of the eastbound carriageway with part of the top of his head sliced off. The whole sight was horrendous.

It turned out both coach drivers were still alive but trapped in the wreckage. The fire brigade were absolute heroes and spent several hours cutting them free. They were both still alive when they eventually got them out, and that was entirely due to the expertise and dedication of the fire service. The London ambulance service dealt with everyone else. There was every type of injury you could think of. The major incident plan swung into operation, the air ambulance and doctors came to the scene and it worked very well.

At the end of it all there were only four fatalities. I do not know how many serious injuries there were, but it was an awful lot. Apart from the driver of the van and his young passenger, the tour guide on the American coach was found dead among the tangled wreckage of what had been the steps up into the coach. She was not found for ages afterwards when they started untangling all the mess. The other fatality was an elderly American gentleman who suffered a heart attack during the accident.

The sight of the accident was very traumatic and while you just get on with it at the time, no matter how experienced you are, it will always play on your mind when you think about it afterwards. However, the next day in the *Daily Mirror* they ran a large spread about the accident. There were a lot of pictures obviously taken from a helicopter, however, in the centre pages were some very graphic photographs that had been taken by someone right in the middle of the incident.

The pictures showed some terrible sights and must have been awful for members of the families of the deceased and injured. I was furious because although I had not noticed anyone taking pictures I had a very good idea who it was. I approached this person the next time I saw him in work and gave him a piece of my mind. He completely denied it was him, but I knew he always carried a camera in his bag and I was certain he was responsible for the pictures. He obviously got well paid for it by the newspaper, and I assured him that if he ever did that again when I was around, I would shove his camera so far up his backside that the only pictures he could take would be suitable for a medical journal.

This person did leave the job some time later to do something involving photography. At least he could not take pictures of people suffering for the benefit of making money as the result of his privilege as a police officer.

Please can we drive a little slower?

Not long after I had joined the relief, a young Indian man by the name of Ravi Thaper, joined the team. He was a very quiet person and came from a strict Indian family who were very proud of their son joining the police force. There were very few Asian members of the force at the time and it took a lot of courage for Ravi to do this; he would take a lot of abuse from younger members of the public, as well as the odd one or two police officers who were so narrow-minded that they believed that non-white people should not be in the police.

I really liked Ravi's company. He was very intelligent and inspired very interesting topics of conversation in the car. He did, however, have one main problem that held him back slightly: he did not like driving fast. Now, bearing in mind that my job as driver of the area car was to take all the emergency calls direct from Scotland Yard, I had to get to each incident as quickly as possible. My operator's job was to deal with the radio communications and check for the best route in the *A to Z*. This, of course, meant looking down at the map as we sped along.

The first time I had Ravi in the car with me as my operator he suddenly said, 'Andy, do you think we could slow down a little? I am having a little trouble.'

I assumed he meant finding the address in the map book, but that was not the case at all. Suddenly as we raced along Ravi wound down his window and started to be sick. This continued until we reached our destination. By then, Ravi was looking so ill I had to leave him in the car and go and deal with the matter with other officers who had also arrived.

Andy Vick

When I got back to the car, Ravi was so apologetic, and explained that he has a real problem with car-sickness when travelling at speeds of over 40 miles per hour. That put paid to Ravi being operator very often and he spent most of his service driving panda cars. About ten years later poor Ravi suffered a medical problem and had to leave the force. A real shame, as he was really nice guy.

My slowest chase ever

THE LOVE OF ALL AREA car drivers is to get behind a stolen vehicle and chase them until they realise they cannot get away from the expert driving, then give themselves up. Well, that's what is supposed to happen, but rarely does.

One of my strangest chases involved a stolen motorbike – a Honda 50cc at that. The bike had been report stolen during the night, and in the early hours of the morning, as I drove up the high street with Ian Chawner, there was the bike driving along at about 10 miles per hour. I pulled up alongside it and Ian opened his window and told the driver to pull over.

'F*** off,' was his reply and he kicked out at the door of the police car.

At one point he was going so slow that Ian had hold of his arm, trying to stop him, but he just kept kicking the car and swearing.

It was about 3.00 a.m. and there was no one about, but he just kept going all the way up the high street. As we got to the junction with Falling Lane he made a dart for it, mounting the pavement and heading for a new estate being built, which had a tunnel at one end that a bike but not a car could go through.

I shot off at speed and got on the road towards the tunnel to see the bike heading towards the entrance. The bike was still going very slowly. I decided to get past the bike and block him from getting up the pavement and into the tunnel itself. As I accelerated to go past him, he must have realised what I was trying to do so he pulled over right in my path. I braked but hit him quite hard in the back wheel and sent him flying over the handlebars, and he went head first into the rear doors of a parked Ford transit van. Amazingly, he got up and decided he wanted to fight the two of us. He was absolutely blotto with drink, and after a small struggle he was handcuffed and taken to the nick.

The funniest part was he in fact owned the bike and had reported it stolen. However, because he was so drunk he had just forgotten where he had parked it. When he left to go home after a 'lock-in' at his local, he found the bike, forgot he reported it stolen and had tried to go home until we came along. In the end, when he was sober he apologised but found him self charged with a drink–drive offence. So much for a high-speed chase: at least he did not get away!

One that did get away

For a period of time around Hayes, someone was stealing cars, joyriding in them and committing crime before burning them out in the Church Road area. It was becoming a really problem to us.

One night, as I sat at traffic lights at the Grapes public house with Roger Ferguson as my operator, I saw a Ford Escort, two cars ahead, which had been reported stolen that night. I told Roger to let every one know on the local personal radio, to make their way in our direction and we would follow at a distance not to spook them and set off a chase too early without help nearby. This would give us more chance to catch them.

As we turned off the Uxbridge Road into Church Road a call came on the main set about us following the stolen car. As Roger picked up the handset to talk to Information Room, the coiled lead of the set flicked on the blue light switch. So off goes the stolen car at great speed followed by us with Roger now giving the commentary. The car suddenly swung into a set of gates into Barra Hall Park and went tearing across the open park area. I followed and realised we were heading towards the church and a favourite bail out point in Church Walk.

As we flew towards the exit at Church Walk I suddenly saw the Escort hit something, it momentarily stopped before carrying on through the gate and turned left into a narrow lane. it was then I realised the Escort had hit the gates and the left hand one was now sticking out and pointing directly at me as we flew towards its.

I started to brake but nothing happened, I then realised I was on wet grass. I had let the red mist get hold of me and I had given no thought to what surface I was on. The more braking I did the worse it got. Then suddenly there was a loud thud and we came to an abrupt stop. The large park gate was embedded half way into the engine compartment of the Rover. We both got out and ran into the lane and found the escort abandoned and completely blocking the lane so nothing could get pass it. The baddies were long gone.

The Rover was a mess and has to be towed away. It was not until I went there in day light and saw how many metal park benches, large trees and other obstacles I had managed to miss more by luck than judgement. That taught me a lesson about the red mist syndrome I have never forgotten to this day.

Yet another injury

Getting injured now and again is something that comes with the territory of being in the old bill, and you have to accept that at some time or another you might get injured. This is one such story.

Around the end of November 1985, we were having a lot of problems with thefts from motor vehicles in the car park of what was then called the Post House hotel. We had plain-clothes officers watching the car park from the hotel rooms. Just after midnight the guys in the hotel noticed a vehicle in the car park acting suspiciously.

All available units made their way and surrounded the hotel as best as possible without being spotted. I parked the area car under the M4 motorway bridge and climbed up the concrete slope where I could see everything that was going on. Ian Chawner, who was with me, crept towards the front fence. I saw a figure smash the window of a large Volvo and the figure then climb into the car.

I instructed all units to move in and made my way quickly to the driver's side of the Volvo. There was a boy of about eighteen years of age lying across the front seats trying to remove the car stereo. I pulled open the door and yelled at him that he was nicked; he turned on his back and kicked out with both his legs and squashed my knees against the door pillar. The pain was unbelievable and I fell to the floor.

As I pulled myself back up I saw the youth trying to get out the passenger door and was blocked by Ian; he just head butted Ian and run off across the front lawn of the hotel. I went after him determined to get him. Halfway across the front lawn I fell on the floor with my left knee looking decidedly not right at all.

Andy Vick

Suddenly the police force's answer to Linford Christie flew past me and seconds later on my radio I heard the man had been detained. Then, like a man possessed, I got up and hopped on one leg around to the back of the hotel where the car thief was lying on his back on the floor. I saw red and jumped right on top of him threatening to bash his brains in. I was in horrendous pain and it as his fault. I wanted to give him some too. Fortunately, the boys pulled me off him before I did anything that I was likely to regret. I felt it would have been worth it though. I ended up with my kneecap out of place and a few weeks off work.

Now I know I am getting old

THERE IS A SAYING IN the force, which is that you know you are getting older when you see how young the recruits are looking. Well, this came true for me when I met another PC called Russell Williams.

Russell was based at Kensington police station and I was still at West Drayton. We were both seconded to a marked vehicle that was being run 24 hours a day during the Royal Tournament at Earls Court. Everyone in the vehicle was armed and there were four of us in all. This particular day was quiet and as I knew that Russell was from my hometown, we spent quite a bit of time talking about the place, and obviously made reference to the fact that I had spent the first five years of my service in Gwent.

I was sat in the back of the car and Russell was in the front passenger seat. He turned and looked at me and said, 'I remember you; you used to drive a panda car around Ringland didn't you?' (Ringland was an area of Newport.)

I said laughingly, 'You have a good memory! What did I do, arrest you for something?'

He replied, 'As a matter of fact you did, sort of. I thought I recognised your face from somewhere.' He then told me when he was quite young and out on an estate with a friend. They had with them an air pistol. I had been called there by a member of the public who had seen them shooting the air pistol on nearby wasteland. Straight away I remembered it all.

Russell went on to say that I gave them both a good telling off that scared them to death and they were convinced they were going to prison. Instead, I took them both home to their respective parents and

Andy Vick

told them out of the boys' earshot what had occurred and exactly how much trouble they would be in if I were to take them into the police station. I also told them I had read the riot act to the boys and got one of the fathers to sign a disclaimer for the air pistol so I could dispose of it correctly.

I left both boys with there parents and thought no more of it until this day.

Russell told me he got a right old slap and was ranted at by his father. But it was the best thing that could have happened to him. We had a great laugh about it, but God, did I feel old.

Inspector Gumbleton

There was no way I could go through stories from West Drayton with out mentioning Tony Gumbleton. Tony was a very outspoken, very direct and very rarely wrong on any matter on which he stood his ground. He was an exceptional police officer and one of the best inspectors I ever worked for. He had an amazing photographic memory and would always get to calls before you.

Night duty was amazing because a night would not go by without him instigating a car chase with a lost or stolen car or catching a couple of burglars in the process of committing the burglary. I devised a great system on nights: I would just follow him everywhere he went and got on board whatever it was he came across. It proved very productive. There seemed to be nothing that fazed him and he fought for his officers tooth and nail with senior officers

The one incident I remember the most happened on the Uxbridge Road and the major junction called the Grapes. We were on night duty and just after midnight we received a radio call relating to a car just being stolen from the Hayes area. The registration number and make of car was given out by the radio operator.

Almost immediately, Inspector Gumbleton was on the radio saying, 'I am sitting behind this vehicle at the traffic lights, junction of Lansbury Drive and Uxbridge Road. The car has two young white males inside and is indicating to turn left on to the Uxbridge Road towards Southall.'

Inspector Gumbleton was driving an unmarked police car but the people in the stolen car must have spotted his uniform. It suddenly took off from the lights at speed and roared off eastbound on the Uxbridge Road.

I was only a couple of miles further west on the Uxbridge Road heading towards Inspector Gumbleton. I quickly set off to catch him up. He was giving a running commentary of where the car was going. It was remaining on the Uxbridge Road but driving at tremendous speed towards the Grapes junction. The junction was a crossroads in those days, and north of it is Yeading Lane and south of it Coldharbour Lane. It was always a busy junction day or night and Inspector Gumbleton warned everyone that the stolen car was slowing down for nothing or nobody.

I could see the inspector's car ahead of me in the distance, but suddenly I heard a huge explosion and I could see a big cloud of dust rising. We caught up with them at the junction where there had been a massive crash.

An elderly gentleman in an Austin Allegro was travelling home and was going through the lights that were on green for him. As he went through the centre of the junction, he was hit, driver's-side on, by the stolen car with the front of the stolen car embedding itself into the driver's door of the Allegro before bouncing away, and spinning off down the road.

The driver of the stolen car actually got out and ran away. When Inspector Gumbleton got to the Allegro it was a total mess, completely smashed up with the driver trapped inside. We arrived seconds later and I found the passenger of the stolen car still sitting in the seat with the left half of his face hanging off from where his faced had smashed into the dashboard when the two cars collided with each other.

The fire brigade and ambulance got the driver out of the wreckage but he was dead as a result of severe internal injuries. The passenger of the stolen car told us who he was straight away, and also the name of the driver. They were both thirteen years of age and from a council-run secure home which was situated in Coldharbour Lane, not more than 300 yards from the scene of the accident.

I went straight around to the home and up to the boy's room. He was not there but his window was open and it led out onto a roof with access down to the ground. I sat there with another colleague and waited. Ten minutes later the boy climbed back in through the window and I grabbed hold of him. He tried fighting his way out and got a broken nose for his trouble. He acted like nothing had happened, claiming he had been out with a girlfriend. I arrested him and he ended up in court, but because of his age was sent to what was a more secure council home and stayed there until he was old enough for a young offenders' unit. The passenger lost the sight of his left eye and his looks for good. He was dealt with for allowing himself to be carried in a stolen vehicle and got nothing more than a fine.

Inspector Gumbleton was only yards behind the stolen car and witnessed a horrendous crash. It must have been something terrible to witness but he dealt with the whole incident expertly and was completely professional in everything he did. He was an officer who should have gone a lot further in rank, but he did not fit in with some senior officers' ideas of how an inspector should carry on at that rank and above. Because of their ridiculous ideas, a first-class officer stayed in the same rank right until the end of service. He was always in uniform and always working shifts, including nights. He spoke his mind and people higher up did not like him for it. It was a godsend for the uniformed teams to have him, so they were the lucky ones. The senior management lost out and what a great loss it was.

I have a story, which should come later in the book but fits in nicely here about Tony Gumbleton. I had left West Drayton and joined the dog section; Inspector G had been forced to move to Fulham because the management of Hayes could not cope with him and his hard work. The same thing happened at Fulham. He took it by storm. The troops loved him but management soon wanted rid of him because he worked to hard and cost them too much money.

They put him in an office looking after home beats and special constables, thinking that would keep him out of trouble and stop him arresting people. How wrong they were. One night duty on the dog van we took a call to suspects on shout at a shop in Fulham Road. As we raced there, we were almost forced off the road by a marked carrier van, which we thought was the territorial support group.

When we arrive on scene, I found it was Inspector G and his specials that he used to have out on nights every Friday and Saturday on a rowdy patrol. Guess who nicked the prisoners? There was no way they were ever going to stop him and they didn't! He ended up putting Brixton in its place, somewhere most inspectors were too scared to be posted. He loved it.

Don't jump

On the odd occasion, I would be acting sergeant on the relief if we were short of a sergeant for one reason or the other. This was no great problem; it just meant making sure everyone was posted to a beat or to a car for the shift, booking them on and off duty, and being available to help out as much as possible. There were several of us on the relief with a bit of service behind us and we used to do this between us as and when required.

One night I was playing sergeant and I was out and about driving X-Ray 7. I suddenly heard my shoulder number being called very quietly over the radio by Colin Hale. I answered him and he told me he had a problem. He had been informed by a member of the public that there was a woman on the M25 railway bridge on the A4 at Colnebrook acting strangely and he was concerned for her welfare. Colin had arrived there to find she had climbed over the railing on the bridge and was going to jump off and kill herself. I made my way there and on my way I got other officers to go to both ends of the bridge to stop any vehicle passing Colin and the woman.

I parked my car a little distance away and walked slowly towards Colin while trying to stay out of view of the woman. When I got to Colin he told me that the woman intended to jump off the bridge when a large HGV came past on the M25 with the intention of landing in front of it, to commit suicide. I immediately contacted Hayes control room and asked them to get a traffic car on the M25 to stop traffic coming northbound towards the woman. This was done fairly quickly as a traffic car was near the M3 when the request was made.

Colin was doing a fantastic job with the woman; he was managing to keep her talking and every time she made a move as if to jump, he managed to attract her attention and distract her long enough to stop her from jumping. Very shortly, there was no traffic coming through at all. Another experienced PC, Brian Houston, was driving X-Ray 6. He came up with an idea and suggested bringing up three HGV vehicles from the roadblock on the M25.

He wanted to bring them up and park them right underneath the area where the lady was threatening to jump. If she did then jump she would only fall onto the roofs of the HGVs and was unlikely to cause herself serious injury or death. We decided this was a great idea and shortly afterwards Brian arrived escorting three large HGVs. They drove very slowly. The lady at first did not realise what was happening. When she saw the lorries were manoeuvring right below her she became hysterical and knew we were trying to stop her from falling. She started raging at Colin, which meant she took her eyes off me.

I started crawling behind some cars to get nearer to her. She was focused on Colin, saying he had lied to her and that men were all the same. I realised then that she was moving away from the lorries towards the opposite carriageway. This brought her nearer to me. She still, however, stayed focused on Colin and I had managed to get up against the bridge railings within reach of her. She then suddenly shouted something out and went to jump. As she did, I jumped up straight and grabbed for her. I realised I had her but something was not right.

Colin was with me in a second and took some of the weight from me. I then realised that I had in fact grabbed the woman by the breasts. As she went to jump her top had come up and as I grabbed her I had two handfuls of this woman's bra and breasts. We managed to pull her backwards over the railings and she kept struggling and we put her on her back on the floor and held her down. It was then I realised I was still holding on tight to her breasts and quickly had to release her and pull down her top down to cover her up.

The lady eventually calmed down and was taken to hospital. The cause of her attempted suicide was her husband's infidelity. I was convinced it was only a matter of time before I received a complaint of indecent assault after I grabbed her breasts. It never came, so hopefully if she was aware of what I had done she had forgiven my indiscretion and had just been grateful that we had saved her life. She received treatment and counselling and I believe she recovered fully from her ordeal.

To bring my time at West Drayton to a close, there is another name I cannot miss out and that is my very dear friend Michael Wise. Michael is currently a superintendent at Kensington and Chelsea. Most of us call him Mick, but as an aunt of his once said to my wife when she called him Mick, 'Well you would not call my Richard, Dick'!

Sorry, that is an in-house family joke that I just had to get into this book.

He joined our relief just a short time before I left to join the dog section. As a result, I never really had the pleasure of working a lot with him. But despite that, my wife and I became very good friends with Mick and his wife Dawn. They have two wonderful children, Rebecca and Jonathan, and they are our adopted family in London. We have spent virtually all our Christmas Days with them in the last sixteen years. I mention them because there have been times, especially in the last ten years of my service, where I really do not know how I would have survived without them. They are such wonderful people and all of them have played such an important part in my life that I could not write this book without saying thank you to them.

The dog section years

During my five years at West Drayton, I worked a lot with the dog section. It was quite normal for me to have a handler and dog in the back of my area car when we did a week of night duty. It made sense to have the emergency car turn up, normally first, to every call and to have the ability to use the dog immediately if required rather than have to wait for one to arrive. The dog was a fantastic tool to have at our disposal and the results proved it. I got very interested in the dog section and decided that this was to be my next career move.

One of the things you had to do in order to get yourself known to the section was to offer to help out during some of the training exercises that the handlers put their dogs through on a very regular basis to keep the dogs up to scratch. I learnt very quickly that everything that a dog could do – searching, tracking or chasing – was purely a huge game to them, but I can assure you it does not feel like a game when it is you they are searching for or chasing. Before I knew it, I found myself playing the criminal on a regular basis on nights.

In the early hours of the morning we would go to a local trading estate and set up some sort of training exercise for the dogs on nights with us. I can honestly say that hiding from a dog and then waiting for it to come and find you is not for the faint-hearted. Even when I knew the dog could not actually get at me, the bloody things always had a good try at getting past the barrier between me and the dog, and it was terrifying.

I progressed to having my arm padded up and running off for the dog to chase me and take me down by the arm. The first time I did, I thought this was madness. My arm was padded with loads of bandages and I was told to run towards a set point in the distance. I was advised to look ahead and hold my arm out as straight as possible. Don't look back they said and what ever you do don't turn your body towards the dog. They also said if I hit the deck hard, and the dog let go for any reason, I was to make sure I fed my arm back into his mouth so he does not get chance to bite you any where else!

So off I went and I immediately heard the handler's voice: 'Police dog and handler: stand still or I will send the dog.'

Oh shit, I really wanted to stop, but just concentrated ahead, and then I heard the thunder of feet as the dog came after me, the thunder of feet quickly became heavy panting and snarling followed by a low deep growl and then *Bang!* It was like being hit by a train and I went face first into the hard ground. My right arm was firmly held in the dog's jaws and he was biting harder and harder. Even through all the bandages I could feel the grip like a vice, getting tighter.

The handler joined us and called the dog off. The dog let go and stood right in front of me with saliva drooling from his mouth and I could tell by the look of him he had enjoyed it and was willing me to get up and run again. I did not move until he was back on the lead. When the bandages were taken off my arm they were already marked, even through all that padding. I wondered what would happen to an unprotected arm: it did not bear thinking about. The more I trained with the dogs the more I was determined to become a handler. They are amazing animals and the things they were capable of achieving were fantastic to see.

I'M IN

I EVENTUALLY PASSED THE DOG section selection board in the summer of 1989 and a short time later, was sent on a suitability course at the dog school in Keston, near Biggin Hill in Kent. This course lasted two weeks and was aimed at making sure you were suitable to be a handler. We learnt the basics of handling dogs, basic obedience training and how to groom and look after a dog correctly.

I passed the course and returned to West Drayton to wait for my posting to the section. In September 1989 I was finally posted onto the then 6 area dog section based at Norwood Green near Southall. This was my first bit of luck, remaining on the area that I knew so well. I then went back to the dog school to meet the litter of puppies from where my allocated puppy was to come from.

The litter was from the 'O' litter of 1989, which meant that all of the pups would have a name beginning with the letter 'O'. I was with five other handlers, three of whom were experienced officers who all had dogs in the section already, but whose dogs were due for retirement so they were being allocated three new pups. The other three of us were novices.

In the litter were four pups to be allocated, and two of the handlers were to get gift dogs. These were dogs that were older and had been given to the school by members of the public, and I really did not want to get one of the gift dogs as a puppy would suit me better. What also coloured my choice was that the litter was from a breeding bitch called Lacy who I knew very well as she was handled by John Clemance, one of the dog sergeants at Norwood Green.

On the three-day allocation course I discovered that I was to get allocated one of the bitch puppies with the name of Metpol Octavia. It was a real joy meeting the litter for the first time and we spent the next two days getting to know these eight-week-old bundles of fur. It was very hard to ever imagine that any of them would ever be working police dogs. Indeed, there was a long process to go through before that could happen but at least it was the start.

At the end of the third day we were allowed to take the dog's home. I had already prepared a covered secure compound outside, in the back garden of my house. Inside was the large green kennel supplied by the job for the dog to live in. We were warned that the dogs should live outside and that they would be very noisy for the first few nights until they get used to their new surroundings and that under no circumstances were we to give in and bring the dogs indoors.

The next step was the journey home from the dog school. This was about an hour-and-a-half journey by car. I had bought the car specially, and my dog vehicle was a Ford Fiesta hatchback. I had kitted the back out with a dog box to keep the dog safe and secure. We had spent some time over the previous couple of days putting the pups in the car and driving slowly around in the car park to get them used to the vehicle and the pup seemed fine.

This all changed when it was time to head for home at the end of day three; as soon as we drove out of the school gates the noise of a screaming banshee came from the rear of the car, and despite stopping several times to make sure she was OK, it continued all the way home and there was nothing I could do to stop it. It really made me concerned for what I could expect that night from the compound.

Just prior to getting home, I stopped off at my wife's place of work to show her the pup. Paula worked at a large airport hotel and she fell in love with her, as did all the other girls working on reception. They loved her and the dog lapped up all the attention. I left for home and, once there, started to settle her in, introducing her to her kennel and compound. A tip given to us by the puppy sergeant at the school was to wear an old jumper while you were settling the dog in, and then when you left the dog in the kennel/compound, leave the jumper in the kennel for the dog to sleep on, as well as her bedding, and the smell of you on the jumper would keep her happy. I was very sceptical but thought I might as well try it.

I wore the jumper all afternoon and evening while spending as much time as I could with her. I went and introduced her to all the neighbours and apologised in advance for the noise I was expecting her to make. They were all very taken with the pup too and said not to worry as they understood. Well, late that night, after the dog had been spoiled rotten all evening, by my wife, I put her out in the compound and into her kennel with the jumper and left her secure in there.

She immediately started whimpering and I thought this was the start of it, and assumed it would be only a short time before the raving banshee noise began. Then the whimpering stopped and I spent the rest of the night worrying about why I could hear no noise from her and had no sleep at all thinking there was something wrong. I got up numerous times in the night to look through the kitchen window. Each time, I could see her quite happily wandering around the compound or fast asleep without a care in the world.

This was how it was to be for the rest of her life. This dog was born to be a police dog and for the next eight years, never ceased to amaze me with what she was capable of doing. I was not a natural dog-handler – far from it. She, however, was a natural, and I always said that by the time she was three years old, she only needed me to open the dog van doors for her; once she was out she worked out the rest for herself. I am also sure that if I had shown her how, she would have learned how to open the van doors.

There was, however, no way was I going to walk the streets of London calling out the name 'Octavia': can you imagine the reaction of hardened criminal and local yobs.

We were allowed to give the dogs unofficial names and I decided to let my wife Paula select a suitable one for the pup. She decided to go for a traditional Welsh name and as a result 'Metpol Octavia' became known by everyone as Tegan and her life as a police dog in the Metropolitan Police began.

During my time in the section Tegan surpassed all my expectations, and for a little over seven-and-a-half years, she was a loyal partner. She was amazing to work with and all the success we had during her working life was down to her. Because she was a fairly small dog, the only defect in her ability was that she did not have a very hard bite but this never really proved to be too much of a problem.

The remainder of the essential exercises she had to complete, such as tracking, finding property and searching for suspects, were always exceptionally good and more than made up for her not having a hard bite. She could, however, turn it on when she required to and twice came to my rescue. She was very defensive of me and sensed situations very well.

The first year of my service within the dog section was spent doing what was commonly known as 'puppy-walking'; this was basically spending my working days at the dog section office manning up on the dog vans and helping with anything and everything that needed doing. It also meant I was able to commit a lot of time to my dog. She would come to work with me every day, and this helped to get her used to mixing with people and getting her used to normal everyday things like heavy traffic in the street. She was also able to have contact with lots other police dogs, including her mother Lacy, who was also at the office every day.

DURING THIS FIRST YEAR, WE both went to the dog school for one day every month for the dog's progress to be assessed. She developed very quickly, especially her obedience. This just seemed to be bred into her and I had a very easy time teaching her the basic obedience exercises. With the guidance of the puppy sergeant, by the time she was four months old she was happily responding to the commands of 'sit' and 'down'.

One of the best things she learnt was to go to toilet on command. I thought it was a wind-up when told that by repetition of the command 'empty' when she was young and naturally going to toilet, she would learn to go when instructed. But it really did work and pretty soon she would go off and 'empty' when told. This was to be essential when she was working so that you could get her to go before starting a search to save any embarrassment where searching someone's house.

As she got older, she was introduced to the skills of tracking and searching both for property and people. Again, she picked this up fairly easily; I was the one who had trouble grasping the art of tracking and was holding her back, but eventually I cracked it and things progressed well from there. As I mentioned earlier, her only problem was her weak bite on a chase. Her actual chase after the criminal was fine; it was the actual final attack of the arm that was the problem. She would always just get a front-tooth bite which was all teeth and no jaw. This meant she could not hang onto the first bite and would need to come off the arm and readjust for the second bite.

In January 1991, we started a fourteen-week basic course at the dog school. I really enjoyed this course and Tegan progressed well through all the various stages of training. The only down side to the whole course was when, in the last week, her brother, Timber, injured a leg very badly and was never to become a police dog. I had become very good friends with Timber's handler, Andy Wood, and we all felt a real sense of loss when Timber had to be retired. Andy went on to have several gift dogs during the time I had just the one. He is still dog-handling to this day.

In March 1991 I passed out of the dog school and was ready to start working as a handler on 'B' relief at Norwood Green. And so started just over six years of a great partnership where I spent more time with Tegan than I did with my wife. Tegan worked until she was nearly eight years old and then lived happily at our home until she was the good old age of thirteen-and-a-half. At that age she was still a sharp as a button but her back legs went and she was in real pain. I had to have her put to sleep and it broke our hearts. I have many stories relating to the time we spent working together, here a just a few of them.

The wrong dog

The 14-week course was very hard work but great fun. Working outdoors all the time in the countryside or some old building gave the dog's lots of environments to get used to. One environment was a large shopping centre in Croydon. We went there one late turn to work the dogs in the underground service areas where there would be lots of scent and distractions to make the dogs really work.

We always travelled about in large police kennel vans that housed all six dogs, and us with a civilian driver. We arrived there just after closing time and set about with a few hours training. At some point we stopped for a tea break and we all left the dogs in various places, some in the van and some outside. I had left Tegan in the down position on top of a large concrete block that was part of a delivery bay directly opposite our van, where I could keep my eye on her to make sure she stayed in the position I left her in; this was a normal training aid for the down position.

I was sitting in the van with Andy Wood and Keith Goodenough (our instructor). The others were doing their own thing nearby. I was suddenly aware of one of the experienced handlers, John Arbour, standing in front of my dog eating a sandwich. All three of us then watched as John started tempting my dog by trying to get her to take a piece of sandwich. I should say that police dogs eventually got trained in food refusal to stop them being given something by a suspect they might be searching for. I had not even tried food refusal with Tegan but John was well advanced in food refusal with his dog.

Every time he would offer Tegan the food she would try to take it, John would smack her on the muzzle.

I said to Keith, 'What on earth is he doing to my dog?'

Keith did not have a clue. I got out of the van and said, 'What the bloody hell are you doing John?'

He replied 'Practising food refusal. What does it bloody look like?'

I looked at him in amazement as he hit Tegan on the muzzle again.

I said 'You're out of order – leave the dog alone.'

He looked at me a bit oddly and said, 'Mind your own business. Look after your own dog and I will take care of mine; he is trained in food refusal but for some reason he keeps trying to take it.'

Then I realised he thought Tegan was his dog. They were both from the same litter but his was a male weighing 100lbs and mine was a little bitch weighing 75lbs. No comparison whatsoever. He again hit her on the nose.

I said 'John if you want to practice food refusal on your dog, then get the bloody thing out of the van and do it, but leave mine alone.'

He looked at Tegan, then me, walked over to the van and looked in the cages and at Andy and Keith laughing their heads off. John's face was an absolute picture; he just kept looking at Tegan and then his dog in the van. He was so embarrassed, but we didn't tell too many people at the dog school about the experienced dog-handler's mistake. Not much!

Close to home

Only a month after starting the basic course at the dog school, an incident occurred that made me realise what an asset Tegan was going to be to me as a partner. On a Saturday afternoon in February 1991, I was off duty at home having just returned from walking her. I had showered and was getting dressed in my bedroom when I noticed a black male acting strangely close to the rear of a house directly opposite my home. This cottage was set in a plot of land with no other houses near it. I knew the owners were away on holiday. I got dressed as quick as I could and got Tegan from my back garden and went straight across the road.

The man was nowhere to be seen and so I made my way through a side gate to the rear of the house. I could see straight away that the garden patio table had been moved to under the kitchen window and that there were jemmy marks of some kind around the window frame. Even though Tegan was not fully trained she had done quite a bit of search training, or seeking as we called it. So I gave her the command 'Find him' and off she went nose to the ground down the garden. She stopped at a three-foot fence at the very end of the garden, this backed onto open fields and she began barking and jumping up.

This was a good sign as suspects climbing over fences leave residual scent on the fence. I put her over the fence and off she went again and tracked for about seventy-five yards into a small wooded area. When I reached her she was trying to get into a large bramble bush. When she could not force her way in she started barking. At this point the same man I had seen earlier stood up and asked me to call the dog off. I kept the man there until local officers who had been called by my wife joined us. He was arrested for attempted burglary and at the police station items from other homes he had earlier burgled were recovered.

What a great start, Tegan was to be the best piece of equipment I was ever to get as a police officer.

As a dog-handler, night duty was by far the best time for working the dog and making best use of their talents. I loved nights and so did Tegan. She steadily got used to being a working dog and her skills improved with age. Her chasing did get better but she always had a front-tooth bite. She learnt that she was not big enough to give a full bite to stop someone too big, so she got around this by biting and coming off the arm then biting again. She would do this with just her large front teeth. This would really hurt any suspect who she was forced to bite; it also used to tear their clothing. It was not uncommon to find her detaining a suspect who looked like he had been in a bomb blast because all his clothes were torn.

She was, however, very honest and only bit a suspect if the suspect showed aggression towards her or me. Some dogs have the most incredible bites that really hurt, even with padding on, but one night duty, before Tegan was fully trained I saw first-hand what injuries, a full-blooded attack on a person can cause.

I was manning up on night duty driving the dog van with another handler. In the early hours of the morning another dog van got involved in the chase of a stolen vehicle around west London that eventually ended up with the driver decamping from the vehicle into a park on the edges of Southall and Ealing. Unfortunately for the driver, Kevin Siddle and his dog, who I think was called Floyd, were right behind him.

Kevin challenged the driver as he ran off. Now at this point, anyone who runs from a dog especially in large open spaces must want his head tested. However, to Kevin's surprise, not only did the man not stop running but he also put out his right arm just as padded-up officers would do when training the dog to chase. The dog must have thought it was his birthday when Kevin sent him off with the words 'Stop him'.

Apparently, the chase lasted seconds and the dog caught him and locked on to the suspect's right arm following a full-blown leap. As the dog locked his teeth around the arm the suspect decided to stop dead in his tracks with the result that the momentum of the dog continued forward; unfortunately for the suspect the dog just held on and as his weight pulled him forward, he came off the suspect's right arm, still with a large chunk of muscle, ripped from the arm, in his mouth.

When we arrived there were local officers giving him first aid, his arm was a mess. I think he must have been on drugs of some kind as he did not seem at all bothered that a large chunk of his right arm was now missing. When he was asked why he had not stopped and why he had put his arm out, he told officers that he had seen it done on a television programme and thought it was meant to put the dog off. How wrong can you be? I realised then just how much damage a dog can do to a human being.

Conan the destroyer

The padding up for a dog to chase you is always scary, but the scariest of all was playing criminal for a dog called Conan. This dog was handled by a very good handler called Tim Rees. Conan was a gift dog to the force but in my opinion he was one of the best police dogs I ever had the pleasure of working with. His sheer presence was enough, but put him to work and he was unbelievable. The best thing of all was his criminal work. I had the pleasure of working with Tim and Conan a lot, but even though he knew me well, it still did not stop him giving me the scariest time of my life. Here is what happened.

One summer we were doing a display at a large village fete. We used to do this quite often through the summer. The grand end to the display was always the criminal work with lots of chasing followed by stick and gun attacks for the dogs to deal with. The crowd used to love seeing the dogs flying at the criminal as they fired guns at them.

Guns always really got the dogs going and the attacks were always pretty impressive. The big finish was always the bank robber with a sawn-off shotgun and the big-hitting Conan was normally the dog to do it to the sound of the theme music from the film *Jaws* being played over the tannoy system. The crowd used to love it.

Regrettably, I was to be the shotgun criminal for Conan in the big finish. I was scared to death but tried not to show it. Come the grand finish, I stepped into the arena with masses of padding on my right arm to the sounds of *Jaws* echoing around the arena. I was dressed all in black wearing a crash helmet and carrying a sawn-off shotgun. As I stepped in I could see Conan at the other end already almost pulling Tim off his feet to get at me.

Tim started shouting the usual warnings of put the gun down and as he did so I let off a round with a big boom. I looked through the cloud of smoke and saw this massive hairy Exocet missile hurtling towards me. I knew I was in trouble; I could see from his demeanour that this was going to hurt. As Conan got about ten feet away I let off the second shot and before the smoke cleared he hit me. I thought a wall had come down on me. He put me flat on my back and had my arm fully in his mouth. He was snarling and growling like mad. I felt my arm going up over my head and he started dragging my fourteen-stone frame around the arena like I was a rag doll.

Eventually, Tim got to me and started yelling at Conan to 'leave', which meant he should have let go of my arm. No chance; he just bit even harder and pulled me even more. The more Tim tried to get him off, the harder he bit and the more he pulled. I thought I was in real trouble here. I could feel my arm going numb and I could have quite easily passed out with the pain. Then I felt Tim pulling the crash helmet off and wondered what the hell was going on. Then I realised Tim was bashing Conan on the head with it to try and get him to let go of my arm. It worked eventually, and the feeling of relief as the pressure around my arm released was wonderful.

The crowd were clapping and cheering and thought it was all part of the show, they loved it. Tim was concerned and checked I was OK, as I stayed there on one knee getting my senses back I looked at Conan sitting nicely like a good boy next to Tim's leg, and I swear blind the big sod winked at me and grinned. I tried to act the big brave copper and we walked off to huge applause. I had survived – only just – what must have been just about as bad as a shark attack in *Jaws*. *Never again* I said to myself, *never again!*

Don't mess with me

One afternoon in September 1991, a robbery took place at a small village post office in West Drayton. Witnesses to the offences identified the suspect as a local druggie who lived fairly close by in the village. The suspect was well-known to the police and was also known to be HIV-positive. Normally, when arrested, he became very violent and would spit at and try to bite police officers, and had stated that before he died of Aids he would give a police officer Aids as revenge.

Officers had attempted to get a reply at his door. They had tried forcing it but it had been strengthened and was proving difficult to gain entry. One of the officers had suggested climbing in through a large window accessed via the porch roof, and a plan was devised for Tegan, me and the local officer to get in this way. We got Tegan up on the roof easily by lifting her up on a large riot shield and she jumped the rest of the way. We then followed.

I knew because of the violence normally shown by the suspect I had to be quick to back her up. I put her in and sent her off with a 'find him', and before I could get through the window she was barking like mad. I got to her as quick as I could. In the living room I found her pinning the suspect in an armchair. His face was a picture. Unknown to us he had a great fear of dogs and was sat there petrified.

Tegan had her hind legs on the floor, her front legs on his chest and she was snarling and slobbering white drool all over his face. You could tell she was looking at him and saying, 'Don't mess with me, just you give me an excuse to bite you.' He could not speak, he was so scared. In his left hand was a cannabis reefer he had just been about to smoke and on the table was a large knife and the proceeds of the robbery at the post office. Also cowering in the corner was a second male who turned out to be an accomplice who had acted as some sort of look out for him.

I could tell Tegan had really enjoyed that one and it was an excellent result all round with no officers put in any danger.

How embarrassing

One night duty in June 1992, I was working on a van with another handler when we got called to an address in Ealing, West London, where officers believed that they still had suspects on premises at a residential house. When we arrived it was about 1.00 a.m. and the local officers explained that a next-door neighbour had seen two males breaking in by forcing the front window of the premises. Police had caught one at the rear as he was attempting to leave and they believed that a second one may be still inside. The house itself was a very large townhouse in a very expensive part of Ealing and was four floors in total.

With the house surrounded by police and my colleague having gone off to check the rear gardens I got the dog ready to go into the premises. I had to enter through the front window and so, after shouting the usual challenge of 'police dog and handler – come out now or I will send in the dog', I had Tegan bouncing around desperate to get inside.

This challenge was always the switch to put the dogs into seeking mode; they all loved it and Tegan was no exception. So I picked her up and put her in through the window with her legs going ten to the dozen to get started. I placed her in and onto what I thought was some sort of table just inside the window. Almost immediately, I heard a horrible scraping noise – almost deep gouging – and then the dog landed on the floor. I switched on my touch and looked inside and saw that the top of the table was badly scratched from her claws and remember hoping that it was not an expensive piece of furniture. I watched Tegan search the room and then climbed in through the window followed by a local officer assisting me.

As soon as I got inside, I switched on the room lights and my heart sank. Not only did the piece of furniture look expensive, it also looked like it was probably an antique type of writing desk. To make it worse, on top of the desk were photographs that had been knocked over as either she or the burglars had climbed through. I picked the biggest one up off the floor and again thought, *Oh no.* In the picture was a gentleman in very high-ranking looking military uniform receiving a medal from the Queen at Buckingham Palace.

I checked other photos and realised the man in the uniform was obviously the owner of the house. I thought, *well never mind, let's just find the second burglar, which will help to make up for the damage caused to the desk.*

So the search commenced. Tegan was very excited all over the ground floor of the house, and there was obviously a lot of residual scent from the burglars as she took quite some time to clear all the rooms. I remember thinking to myself that I hoped she did not get too excited and decide to have a pee while she was searching! This did not happen very often, but in places such as this it was dog-handler's big dread. As for the worry of her deciding to have a more solid toilet moment whilst searching – well that had never happened, so it never ever bothered me.

Having cleared the ground floor and basement, I sent her off up the first flight of stairs. I remained at the bottom with the local officer. This gave her a free reign to search just on human scent already there rather than our scent mixing with it and making it more difficult for her. I could hear her running around panting; the floor was obviously wooden and I could hear exactly where she was searching.

One thing she always did when locating a suspect who was hidden was to stop and not move. Colleagues who were hiding for her to find during training had told me it is almost if she was holding her breath and listening just to confirm what her sense of smell was telling her. When she was 100 per cent certain she had found someone she would then start barking for me to know she had located them. Well, everything suddenly went very quiet. I told the local officer that I thought she had found someone and to wait for the barking to start. It only took about ten seconds or so normally but the silence went on for

You're Nicked My Son

longer. I was a bit confused at this but then suddenly she was running around searching like mad again.

I could not really work out what had gone on and had started to walk up the stairs when suddenly the most horrendous smell hit me, straight up my nose, and I realised she must have decided to have a shit as she was so excited. My worst fears were confirmed when I walked into a very nice television room with beautiful wooden flooring and smack in the middle was one of the biggest piles of dog shit I had ever seen. I did not think that amount of shit could have possibly come out of one dog. It made me gag and the poor local guy with me was nearly sick.

As soon as Tegan had finished searching, I left the dog lying down at the bottom of the next flight of stairs to secure them. I then went and searched out kitchen roll, plastic bags and soapy water to clean it all up. I had to get rid of the smell before we were able to continue as it was so horrendous. So with the shit from hell cleaned up, we pressed on in the knowledge that nothing else could go wrong.

The third floor was searched with no trace of any suspect so the top floor was looking good. I sent her off again with a challenge before hand to wind her up a bit, and off she went. Again, I could here her running around on the wooden floors and then, suddenly, silence followed by a low growl which very quickly turned into a very aggressive bark and again deep low growling. Again I thought *that's odd; she has obviously found some one but it also sounds like she has got hold of him.* I assumed he must have been aggressive and she had bitten him.

I ran up the stairs shouting, 'Good girl, stop him,' to encourage her to hang onto him. I followed the sound and ran into the bedroom followed by the local guy ready to grab to suspect. I stopped in my tracks as soon as I entered the room. There on top of this huge double bed was Tegan, killing a large child's doll as if it was someone trying to kill her. She had its head in her mouth and was throwing it from side to side doing her best to rip its head off.

I yelled at her to leave, the command to drop what she had and come back to me. She normally did this instantly. But not this time, she just would not leave that doll alone and I had to grab her by the collar and pull it from her. The doll's head was destroyed by her teeth and this also looked like a very expensive antique. How on earth was I going to explain this?

Well, I finished the search and no second suspect was found. It later transpired that he had got out of the house before the one who had got caught. I completed the necessary paperwork regarding the damage Tegan had caused in the house and waited for the fallout and complaint from the house owner. It never came. I can only assume the Met paid him compensation or he was just happy with police catching the guys who broke into his house.

What had got into the dog that night, I will never know. She had searched many houses before that particular search. She never behaved like that before and never did it again after. What is it they say? Never work with kids or animals!

You're Nicked My Son

POLICE TRAINING CENTRE, WALES
Class 2 — 14th March, 1977 to the 20th May, 1977

My official class photograph from training school in May 1977 (I'm the good looking one, back row far left) !!!!!!!!!!!!!!!!!!!!!!!

Andy Vick

Maurice Gibb of the Bee Gee's under protection at Heathrow.

You're Nicked My Son

The aftermath of the fatal M4 car crash in June 1986

Andy Vick

Tegan with her two sisters and brother taken on her 9 month puppy course at the dog training school at Keston in Kent.

Tegan aged 12 months old

Andy Vick

Armed robber Malcolm Parker detained after he was ambushed by SO19 and the Flying Squad following the robbery at Ladbrokes in Headington.

You're Nicked My Son

Parker is finally in custody after a year long investigation

Andy Vick

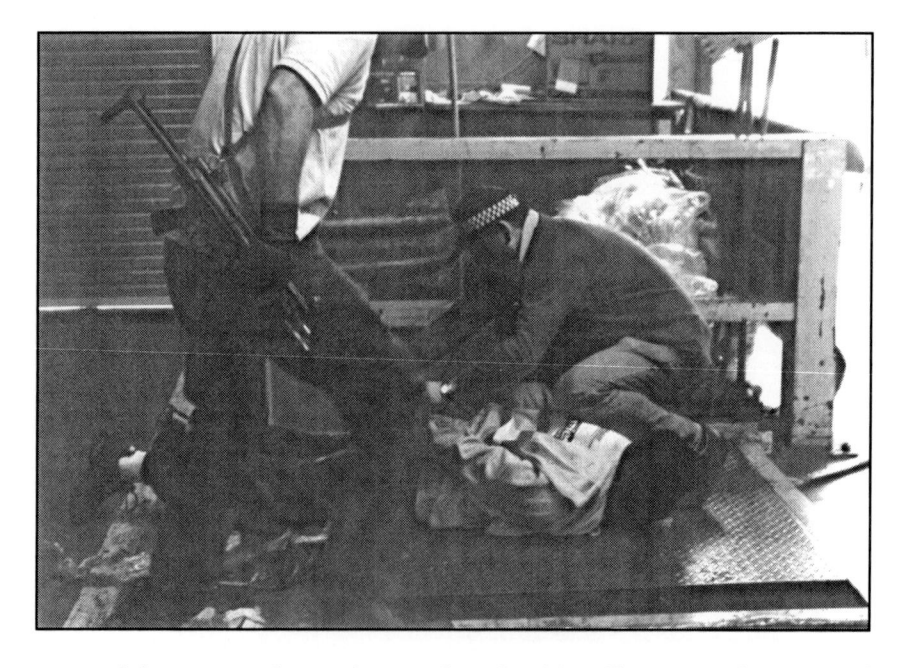

One of the suspects being detained at the 44 million pound attempted bullion robbery at London Heathrow Airport.

You're Nicked My Son

IN THE INNER LONDON AREA AND IN THE METROPOLITAN POLICE DISTRICT

Bow Street Magistrates' Court (Code 2641

To each and all of the Constables of the Metropolitan Police Force

ACCUSED: Ronald Arthur BIGGS

ADDRESS: No fixed abode

ALLEGED OFFENCE: That he being a prisoner in H.M.Prison Wandsworth serving sentences of 25 and 30 years imprisonment (concurrent) passed upon him at the Assizes of the County of Buckingham on the 16th April 1964, upon conviction of a) conspiracy to stop mail with intent to rob the said mail and b) robbery with aggravation and having escaped from the said prison on the 8th July 1965 is unlawfully at large from the said prison in which he is required to be detained after being convicted of the said offences. Pursuant to Section 72 of the Criminal Justice Act, 1967

Information on oath having this day been laid before me, the undersigned, by D.S.Wilson.

that the accused committed the offence of which particulars are given above.

DIRECTION: You, the said Constables, are hereby required to arrest the accused and to bring the accused before the above Magistrates' Court immediately, ~~unless the accused is released on bail as directed below.~~

BAIL: ~~On arrest, after complying with the condition(s) specified in Schedule I hereto, the accused shall be released on bail, subject to the condition(s) specified in Schedule II hereto, and with a duty to surrender to the custody of the above Magistrates' Court at the hour of ten in the forenoon of the next day upon which such Court is open on   at~~

~~SCHEDULE I~~
~~Conditions to be complied with before release on bail~~
~~To provide   suret   in the sum of £   (each) to secure the accused's surrender to custody at the time and place appointed.~~

~~SCHEDULE II~~
~~Conditions to be complied with after release on bail~~

Date: 27th July 1990.

M.C.A. 4
WARRANT
First Instance
M.P.81(E)

Metropolitan Stipendiary Magistrate
~~Justice of the Peace for the Inner London Area~~

(annotation: 9.05am 7th MAY 2001)

A copy of the arrest warrant issued for Ronnie Biggs and executed on the plane at Northolt RAF on his return from Brazil on 7th May 2001

SLIPPER
OF THE YARD

Jack Slipper

> To Andy,
> With my best wishes. I can assure you that I will never forget that DRIVE to Scotland Yard. You "topped up" my poxious Squad Driver's well & truly. Once again Thanks
>
> Jack Slipper
> Ex Det ch. Supt
> of the Flying Squad

SIDGWICK & JACKSON
LONDON

The inscription written in my copy of 'Slipper of the Yard' by Jack Slipper

You're Nicked My Son

The Ronnie Biggs arrest team- May 2001

Tegan to the rescue

AT AROUND 3.00 A.M. ONE Saturday night duty in November 1994, I was on a dog van with another handler, Martin Game. We had spent several hours in and around the Uxbridge area trying to help local officers catch up with a stolen vehicle that had spent all evening travelling through Thames Valley and the Met area of West London, committing crime both from vehicles and burglary. They seemed to have a charmed life and just kept one step ahead of police at all times.

It was at this time we received a request from Thames Valley police to assist some of their units to search for two or three males who had been disturbed trying to steal a car in Chalfont St Peter. The suspects had decamped into a large wooded area just off the A413 at Gravel Hill, and it was believed that they were the same lot we had been chasing for hours.

We arrived on scene and were met by local officers who pointed out two separate places where the suspects had fled into the woods. The first place of entry was where a fence had fallen down and which led instantly into thick woodland and the second was a recognised pathway. Martin took this path with his dog, Toby, and I was to start from the broken-down fence. Martin set off with Toby on a tracking line accompanied by a local officer. I waited a minute or so to allow them to get clear and then got Tegan out of the van. I sat her at the broken fence and issued the usual challenge of 'police dog and handler come out or I will send in the dog'; I then released her into the woods.

In less than a minute she was barking loudly and I found her less that twenty yards from the road with a male tucked into very deep undergrowth. I called her to me and ordered the male to get himself

You're Nicked My Son

out of the bushes. He came out very compliant, and I walked him out to the road where the local officer identified him as one of the men who had run away. He was arrested and placed in the police car.

I continued the search of the wooded area and, having cleared it, I then tried to call Martin on the radio to let him know I had found one of the suspects. It was then we discovered that the area was a bit of a black spot for police radios, so I decided to follow the path Martin had taken to give him a hand. I had to go on my own as the local officer had to take the prisoner away. I let Tegan off and kept guiding her into the wooded area to the left and right, mainly checking for any property that may have been discarded by the suspects who had run this way.

The path and woods opened out into a large clearing. At the far end was a large building fenced off with a mixture of wooden and wire fencing. I later discovered it was a scout hut. At the other side of the hut was a large car park. Unknown to me at this time, Martin and Toby had tracked right through to this car park and were busy searching over there. Around the edge of the fencing was a ditch with a high bank around it. The ditch was not visible to me as I walked towards it. As we approached the compound fence, it was on my left as I followed the path Martin had taken.

I suddenly saw Tegan's head come up and she was obviously air-scenting something, I thought possibly a fox. I gave her a 'good girl, find him' and off she went in circles trying to pin down where the scent was coming from. Then she was up the bank and out of my sight and into the ditch; seconds later she was barking like mad.

I climbed up the bank and from the top of the ditch which was about two foot deep; I could see Tegan was bouncing all over a male lying face down in the ditch. Even with the dog all over him he was not moving.

I called her away from him and called out that I was a police officer and for him to stand up. He did not move. I repeated this several times but he still did not move. I was a bit uneasy of approaching him, as it meant climbing down a slippery bank, but I also had some concerns for his welfare. There was no water in this ditch but I still feared he may have been injured. I tried calling Martin again but the radio still did not appear to be working.

I decided I had no choice and made my way into the ditch carefully. So with handcuffs in hand, I made my way down; suddenly the male half-turned and kicked out with his legs. This toppled me over and I hit an upright section of the wooden fence with the left side of my chest as I fell. I immediately knew I was in trouble as I felt all the wind burst out of me as I hit the ground. I could not move and was winded and in real pain. I was waiting for the male to get up and kick the living daylights out of me, but I then saw that Tegan was on his back growling and snarling and she had him by the back of the neck.

He was screaming as she bit him, and every so often she would pull backwards with a lump of his jumper and shirt in her mouth. This had the effect of pulling his head back and strangling the man. Then she would bite his neck again. As I got some breath back, I kept encouraging Tegan to keep doing it with a 'good girl, stop him' in as aggressive a voice as I could manage. This kept her at his neck. I was in a lot of pain in my chest and side but knew I had to do something before the dog got tired. I managed to find my handcuffs, got to my knees and got over to the male, who was still face down with Tegan on his neck. I lay my full weight on top of him and told him to put his hands behind his back. All I got was a choking reply, and he did as he was told. I then managed to handcuff him in a fashion and felt a little relieved that I now had some sort of control of him.

Next, I told him that I was going to stand up and call the dog off him. I warned him that if he made any attempt to get up without me telling him to do so, I would set the dog back on him. I called Tegan off and she released his neck. I knew she was going to need a rest so I lay her down at the man's head so she was looking directly at him and he could feel her panting all over him; more as a fear factor for him, really.

This had been going on now for some five minutes or so. I was in real pain and guessed I must have cracked a rib or two. I again tried the radio but with no effect. I could not get the man out of the ditch myself and did not want to let him know that I was injured. So once Tegan had rested I thought the only other way I might get Martin's attention, as he was hopefully close by, was for him to hear Tegan barking. So after she had rested for a minute or two, I got her to sit and then whispered the command of 'speak' to her. This set her off in a mad barking mode. I did this several times over the next two or three minutes.

You're Nicked My Son

Fortunately, Martin did hear the barking and assumed I was somewhere close by with another suspect. He tried the radio also without success. However, there was a traffic car in the car park and he told them I was somewhere close possibly with a prisoner and asked them to search one way while he went the other. The traffic car drove into the scout hut compound and managed to pick me up in the headlights of the car as they drove around. They joined me shortly afterwards and arrested the male who was also identified as one other the car thieves.

It later transpired that there had indeed been three suspects. Martin and Toby had tracked along the path, past the scout hut, out onto the car park and right to the far corner where the track disappeared. It seems the third male had got into a car and left the scene. Martin had been double-checking the car park when he heard Tegan barking.

In all, I was in the ditch for about ten minutes totally unable to do anything; had it not been for Tegan I have no doubt that the suspect would have got up and given me a good kicking in that ditch. She did a fantastic job that night. I ended up with a couple of cracked ribs and bruises, but it could have been a lot worse.

Tegan's finest hour

In the early hours of the morning of Friday 16 July 1993, I was working a dog van with a very experienced dog-handler, Frank Malton, and his dog Sabre, when we were called by Ealing officers to assist them at a burglary. Suspects had been disturbed inside the pub by the landlord; he was savagely attacked and the suspects made off when they had finished attacking him. They left having stolen a large sum of cash from gaming machines inside the pub.

The pub was called the Halfway House and was situated on the Uxbridge Road close to Ealing Broadway. Frank suggested I try Tegan on a hard surface track from the rear of the premises. Tracking on hard surfaces such as pavements can be very difficult as it is only the suspect's shoes on the concrete leaving a very light trace. During the daytime in a busy street this would be an impossible task. However this was 3.30 a.m. in the morning and the pavement and roads would be virtually empty, so it was well worth a go.

I put Tegan into her harness and line and off we went. She went around in a few circles at the rear door of the pub then bang: nose down and off. She took me across the road and into a multi-storey car park. As she tracked towards a large wall in front of me, I heard the sounds of movement on the other side of the wall. Local officers shouted on the radio that suspects had run out of a back garden and they gave chase. We had obviously flushed them out of hiding. The local officers chased the suspects into a nearby road and lost them again in gardens.

Frank and I set about searching a side of the street each. In the second garden I noticed Tegan pulling at something. When I reached her I saw she was pulling off a torn piece of jacket sleeve that had caught on the gate lock, a positive indication that the suspects had been through the garden. I carried on the search through the gardens on my side of the road. About three houses down, Tegan was out of my sight when I heard her growling. I could see she was trying to pull something white from out of the bushes. I tried encouraging her to bring it to me but she was not able to do so. I went and looked myself and realised why she could not pick it up and bring it back to me: the item was a cloth money bag containing a large amount of coins and tokens (later found to be just over £1,000 in coins).

A local resident then told us he believed that he saw at least one of the suspects run from his garden and down the road and he believes he may have entered a house, although he could not say exactly which one. So again, I harnessed up Tegan and put her to track from his gate. She tracked down the footpath for a short time then crossed over to the other side of the road and stopped and circled outside number 3. She found no other track from here. This had to be the house he went into.

Intelligence checks with the local station showed this address to be very well-known to the police for criminality reasons. Frank and Sabre went and searched the address with local officers but found no one there. Frank was certain we had the right address and suggested everyone make as if we were giving up the search. Leaving two officers in an unmarked car to keep an eye on the address, everyone else moved a little distance away.

Still convinced they were still in the area; Frank suggested we check some back doubles around the streets. He found an alleyway that led to the rear gardens of the street where we had searched. He suggested I give Tegan a run through the gardens so I sent her off and she did her usual bomb around, jumping the small garden fencing of her own accord. About five gardens away she was getting very agitated and I thought she was about to bark to tell me she had located some one. She didn't, and I joined her and saw a large area of flattened vegetation where quite a few people had obviously been lying down.

This was about six gardens from the rear garden of the house we had searched. Frank got Sabre from the van and remained in the back gardens. I went back to the front and met up with the local guys, and we went back to the front door but got no reply. Someone could be heard on the stairs and so we forced entry by kicking open the front door.

As we kicked open the front door I could hear Frank challenging someone at the rear. The suspect was attempting to get out the back again but was prevented from doing so by Frank, Sabre and the local officers. Then one of the guys at the back called over the radio, 'all officers beware: he is armed with a knife.'

As he did so, the suspect ran back towards us and rushed up the stairs. I had missed a chance to take him with the dog as all the local guys were in front of me having just forced the front door. We secured the house downstairs and I then went to the bottom of the staircase and tried to get the suspect to speak to me. Upstairs was in total darkness. I got no reply but kept trying to make contact.

In the darkness it was very unsafe to make a move without knowing where the suspect was. I then tried a challenge, threatening to send the dog up, something I did not really want to do just yet, as a knife was a very serious threat to a dog if it got hold of a suspect. It would have been very easy for him to stab the dog when it got hold of his arm.

Suddenly, the suspect appeared at the top of the stairs with his right hand behind his back. Tegan went ballistic at the sight of him and I had to hold her really tightly by the collar. This was just what I needed to get her into an attack mode, to try and take him out if given the chance. (Tegan was also trained as a firearms team support dog. We had practised in training for the situation of attacking a standing criminal, but not having to send up her a flight of stairs in order to do it so. I was not sure how she would react to this situation.)

I gave the suspect firm instructions to come down the stairs slowly showing his hands or I would send the dog. The guy just looked at me then Tegan and said, 'F*** you, I'm going to get my shooter.'

He then turned and ran. I immediately released Tegan and she flew up the stairs; I followed right behind her. As I got to the landing the suspect was trying to open a bedroom door that appeared to be locked. He suddenly turned to face me and as he did so Tegan launched herself at him, hitting him at stomach height and he fell backwards. I jumped on top of him and, following a very violent fight, he was handcuffed and arrested.

As we tried to stand him up I realised Tegan still had his left wrist in her mouth and did not seem to want to let it go. The suspect was completely oblivious to the pain and to her on his hand. I called her off and she let his wrist go.

Fingerprints and DNA later proved positively that the suspect was the person who had broken into the pub. He also turned out to be a one-man crime wave and his arrest virtually solved Ealing's entire burglary problem in one swoop. He subsequently received a long term of imprisonment.

As you can imagine, I was extremely happy with the way Tegan had performed that night. The whole incident, from start to finish, lasted over an hour and forty minutes. It was mainly down to Frank's insistence that we keep searching and Tegan's ability, which never ceased to amaze me that we got the result that we did.

To add to her achievement, in the following October I took part in the 6 area police dog trials at Imber Court sports ground. Here all the dogs in the area compete against one another in all aspects of police dog skills from searching to dealing with armed suspects. There are three categories, which are broken down into several different elements. For example, the nose-work element involved searching for suspects and property and also tracking on hard and soft surfaces. At the end of two days of trials I was thrilled to find out that Tegan had won the whole competition outright.

At the end of the day we had a presentation of various awards, with Tegan receiving two awards in total. The final bit of the presentation was a complete and utter surprise to me. The dog inspector, Chris Sevier, stood up to announce the winner of the action dog of the year award for 6 area dog section. He then started to read out the details of the winning incident. It took me a little while to realise he was reading out the details of the job at the Halfway House pub, in Ealing and that Tegan was going to get the action dog of the year award as well. It was a great thrill to receive that award, and for me went a long way to justifying all the hard work involved in bringing out what was just so natural to Tegan.

Windsor Castle

A REALLY FUNNY STORY I have got to mention happened while I was on the dog section, and is not really anything to do with me, but I think it is worth putting in as I found it so funny.

At about 11.00 p.m. on 20th November 1992, a large fire at Windsor Castle caused such a serious amount of damage that the total cost of repair and restoration amounted to around £40 million pounds. The castle is policed by the Met despite the fact that it is in the Thames Valley police area. As a result of the fire, two dog-handlers from my office at Norwood Green were called to attend the castle urgently.

Phil 'Golly' Green and Clive Smith were probably the two most senior PCs on the unit and they were posted together on night duty. They duly turned up at Windsor Castle and identified themselves to the duty officer. As you can imagine, all hell was breaking loose around the castle grounds. When they arrived the fire was blazing away and the fire brigade was fighting to get it under control.

Phil and Clive were told to park the dog van up in a spot that gave them a first-class view of everything that was going on. Their job was to stay with the van and all the priceless paintings and furniture, being removed from the castle to prevent them from being destroyed, would be stacked up around the van. Their job was to protect all the paintings and furniture with the dogs until such a time they could get vans there to take it all away to a secure site. Within a very short space of time the entire van was surrounded by these amazing paintings of all shapes and sizes, along with some very grand furniture.

At some point they are both stood close to the van watching the castle blazing away and commenting on how much damage it was going to cause. Clive was suddenly aware of someone stood fairly close to him, obviously looking at the fire as well. With out even taking his eyes away from the fire, Clive piped up with, 'A right f***ing mess this is going to be.'

At this point Phil looked to his right and passed Clive to see who it was standing near to them, and to his horror he realised it was the Queen herself.

She was stood there in a scarf, long coat and Wellington boots. Without looking around she replied, 'Yes it is, officer; yes it is!'

She then walked off.

It was later the next morning that Golly was relaying this story to all in the office. It was the only time in his whole career that Clive was ever lost for words. Ah well; at least he did not lose his head!

Firearms support dogs

Apart from the normal everyday policing a dog is used for, most dogs also eventually tend to specialise in some other police dog-related exercise. Some dogs train as human remains recovery dogs, which are used to search for missing people and for buried bodies, and are a very successful tool in a major enquiry.

Some also specialise in the recovery of firearms and ammunition. In the Met, general police duty dogs, as they were known, did not get involved in the search for drugs or explosives – this was done by a separate wing of the dog section. The main additional use for a police dog is to be trained to work with the specialist firearms teams, otherwise known as SO19. These were the highly trained firearms officers who did all the serious work against the really big villains and terrorists that plagued London.

I really liked the idea of getting Tegan to move on to become a firearms support dog and noted my interest at a very early stage. However, it was not an easy thing to get to do. First, the dog had to get some experience and show she was up to the grade. When the dog inspector decided that a dog may be suitable, you would then have to go on an assessment day to test the dog and the handler, as both had to be the right calibre. There were several things that the dog had to be able to do.

The main thing was that the dog had to be a quiet searching dog. A lot of dogs get very excited when searching for suspects. They would very often whine or growl as they searched. This, of course, gave away any form of surprise as any suspect, hiding with a gun, would know exactly where the police were because of the dog's noise.

The dog's obedience had to be exceptional and the most important thing of all was that the dogs had to be able to be handled by other officers. This was because in houses or tight spaces the firearms team would at times be very close to the dog, and sometimes would take hold of them to guide them into the right search area. It used to cause a bit of a stir if a member of the firearms team got bitten by one of our dogs.

We went off for an assessment day and Tegan passed with flying colours, as usual. The only problem was her bite on the chasing a criminal, but her attributes in all the other disciplines got her through. Those that passed the course were sent away with ideas of things to try with their dogs to make the eventual four-week course go a little easier. The course was known to be very demanding, and hard on both handler and dog, but I was really looking forward to it.

Something I really wanted to be able to do with Tegan was to give her commands by hand signals rather than voice. This would be a great help when searching with the firearm teams because it kept things silent. Over a period of time I had taught her to sit, lie down and stand still just by hand signals, and it worked well. I decided, however that I wanted to push this a little further.

One of the exercises she would have to learn would be for her to be sent out into an open area, for instance a field. The dog would have to go away from the handler in a direct straight line. The idea was to simulate an armed suspect from a distance, where it might not be safe to approach in case he had a weapon. The dog would have to be sent out over a distance of anything up fifty yards away, and past the suspect. It would then be made to lie down on the ground a few yards away. This then gave the suspect something else to worry about. The suspect would then be given instructions to walk towards the police with his arms outstretched, made to stop as he got closer, and to turn around 360 degrees so that police could see he was not armed. He would then continue walking under police direction until he was close enough to be dealt with.

All the time the suspect was walking, the dog would be instructed to walk a short distance behind him, the idea being that if he ran or tried to do anything, the dog would be close enough to deal with him. A couple of other experienced handlers had worked out a set of hand signals to control their dogs in these circumstances and this stopped them having to shout commands to the dog above the officer who was shouting the instruction to the suspect. It also meant it kept the suspect wondering what the dog was doing. By the time I went on the course, I had managed to achieve this to great success thanks to Tegan's ability to pick things up very quickly.

As part of the key to show the dog that things were different when working with the firearms teams, and that she had different tasks to perform, we were all kitted out with exactly the same equipment as the teams would wear: black coveralls, boots and ballistic helmets etc. The only thing we did not have was a gun. It was then a ritual that at every job you went to with the teams, you would put your kit on at the same time as the team and the dog then realised that this was firearms work and not general police work.

The main use of a dog to a team was the searching and clearing of premises where a suspect may be hiding. At the time, the core work of the teams was early-morning raids to arrest wanted armed criminals. The normal event would be for the front door to be forced open, and a challenge put in by armed officers for the suspects to come out. If no one showed themselves, room by room, floor by floor in a well-rehearsed method, the dog would search for any suspects hiding.

It was my job to call a room as being clear after Tegan had searched it. It was a big responsibility because after I called it as being clear, members of the team would then search the room. Fortunately, I never made a wrong call. This was mainly due to Tegan, whose indications were always spot on.

OTHER PARTS OF THE COURSE must have been really strange for the dogs. They had to get used to a form of abseiling, where they would be put into a special harness and lowered off a roof from various different heights. This was to allow us to get dogs in into any positions required during an armed operation. Most dogs take to it after the first drop over a ledge; Tegan tried digging her claws into the roof on the first time she tried it but after that she was fine.

The dogs also had to get used to going up in the force helicopter. I loved flying but was a bit unsure how the dog would take to it, especially in a helicopter. It was making a horrendous noise and there was a downdraft as we approached it, but I think if you put any type of white vehicle with a red stripe down it in front of a police dog, they would happily get into it as they knew it was work time. Off we went for a flight around the Surrey countryside and Tegan loved it, happily looking out of the window. Another test passed, and she went from strength to strength.

During the course we spent a lot of time practising the searching of premises. With one or two dogs doing the searching, the rest of the guys on the course would play the part of the firearms teams. We had deactivated weapons or wooden guns to hold and would carry out the search as closely as possible to real life. This was all part of the method of getting the dogs to work to the correct standards.

Even in training, if you made the wrong judgement call as a result of the dog's indications, or the dog failed to locate the suspect who was hiding, you would fail the course. It was very strict and rightly so: a wrong call could cost an officer his life. We completed the course, and in September 1993 Tegan became one of only thirty-two dogs out of over 300 in the Met at that time to be a firearms support dog.

SHORTLY AFTER FINISHING THE COURSE my first job with the firearms teams was a domestic related siege, at a house in Dagenham. A man was in the upstairs part of this house and had held his ex-girlfriend and her new boyfriend at gunpoint. The girl managed to escape out of a window and call the police. There was another, more experienced handler there also and normally he would have taken the lead role. He had, however, arrived first and been directed to the rear of the house to cover a possible escape route with a couple of armed officers.

After quite some time the male hostage was released leaving just the suspect inside. This suspect was a South African ex-soldier and had a rifle of some sort that was believed to be a real gun. I spent quite some time in the front garden with Tegan. Eventually, the man came to the top of the stairs which went directly up from the front door. He had put the rifle down on the floor but was refusing to come down. I moved up to the front door with the dog and was positioned right behind the front member of the firearms team.

The dog now had sight of the suspect, who was ranting and raving and it was really winding her up and she was eager to get at him. I was asked by the team sergeant if the dog would be able to take him out at the top of the stairs as a standing-still suspect. Attacking a suspect who is standing still is against all normal police dog training. Normally, under Home Office guidelines a dog is trained to circle, bark and detain a suspect who has, to all intents and purposes, given up. The stand-off exercise as it is called is something a police dog must be able to be able to do to stay licensed as a police dog. Tegan was good at circling and detaining a suspect, but I was not sure how she would react to being sent at a standing criminal as a straightforward attack, especially up a flight of stairs. But I told the sergeant I was prepared to give it a try.

Before it came to that, the suspect stated he wanted to give himself up. He was given instructions by the firearms officers as to exactly what he had to do, and he was then instructed to come down the stairs and out into the front garden. It was a fairly confined space near the doorway and I had moved back to the front gate making sure Tegan had sight of the suspect at all times. As the firearms guys backed away from the doorway to give him room to come out onto the footpath, he suddenly bolted knowing full well they could not shoot him.

He went over a small hedge and onto the road directly in Tegan's line of sight. I released her with a loud 'stand still and stop him'. The 'stand still' was to make sure all police officers stayed still, and the 'stop him' to let Tegan know he was hers for the taking. Off she went and as she lined up to take his right arm, he looked around at her. This caused him to trip over and she jumped on top of him, closely followed by numerous members of the team.

I could not see Tegan as she was underneath a pile of bodies. As they slowly stood up one by one, I saw the dog on the bottom of the pile with the suspect's right bum cheek gripped firmly in her mouth. The suspect was screaming in pain and I left Tegan biting his arse until he was securely handcuffed, then I called her off him. He had a big rip in his jeans and two large puncture wounds in his backside.

That was the least of his troubles. The rifle recovered in the flat was real and was loaded with real ammunition. He would be dining at Her Majesty's pleasure for some considerable time now, and was likely to be deported back to South Africa after his sentence was complete. For Tegan it was an excellent first firearms incident and I was very pleased with the praise given to her by the team during the debriefing afterwards.

THERE HAD BEEN A FEW occasions when the dog or handler had made the wrong call in real-life situations, but fortunately nothing serious had happened as a result. However, this led some of the firearms officers on the teams to totally distrust the dogs. I was fortunate that because of Tegan's temperament and abilities, most of the teams got to enjoy working with her.

A couple of teams got used to her so much that they would actually phone me directly and ask for me to be used on operations they were involved in. But a couple of the teams did not like police dogs at any firearms incidents and considered them a waste of time; something that got in the way and was likely to bite them. One team in particular, Grey team rarely used the support dogs at all. If you got called to an incident by information room, Grey team would normally leave you out of the briefing all together and then stick you on some outer cordon out of the way. Two members of the team in particular were really anti-dog so working with them was a real pain. One such time could have proved fatal for one member of the team. This is the story.

On Friday 10th February 1995 I was called out in the early hours of the morning and went to a briefing at Harlesden police station at 3.00 a.m. When I arrived there I realised it was with Grey team and I really was not looking forward to it. Then I saw a guy called Phil who I had known quite some time. He was member of another team and I believe was manning up on Grey team as they were short of numbers. Phil was a very experienced firearms officer and his team normally used the dogs correctly, so I felt a bit happier.

We were to go to an address that was a house split into four floors, all self-contained flats. Information had been received that in the top flat which was converted from the loft was a male, who was on the run from prison where he had been serving time for armed robbery. The man was also believed to have a firearm with him and he had committed several armed robberies while on the run.

The premises were entered at about 4.00 a.m. and containments put in around the surrounding streets. A quiet entry was made through the main door of the house, then the front door to the top flat was forced open and a challenge of armed police shouted out, instructing all occupiers to come out with their hands visible.

The flat itself was difficult to enter. On forcing the flat door we were immediately confronted by a steep staircase of about fifteen steps. Then there was a very small landing area where there was a door to a room directly in front of you. The landing then seemed to double back on itself over our heads so that it was impossible to see anything else. After several requests for the occupiers to come out, two black females, one with a baby, eventually showed themselves and came down the stairs.

When questioned, they denied there was anyone else in the flat. Several more challenges were made by the team. Thanks to Phil being there, I was up on the third floor landing near to the door of the flat and I could see the situation on the stairs. Phil asked me what I thought in relation to putting the dog in to search. I said I thought the best thing to do was to send her up the stairs and direct her through the room directly in front of the stairs and see what happens. If she clears it, then I will direct her onto the landing above us and place her there to cover that danger area. The team could then move up into the cleared room and we could work out our next move from there.

Phil was happy with that, although some of Grey team obviously were not and there were a few mutterings from them of 'a waste of bloody time'. Fortunately, Phil seemed to have the final say and I sent the dog off up the stairs where she went straight into the room out of our sight. I could hear her padding around and a couple of times she went quiet and I thought she might have something. But a few minutes later she appeared at the door and looked at me.

'Well,' Phil said 'What's your call?'

'I am happy the room is clear,' I said.

I then used hand signals to get her to lie down on the landing where she was looking directly along the landing area that was blind to us. Any movement by anyone, and she would hear and react to it. The team moved up the stairs slowly into the room that turned out to be the main bedroom. They cleared it manually and I joined them. The occupants had obviously just got out of the bed; the fresh scent there had been what made Tegan go quiet until she had worked out there was no one in the room.

The team were then chomping at the bit to move on. Across onto the next landing were two doors on the left side and a sliding door at the end of the landing. The difficulty we had was caused by the fact that there was a large bicycle resting up against the banister. This left hardly any room to pass. I suggested letting the dog check out the landing and see what response we got.

The reason for this was that the longer someone is hiding, the more their scent permeated and travelled from their hiding place. Even with the doors shut I should get some sort of indication from the dog. It was even possible she could hear them if they moved slightly. Again Phil agreed, much to the displeasure of some of the team.

I sent the dog across the landing and she stopped at the first door and sniffed it and moved on. She reached the second door, sniffed at the bottom and stopped totally still. I looked at Phil and said, 'I think there is someone in there mate, definitely.'

He said, 'How can you be so sure?'

I replied, 'Watch the dog.'

With that, Tegan started taking really big snorts of air from under the door, she stopped and looked at me and I signalled her to sit.

I said to Phil, 'We need to move that bike and get someone from the team to approach the door to open it so I can send the dog in there.'

This was normal practice with most teams, the idea being that if the suspect was inside and in the open she could take him on straight away, or if he is hiding she could locate him and the team could control taking him out.

One of the guys who did not like using the dog said, 'OK, take the dog away back down the stairs. We will move the bike into the bedroom we have cleared and get two guys set up on the door. When we are ready to go you can move back to the cleared bedroom door and send her in from there.'

It made sense to make a bit of space so I did as he suggested, but before I got halfway down the stairs I suddenly heard someone shouting 'Support, support, support.'

This shout means someone had made contact with a suspect and wanted help. My heart sank: I thought she had missed someone in the first room and they had popped out in front of the team. I raced back up the stairs to find them in the bedroom I had told them the suspect was in.

It contained only a bed and wardrobe. The wardrobe door was open and sat inside was a black male in his underpants with two firearms officers pointing guns at him. I was absolutely furious. The knobhead who had suggested I make some room by going downstairs, and who did not trust dogs, had gone in the room himself not believing the dog could catch a scent from outside the door. He opened the wardrobe door and got the shock of his life. Had the suspect had a gun in there with him the end result could have been disastrous.

Phil was most apologetic, but I was absolutely seething. We went to a local nick for debriefing and to do the paperwork. The team were very quiet and when I got my chance to have my say I ripped into them with everything I had. I even made an official report to the firearms support dog instructors at the dog school so that they were aware of it for future courses, warning them what they might have to put up with from a minority of firearms officers. Nothing ever happened to me like that again, thank God. Fortunately, there were not many people like that in the firearms team.

Most of them were extremely hard-working and excellent at doing what is a very hard job. Their skills at firearms and tactics are amazing to watch. Unfortunately, you will always get one or two in every bunch who are just complete cowboys who want to be covered in glory. In this story, the officer was lucky not to end up covered in his own blood, either from being shot by the suspect or by being punched in the nose by me.

TEGAN CONSTANTLY DID THINGS THAT amazed me. It was a pleasure not only to watch her work but also to see the other dogs we worked with doing the same. All had different strengths and capabilities. Some of the handlers were so experienced and were on their second or third dogs, and their abilities made it a pleasure to go to work.

Tegan's enthusiasm always kept me going; no matter how cold or wet or tired I was she would just keep working. To hold onto a tracking line and just watch as she tracked over fields, golf courses, etc, sometimes used to make me admire just how intelligent the dogs were. There was only one time that anything ever got the better of her: that was the time she tangled with a police horse.

We were working at a Chelsea football match and I was stood at the main gates talking to a chief inspector I knew. I had the dog in the down position near the kerb and a few feet away was a police horse.

The rider was taking to someone and I noticed the horse was moving back slightly towards Tegan. I moved Tegan away a little but the horse would readjust and start backing towards her.

I moved my dog several times and the horse seemed to give up. Suddenly, there was an almighty howling noise and I felt the lead go tight in my grip and then fly out of my hand completely. I realised Tegan was flying down the road about two feet off the ground. She landed about nine feet away. I ran over to her and she was lying on her side yelping in pain. She seemed to by spinning round in circles on the roadway and as I tried to calm her, she kept biting me. The noise had stopped all the supporters making their way into the ground in their tracks. I was suddenly joined by the horse's rider, He was apologising because he had felt his horse move backwards, and looked around to see what it was doing; he then saw it lash out with one of its rear legs and kick Tegan, who had stood up to get out of its way.

Well, I thought she must be seriously injured and rushed her off to a nearby vet. She stopped biting me but was obviously still in pain as we entered the vet's surgery, and could not walk. The vet examined her and took X-rays, and thankfully found she had taken the kick on the solid muscle around her hind leg area. Had it been anywhere else she would have been seriously injured. Apart from missing work for a week she made a full recovery. I never did like those bloody horses, and neither did she after that.

Central demonstration team

THE DOG SECTION ALSO USED to have a police dog demonstration team. Handlers and their dogs could apply to be considered for the team and if they passed selection they would then be part of the team that would take part in open days, etc. They also took part one year in the Royal Tournament at Earls Court. Unfortunately, due to the usual reasons of cost and man hours, etc, the demonstration team was slowly being stopped from doing these displays and, by the early 1990s, were almost non-existent.

The one thing they were allowed to still take part in was the Met police horse show. This was held every July at the Imber Court Sports Ground near Hampton Court and was a great favourite with the public. The display team always put on a big show at this event. In 1993 I applied to join the central demo team with Tegan. She passed the selection but, as it turned out, the only show we were likely to do was the horse show. There were rumours that this would be the last horse show, again due to cost, so it was most likely the last time the dog section demonstration team would also be able to perform.

So in July 1993 I found myself at Imber Court as part of the team. We did all the usual things, dogs racing over jumps, dogs doing tricks, as well as all the usual things of chasing criminals, etc. There was a huge crowd in the arena and it was a lovely sunny day and everyone was really enjoying the show especially the kids.

The grand finale to the show was to be a great spectacle. We were going to simulate a post office van being robbed by an armed gang. This would be followed by a big chase with lots of gunfire and dogs chasing criminals and biting them. A real winner, we thought, and everyone had their part to play.

Everything started well. We had a bright red Fiesta van that belonged to a handler, Steve Witcomb. It was made up to look like a post office van. Another dog-handler was playing the post office van driver dressed in a post office uniform. The van drove into the arena to the theme of *Postman Pat* being played over the sound system. The driver went around the area holding out a stuffed black and white toy cat just like Jess in the children's programme. The kids in the crowd loved it.

Then a second van drove into the arena full of criminals and they chased the van around a few times and eventually stopped the post office van and kicked out the driver as they pretended to rob it. This was when a police dog van entered with blue lights and siren going, and they chased the robbers around the arena a few times. One of the robbers drove off in the post office van.

This is where the first thing went wrong. As the robber was driving around the arena he was pointing a sawn-off shotgun at the police van. The sawn-off obviously contained only blanks, but these can still be quite lethal if used too close to somebody. As the robber was driving around the arena he let off two rounds from the shotgun. However, he misjudged where he was pointing the shotgun, and when he pulled the trigger he shot off the driver's door mirror and left it in pieces.

Eventually, the robbers ran from their van and were shooting at the police dogs that eventually caught them all. The kids were going mad and seemed to be really enjoying the show. Then suddenly there is a big loud bang, and out of the post office van stepped a robber. He was masked and looking pretty mean and nasty and he had got Jess the cat. He then held the police at bay by threatening to shoot the cat.

The kids in the crowd were now in a state of panic; they were crying and screaming while the adults were laughing. The robber continued to threaten to shoot the cat and even the parents went quiet as they tried to assure the kids that Jess would be alright. Suddenly the police moved in on the robber as the final part of the show.

Completely unrehearsed, the robber suddenly threw Jess up in the air and blasted the cat with the shotgun and ran off chased by the dog and he was caught after a brilliant chase. Jess the cat fell to earth in pieces and all the handlers were in hysterics as none of us had been expecting the cat to get shot; the whole thing seemed very funny until we started to realise there was a very strange air of silence around the arena. This silence was being broken by the sound of children crying and the commentator on the PA system trying to do his best to sound normal as he closed the display. He was obviously trying not to laugh for the benefit of the crowd.

It seems this completely ruined the day for almost every kid at the show. The atmosphere as we left the arena was as if someone had really been killed. I have to say all the handlers thought it was a great end to the show. I believe there were actually some complaints made by parents after their kids were traumatised by seeing Jess the cat executed, but I thought it was a brilliant touch.

That day did turn out to be the last time the display team ever performed so I was even more pleased that it had ended with a bit of a bang!

A man to be admired

In my thirty years' service I was fortunate to meet some exceptional police officers whose skills and devotion to the police force gave you such encouragement to emulate them that it seemed to make the job that much easier to do. When I became a dog-handler, I was fortunate to meet one such man, Jon Gordon.

Jon had been a dog-handler and by pure fate, on 17th December 1983, had changed shifts with a colleague; as a result found himself at the scene of a suspected explosive device following a coded warning by the IRA. Jon was called out from a canteen at a nearby nick to attend the area of Harrods in Knightsbridge and subsequently was walking in the side street when a car bomb exploded, killing two police officers.

Jon was blown off his feet and when he tried to stand up found he could not because of serious injuries to his legs. His dog, Queenie, also was seriously injured and had to be put down there and then. Jon lost both his legs as a result of the bomb. After a very long battle Jon got himself back to work. He initially was based as an office manager at the territorial support group at Alperton traffic garage; some time later he moved to the 6 area dog offices at Norwood Green, which is where I first met him.

I cannot put into words how much admiration I have for Jon. At the time I first met him in late 1989, the Met was full of shirkers who would take the force for a ride at the slightest sign of injury and get themselves medically cast from the force in order to receive large pay awards and larger pensions. Here was Jon, severely injured, yet he got himself back to work and he was a great inspiration to many people.

What was great for me, being a novice handler was that while I was puppy-walking Tegan during her first year, Jon was always in the office and every day as Tegan got older, Jon would have a little snippet of advice to give me. I honestly believe that the success Tegan had was a direct result of all the help I received from Jon.

I spent a lot of time in the office with Jon in that first year and even though he very rarely talked about that awful day at Harrods, just occasionally he would mention something and we would get into a conversation about it, and his story is fascinating to listen to. I desperately tried to persuade him to write a book about his experience but he never wanted to. I would love to relay some of the stories he told me, but will not do so out of respect for Jon.

However, there is something I will write about and that is the disgusting way Jon was eventually treated by certain people within the police. Their behaviour forced him to retire and break contact with everyone in the police.

Every year, on the anniversary of the Harrods bomb, Jon would bring a bottle of champagne into work. At the exact time the bomb had gone off in 1983, Jon would open the champagne and share a drink with those who were in the office with him. This was a way of remembering the officers who died, and obviously meant a lot to Jon. Also in his desk drawer he kept a small bottle of very expensive whisky that had been given to him some time after the bombing. Jon would also have a very small drop of the whisky and then lock it away for another year.

With John Clemence, one of the dog sergeants, the 6 area dog section ran very efficiently and Jon was a very important member of the section and more than pulled his weight. In 1995 there was a change of areas and, as a result, the dog office at Norwood Green was disbanded and the handlers allocated around the Met to other offices.

I went by choice to central London. There was, at the time, concerns as to where Jon would go. He had been told by the then-commissioner, Sir Peter Imbert, that there was a job for him for as long as he wanted. Sir Peter visited the dog office on numerous occasions to see Jon as they knew each other very well.

EVENTUALLY, JON WENT TO THE new area dog office based at Kingsbury near Kenton as their office manager. Unfortunately, the dog inspector there was a real knob head and did not really want Jon there, but he had no choice. This resulted in some resentment and Jon appeared not to be settling in there too well. It then came to a head when the inspector suggested to Jon that he tried to find some sort of local sponsorship in the area to pay Jon's wages, as the inspector claimed the budget did not allow him enough money to have Jon on his staff. Jon apparently reminded him in no uncertain terms and that he was a serving PC and not a civilian and his wages came from central funds. This incident really upset Jon and, on top of a few other things that had been taking place, caused him some distress. He eventually was taken ill as a result of it and was off work for some time.

At some point he returned to the office. When he did so he found his locked drawers had been broken into and all his stuff moved all over the place. Worst of all, his expensive bottle of whisky had been drunk, leaving just the empty bottle. I believe this proved too much for Jon and he suddenly finished work and retired without a retirement party; he left very disillusioned and upset by the way his police service ended.

Jon eventually moved away from London and only kept in touch with a small group of people. The last time I saw Jon was at the funeral of a friend who was dear to both of us. Unfortunately, as I was deeply involved in the funeral on the day, I did not get chance to speak too much with Jon at the service. I was really looking forward to catching up with him at the get together afterwards, but for some reason he never came back with everyone else. That was the last time I would get to see Jon.

In March 2006, I was at the police rehabilitation centre in Goring for some treatment to a neck injury. Jon I knew was living nearby and I intended to try and track him down and pay him a visit. I was woken up at about 7.00 a.m. on the Wednesday morning by a text message from a retired colleague who told me he had just received word that Jon had died the previous day while on holiday in Wales. His death really upset me and I was really mad that I had not made to effort earlier to get in touch with him. A very sad loss; he was such an inspirational man.

Time to leave

THE SAME CHANGE OF AREAS that had caused Jon Gordon's move resulted in my move to work in central London at the dog office at Rochester Row. This resulted in my leaving the dog section just over a year later when Tegan retired. There were several incidents that culminated in my decision to leave, the main one being the overbearing conduct of a senior officer who thought he was God, and everyone had to obey him and live by his rules.

Unfortunately, I was not prepared to do so and we crossed swords and he eventually tried to get me sacked with accusations that, fortunately, he could not substantiate. He was a bully and he used his rank to twist things his way. That was until he tried it on with me and a few others. The story is long but I intent to tell my side of it in this book, so here it is.

I moved to Rochester Row in January 1995. There was about eight of us from Norwood Green who choose to move into town and I found it quite easy to settle in there. Everything was fine there for the first six months or so; I really had little contact with the senior officer in charge who appeared at the office very little and seemed to have the best job in the Met doing absolutely sod all to earn his wages.

I found myself very busy doing firearms support dog work, and this to led my first confrontation with this senior officer. Because of the nature of the work it resulted in long hours and the obvious amount of overtime incurred. After one particular weekend, where I had spent virtually the whole time with a firearms team on a long protracted operation, I returned to work to be called into see this officer. He basically told me I was a money-grabber and that I was causing problems with his budget. As a result he ordered me not to take any calls outside of central London. I tried explaining that the dog was a resource to be called upon to go anywhere the firearms teams needed her, but he threatened me with all sorts if I went off the area without his permission.

The following week I was on night duty. Whenever I booked on duty with information room at the yard, I had to book on as a Trojan (firearms) support handler. This then allowed information room to contact me quickly if we were needed by a firearms team on a call-out. Halfway through the week in the early hours of the morning I got called to go to a firearms incident in East London. I told them on the radio that I could not go as I had been instructed by my senior officer not to leave central London.

A short while later I was told that I was required and had to attend. I again explained that I was under strict instructions not to leave central London. I was immediately instructed to return to the dog office and contact the chief inspector on duty in information room. I did as I was instructed and rang in to information room. I was initially yelled at by the chief inspector, but when I explained fully why I could not go, the chief inspector then ordered me to go and said that he would make sure that my supervisor was aware that I had been ordered to do so by him. So, leaving my partner to cover the area, I took another van off to Dagenham.

I was there for about twenty hours and did not get back in time to do nights the following night. As a result I did not see the senior officer until after I had returned to day duty the next week. He called me into his office and, during a heated exchange he told me that as soon as he had the chance I would be finished in the dog section. I tried to keep out of his way as much as possible after that and things calmed down a little.

I really had just begun the thought process of leaving the section ready for when Tegan retired; I loved the work but just was not happy working for this overbearing senior officer. The rest of the office was fine; wherever you work you get on with some and not others – there are a lot of strong characters in the dog section and sometimes people clash. There was just something that was nagging me and I was considering returning to normal duty.

Then one of the guys I had worked with at Norwood Green got a position on the bombs and drugs dogs unit. Paul was an excellent dog-handler, very experienced. As well as his working dog, he had also been bringing up a puppy called Boz. The pup was now nearly twelve months old and he was huge and all the signs were he was going to be a superb dog.

Going on the bombs and drugs unit meant Paul had to give Boz up to someone else. Because I knew Paul and Boz well, I was offered the chance to take on Boz as my new dog. I had always said that if I had another dog it would have to be from a puppy and at first said no. Eventually I was persuaded to give it a go and one day Paul and the senior officer arrived at my home and handed over the dog to me.

This proved to be a bad idea. Unknown to me, what should have happened was that Boz should have gone to the dog school for a couple of weeks to help break the excellent bond he had with Paul. I should have then spent some time with him at the dog school, feeding him, playing with him and getting him to bond with me. However, just bringing him straight to my house meant he still saw Paul as his handler and did not take to his new surroundings too well.

A few days after he arrived home, my wife tried to take his collar and lead him from the living room to put him out into the kitchen area. As she did he turned on her, knocked her to the floor and went for her face with snarling teeth. Fortunately, I was close by and managed to kick him in the head and then pull him away from her. He fought me all the way into the garden where I struggled to control him. Eventually, I forced him into submission and put him in the compound.

This really distressed my wife and I phoned the dog school for advice. A dog sergeant came the next day and collected Boz and took him to the dog school. It was only then that I found out the correct way Boz should have been reallocated and I was furious. I blamed the senior officer, completely: he should have known better and perhaps did. He just wanted a way to get at me!

I felt really guilty about the dog. We knew Paul and his family loved the dog and wanted it to go to someone they knew would look after it, but there was no way I was taking the dog on and it finally made my mind up to leave the section. (Boz did eventually make a full police dog with the unfortunate reputation for biting police officers as well as criminals.)

So I started making enquiries about spaces for area car drivers at stations I enjoyed working at. My first choice was Hammersmith. I knew the chief superintendent, Mr Cullen, quite well and contacted him. He was going to be looking for an experienced area car driver in a few months' time to replace people he had leaving his division, and told me he would gladly have me. There were still a few months before Tegan was going to retire so I thought it would all work out perfectly. However, the worst was yet to come.

Another one of my friends who moved from Norwood Green to 1 area with me was Martin Game. His dog, Toby, was close to retiring and Martin then had a gift dog that failed to make the grade. As a result he got a hard time from the same senior officer.

However, he got a second gift dog and went off on a course at Imber Court. At the same time we were made aware that budget restraints were causing the office problems and the senior officer had to find a saving of £34,000 (roughly the annual wage bill for a dog handler) halfway through Martin's course, I happened to be down at Imber Court on a day's training when I found Martin in a very distressed state. His dog had failed to make the grade and was to be dropped from the course.

At the end of the day I met Martin for a coffee and he showed me the report from the course instructor which basically said the dog was too weak and not up to standard in all aspects of training. He put no blame on Martin due to the short period of time that he been handling the dog and stated that Martin should be given another course with another dog.

When Martin returned to the office the following Monday, he was blamed by the senior officer for ruining the dog and told that it was likely that he would have to leave the dog section. He was told that he was lazy, produced no work over the previous year, and was a disgrace to the section. He was absolutely devastated and left the office very upset and told to take a few days off.

The effect that this had on Martin, his wife and children was horrendous. Martin, being a very gentle and quite man despite all his size and experience, was too upset to fight it. However, a couple of days later he was called to office to hear his fate. Sensing something was not right he did something that only a handful of people knew about until I wrote this book. Martin went into see the senior officer with a dictaphone running in his top pocket.

The things that person said to Martin were absolutely outrageous and a complete pack of lies. Some of it was very personal and rude, and some of it was so bad that had Martin taken it further I believe the person would have been sacked. I only found out about the tape several weeks after the event when I had left the section.

Martin had it transcribed onto paper and it was horrendous to read. To think that a senior police officer could say such things to another officer really angered me. The person concerned can consider him self very lucky that it was Martin with the tape and not me because I would have slaughtered him with it and taken it all the way.

Martin left that meeting having been told that he was to empty his locker and not come back. He was told to find himself another place to work but to stay away from the office. Martin, I, and a few others went for a drink. He was devastated and nothing we could do seem to help him and I was really concerned for his welfare. Martin told me that the senior officer had used the report from his course to get rid of him. I could not see how, as I had read that report on the Friday at Imber Court and no blame was placed on Martin.

Martin then told me the report shown to him bore no resemblance to the report he had been given. It had been altered blaming him entirely for the dog failing. This was the final straw and he knew he had been set up by the senior officer who wanted to get rid of him. I believe now, as I did then, that this was his get-out clause to save his £34,000 he needed to save on his budget, and saving his budget was really important to him for climbing to the next rank.

Well, that was it for me, and I went head on into conflict with this officer, as did several other handlers. During an office meeting he tried to justify Martin's transfer by saying his work records for the last year were non-existent and the office could not carry someone not pulling his weight. The fact that Martin had spent the last year puppy-walking and hardly on a working dog van might have had something to do with it, but he could not see that and totally blamed Martin. I had worked with Martin for six years at Norwood Green and had crewed vans with him many times, and lazy is something he was not.

After the meeting I went down into the main office and got all of the work records off the shelf. These were records we submitted after each piece of work completed by a dog and were a gauge as to how well each dog was working. However, if you had a pup, you spent very little time on a van working to keep those records building up. This is what had happened to Martin. He wasn't lazy; he just had not had chance to work his dog.

With several people present, I went through the books for the last year and found that Martin was one of about six handlers who were all in the same position because they had not been able to work their dogs. I challenged the senior officer about this but he refused to discuss the matter.

Within a couple of days Martin got himself a place on a relief at Hammersmith. I tried to persuade him he had a good case to put in a grievance against the senior officer, but he had decided to do nothing and just forget about it. That was the type of guy he was: too nice for his own good.

When I submitted a request to leave the section, I was called into his office. Basically a slanging match started where I told him what I thought of his abilities, and he told me exactly what he thought of me and that if he had his way, I would be sacked and not transferring. No love lost there, then. He warned me he would put me in my place before I left the section and, boy, did he try.

Unknown to me someone had told him that I was putting together evidence for Martin to use in a grievance procedure against him and the office. He was told that I had copied the work records, etc, of six handlers as evidence – all untrue. I believe it was said to him as a bit of a wind-up and wind him up it certainly did.

I arrived for work at 6.00 a.m. one morning to work with Dave Whittaker. The senior officer was in and immediately called us into his office. Also, there was a new dog sergeant who had just joined the section. The senior officer made an allegation that I had broken into the personnel filing cabinet, causing criminal damage and then photocopied the records of six officers to give to Martin Game. (The fact that the items he claimed I had taken were available in binders on a shelf in the main office and not locked away mattered not.)

He then said that Dave was also involved by assisting me. I told him that I knew exactly what he was trying to do, and not to involve Dave in this matter, which was between the two of us. He told Dave to wait outside and, when the sergeant had also gone outside with Dave, the inspector smiled at me and said something to the effect of: 'You think you're big enough to take me on do you? Well, you will be lucky to have a job after I have finished with you on this one. I sorted your mate out now it is you turn.'

Well the red mist came down and I was out of my seat and heading across the desk after him. Fortunately, the sergeant came in and stopped it going any further. I was steaming and I was sent out of the office after being told that Dave and I were only allowed to do walking security patrols around Westminster until told otherwise.

I went and apologised to Dave; he was being used by the bully just to make it look like he was not purely picking on me. After that, I walked straight over to Westminster and into Cannon Row police station to speak with the federation representative and asked for an appointment with the chief superintendent in charge of the dog section who I knew was a very fair man and I was sure I would get a fair hearing from him. He eventually spent some time with me and I told him the whole story. I left his office sometime later satisfied that he would deal with it correctly.

I walked back to the office and was again spoken to by the senior officer who demanded to know where I had been. When I told him, he went bright red in the face and demanded to know what right I had to go to the chief superintendent without his permission, and it kicked off again.

Later that day I was sat in the canteen when he appeared with some paper in his hands. He loved writing reports on his computer; it was the only thing I would say he was any good at. Most of it was fiction, unfortunately. I was the only one in the canteen and he stood next to me and said, 'I want you to know what I have put on this report to the chief superintendent; this will be the end of your trouble-making.'

I told him I had nothing to say to him, and on the chief super's instructions I was to avoid confrontation with him; this made him even angrier and he started reading from the paper. He basically said that I was untrustworthy, a liar and should not be trusted ever to work alone.

He also recommended that I be disciplined for my actions. I ignored him; he finished reading the report and stated he was off to see the chief.

The allegation, although completely false, really upset me. I have great professional pride and integrity and the thought that he may cause sufficient waves that might colour my good name really upset me. I decided to take some time off to stay out of his way until the matter was resolved. So, after confirming with Mr Cullen and Hammersmith that I could move there when things were cleared up, I took a few days away. This, in itself, proved to be a bad idea. It all played on my mind so much that I could not sleep. On the weekend I was very snappy with my wife, Paula and then something happened which really made me realise how much the whole incident had got to me.

On the Saturday morning my wife said something to me and I shouted at her and walked out. I have no memory of what happened for the next 24 hours or so until I woke up in a hotel room. I was very scared and did not have a clue where I was and could not really remember anything. Headed notepaper told me I was in a Holiday Inn in Manchester. How the hell did I get here? Then I remembered Paula, but could not remember my phone number. Eventually, things came back and I spoke to her on the phone; she was very worried and obviously upset, but calmly talked to me and gradually things started to make sense.

With her guidance I checked my wallet and found a return train ticket from Birmingham airport, but how did I get there? Paula told me what had happened as I left and that I had taken the car. I realised I must have suffered some sort of breakdown, and with Paula's help, started piecing things together.

I must have looked a right state, but made my way back to Birmingham airport and spent ages walking to numerous car parks and eventually found my car. At the time I had a red Astra estate. I found the car completely unlocked. Then I had a massive panic. In the car, along with all my dog-handling equipment, was a bag that contained all my firearms support dog equipment including two deactivated revolvers that I was authorised to keep for training purposes. What if they were missing? I dived into the car and thankfully everything was still there.

All I wanted to do now was get home to Paula. The journey home was very strange, almost unreal, as I tried to remember what I had done during the time I left the house and then woke up in the hotel and I could not remember a thing. I still do not know what happened to this day. I got back home, and it was all very emotional. Paula had tried every one of our family and friends looking for me and she had a sleepless night of worry.

I went to the doctors on the Monday and told him what had happened. He said it was brought on by the stress of what was happening at work and treated me with the usual pills. I vowed then that the senior officer concerned would not get me into the state again, no matter what, and that the sooner I left the dog section the better.

About a week later I was called to the chief superintendent's office. He told me that he was satisfied that there was no wrongdoing on my behalf and that there was obviously a clash of personalities between me and the senior officer. His report would clear me of any wrongdoing and asked if I still wished to leave to dog section. I told him I did and would like to go as soon as possible to avoid further conflict.

What he said next stunned me.

'When would you like to start at Stoke Newington then PC Vick?'

The look on my face must have said it all.

'Is there something wrong?' he asked me.

Stoke Newington is the last place on earth I would want to work, apart from the travelling aspect it is a complete shit hole of a place.

'Sir, I am going to Hammersmith not Stoke Newington,' I replied.

He looked at the form he had in his hands and said, 'Well your request form shows you have asked for Stoke Newington,' and he showed it me.

Well, it was my photocopied signature on the bottom but the rest of the typed form was completely different from the one I completed. I knew straight away the senior officer had been up to his tricks again.

I explained to the chief that everything was sorted at Hammersmith and Mr Cullen was expecting me, and I had no knowledge of the form for Stoke Newington. He realised something was not right and asked me to leave the room while he telephoned Hammersmith. He called me back in and told me Mr Cullen had confirmed what I said. He was very annoyed and said, 'You start at Hammersmith straight away. I will sort the rest out.'

He then asked me if there was anything else. I told him I wanted the report the senior officer had written about me, calling me a liar and untrustworthy, removed from my file and explained to him the confrontation in the canteen. He looked puzzled and said that in the report he had there, the senior officer rated me very highly and did not want to lose me. It was obvious he was playing games again, and I left it at that. And so off to Hammersmith I went, thank God.

BUT THE STORY DOES NOT end there. At Hammersmith I discovered Martin's recording of the conversation with the senior officer. He had decided to do nothing with it as he was now happy at Hammersmith. I also decided it was best to let things go and cause myself no more stress. I settled in to my new team and was really enjoying it. I found it strange not having the dog with me, but soon got used to it.

Three months after joining, I was due my annual report and one of my sergeants spoke to me as he had to complete it. A couple of days later he came to me for me to read it and sign it. He then said to me, 'Listen Andy if I were you I would ask to see your personnel file; there is something on there you need to see.'

What now? I went to the personnel office and asked to see my file. When I opened it the first thing I saw was a typed report. It was the report saying I was a liar, untrustworthy and should be sacked. The senior officer had obviously managed to swap the reports when my file went to him before Hammersmith.

I went straight to Mr Cullen and as he already knew the full story he went mad. I was all for a full-blown fight now. Mr Cullen calmed me down and told me to go and discuss things with my wife for a couple of days.

Several days later, I went to see Mr Cullen. He then told me my choices. The matter had gone too far to be just a grievance matter, taking into account the problems Martin had also had with the man, a mere grievance process was not the right course of action. It meant a full complaint against the senior officer on various grounds. He warned me that this course of action may result in months of unrest and counter allegations but he was prepared to support me.

Andy Vick

The other option was to trust him to take it to the highest level with the promise that the senior officer would be more closely supervised to ensure he behaves to the correct standards and treats people properly. He again told me to talk it over with my wife and let him know. We decided to leave it with Mr Cullen as I completely trusted what he said and that is what I did. Thankfully, that was the end of it.

I CAN NOW ALSO TELL one other story that relates to this senior and shows just how bad he was. The story involves a very close friend who unfortunately died in May 2004 just a month before he was due to retire. His name was Andrew Lawrence Toole. To his friends he was known as TOOLIE.

Andy was an ex Royal Marine Commando, a very proud Scot from Glasgow and without doubt the proudest man in a uniform I had ever met. He was also the hardest man I ever knew. But the other side of him was a complete gentleman that everyone who knew him loved. The ladies all adored him. I could not write my book without including Andy and I could write a book just on stories, all true about him.

At his funeral there were over 500 people present from all walks of life not just the police service. It was the mark of such an incredible man that he had so many friends but if you became his enemy you were in real trouble.

I first met Andy in 1984 and eventually worked with him as dog handlers at Norwood Green. He was the man to be with if there was trouble and did not suffer fools gladly. He also came to Central London to work at the same time as I did and after the trouble Martin and I, had he became to next target for the same senior officer. What that person does not know is how close he came to being sorted out by Toolie.

There was trouble with Andy's second dog that ended in Andy also leaving the section and returning to normal duty at Uxbridge. Andy firmly blamed everything on the senior officer. One night I was out with Andy and he told me this story and I just have to repeat it.

Andy was in his local pub one evening drinking with some friends, none of which were in the police. As the night went on the conversation got around to the dog section and how much Andy hated the senior officer. Andy got so worked up about it and egged on by his friends he told them all that if the person concerned had been in the Royal

Marines he would have been well and truly sorted out by know. Well the bravado got stronger with each drink and by the time Andy went home he was so fired up that he decided he was going to teach the senior officer a lesson and sort him out.

At Rochester Row there were a few rooms set up with beds. They were used by the guys on a night up town so no one had to drive home. The senior officer had a room of his own and he would use it one or twice a week for personal use. To get there, he had to go down a flight of stairs from the car park in to a fairly dark basement area that led to his room.

Well this night Andy, with too much drink on board decided to go and surprise him and teach him a thing or two. So stupidly Andy got on his motorbike and rode into London. This is itself was a terrible thing for Andy to do. He was very strict about drinking and driving, especially with his motorbike.

However dressed all in black leathers and armed with a baseball bat off he went to the dog office. He then lay in wait for the senior officer to arrive as he normally did in the early hours. Fortunately for him (and Andy really) the senior officer did not turn up and the next thing Andy knew was that he was waking up cold, tired and aching in the basement area.

When he finished the story I could tell Andy was upset. I told him not to worry; the person concerned was not worth getting himself arrested for a serious assault and to just forget him. Andy got a bit angry and said

"I am only really upset that I did the stupid thing of riding my bike after drinking, but I am bloody annoyed that the bastard didn't show up because my god he was going to get everything he deserved from me."

That senior officer does not know how lucky he was he did not turn up at the dog office that night. No one would like to have met TOOLIE at night in a dark alley!!!!!!!

I have no doubts that Andy would have carried his plan out and I dread to think what the outcome would have been. Rightly or wrongly the senior officer was a complete arsehole and would have deserved everything he got and Toolie would have been the man capable of doing it for sure.

Return to Hammersmith

So it was that in January 1996 that I found myself back on relief at Hammersmith. I was really pleased to be going back there. I was very fortunate to find myself attached to a fantastic hard-working relief and I found it really easy to settle back into normal police work after eight years on the dog section.

After a couple of days' settling in, I was posted late turn to drive Foxtrot 2 the area car. My operator was Shaun Dougherty who was still a probationer at the time. We had finished briefing and were in the canteen grabbing a quick cup of tea when suddenly there was an urgent assistance shout over the radio. We only knew that there were some crime squad officers asking for help, and by the noise on the radio they were having a hell of a fight. Over the noise we were able to find out that they were in a shop inside Hammersmith Broadway shopping mall.

Hammersmith Broadway is one of the main arterial roads in west London. It is a large roundabout system with eight roads leading off it. At the very best of times it is extremely busy; at worst it is total gridlock with hardly anything moving. The shopping mall is at ground level; on top is a major bus station and below run the Piccadilly and District tube lines. The main entrance into the shopping mall is on the north side of the roundabout and faces Shepherds Bush Road; this is where the police station is situated, some 500 yards away.

On hearing the urgent assistance call, everybody bailed out of the canteen; Shaun and I were in the car and away before everyone else and as I pulled out of the gates and tried to turn right I realised it would have been quicker to run. The whole length of Shepherds Bush Road to the Broadway was at a standstill.

You're Nicked My Son

The other side of the road was not too bad, so off I went with blue lights and all the noise and blasted up to the Broadway. Because I was on the wrong side of the road, I had to force my way against the traffic on the roundabout itself. This was solid and it looked like I was stuck.

Suddenly, a gap appeared across the three lanes of the roundabout. Across the other side I saw a gap in the fence that would allow me onto the pavement directly outside the entrance to the shopping mall. I went for this gap, up onto the pavement and decided the quickest thing to do to help the crime squad boys who were screaming for help was to drive straight into the shopping mall. It was easily wide enough, and the noise of the two-tones sent shoppers well out of the way. It also gave the crime squad boys notice that help was on its way.

The shop they were in was halfway into the mall on the left of us. As we arrived I noticed the shutters were almost completely down. I dived out of the car, threw myself under the shutters and was confronted by the sight of a demolished shop with all the displays knocked over. There were two crime squad guys fighting on the floor with one of the biggest black guys I had ever seen. He was huge. I piled in with them and as more troops arrived, we managed to get control of him and handcuffed him. We had to use two sets of cuffs linked together just to be able to get them on him.

The suspect had been seen, by the two officers in plain clothes, committing a robbery on a female. They had challenged him and he had run off and the chase ended up in the shop. It was only once things had calmed down a little did I realise that the two-tones on the car were still going and the noise inside the centre was incredible. I went out to the car to find a huge crowd had gathered to see the spectacle of a police car with its blue lights and two-tones on, sitting in the middle of the Broadway Centre.

I actually felt a bit embarrassed and sheepishly drove the car out of the centre and back to the nick. As we were heading back I noticed Shaun had the big grin on his face.

I said, 'What's the matter with you?'

He just grinned and said, 'Do you always drive like that?'

I looked at him and he said, 'Was that legal? Are you allowed to do that, just drive into the middle of a shopping centre?'

I thought he was having a moan about the way I drove and I replied, 'If old bill are in trouble mate, anything is legal to get there and help them. You leave the driving to me and do what you're supposed to do.'

I was really arsey with him. He gave me a big smile and said, 'I'm not having a go. That was brilliant, like being on the *Sweeney*. I have just never done anything like that in a police car I was gob smacked when you went across the pavement.'

The look on his face told me he was being genuine and Shaun and I went on to have many other moments that he was to enjoy as my operator.

The Kung Fu Vicar

The 14th July 1996 is a day I will never forget. It was a Sunday early-turn shift and, being a typical Sunday in the summer, there was hardly anyone on duty. The area car was off the road having broken down overnight and so I was posted to drive the station van. Jon Godfrey, a sergeant on my team, was acting as my operator. If we were to have a busy morning, as some Sundays could be, we were so short of staff that it would be a real problem.

Around midday we took a call to St Paul's Church in Wormholt Road on Shepherds Bush's ground. The call was from the parish priest who stated that he was trying to hold Sunday service there but a male had entered the church and was causing a disturbance. When Jon Godfrey and I arrived there we found the congregation outside.

We spoke with the priest who told us that the male had entered the church and was dressed as a priest. The male approached the priest mid-service and told him that he had been told by God to take over this church. As the priest stood in the pew overlooking his congregation, the male punched him in the face and dragged him out and down to the bottom of the steps.

Other men in the church tried to help but this male attacked them as well. They all left the church leaving the man inside. We were the only officers there – in fact we were they only ones to accept the call. To be on the safe side, I radioed Hammersmith and asked them to try and get another car to back us up. Jon and I entered the church.

The male, who was black with a large afro haircut, was sitting in the middle of a row of seats with his back to us. I tried to call him but he ignored me. As we approached I could see he was sat with his hands clasped together and he appeared to be praying. The other thing I did notice was he was a bit of a man-mountain. Why are these people always so bloody big?

I went into the row of seats from his right and Jon from his left. I tried to speak with him but he appeared oblivious to me. After several minutes of trying to speak with him, I signalled to Jon that I would take his right arm and he should take the left. We would then take him out to the van. Wrong!

As we tried to move him, he resisted. It was like trying to pull a vice apart, his arms were that strong. Then he kicked off and we proceeded to roll around the church, smashing chairs and all sorts as we did so. Jon radioed for urgent assistance, as this male was so strong we had no chance there just being the two of us. Help eventually arrived but not before we had made a bit of a mess of the church. We managed with help to handcuff his hands behind his back and then we dragged him outside to the police van.

This is where we hit our next problem. The Met had just started using the new VW van with a built-in prisoner cage. The design was wrong, however, because the back of the van was quite high and trying to get a struggling prisoner up onto the van and into the cage was very difficult. It meant the prisoner, just prior to getting in the cage, was substantially higher up than you and I felt this was very dangerous.

With help, we managed to force him in and shut the cage door. As he sat there I could see the madness in his eyes; there was something very wrong about this guy!

As we drove back to Hammersmith, the guy was deadly silent in the back. I had some real concerns about him and I said quietly to Jon that I was a bit wary about getting him out of the van as he was that little bit higher up than us. Jon agreed.

I told Jon that when I opened the cage door to let him out, I was going to let him get out of his own accord; I just felt that to lean in to get him out was asking for trouble. I had also decided that if he did not come out of his own accord I would use my baton on his knees to make him come out. We duly arrived into the back yard of the police station.

Jon and I went to the rear of the van, as we did so Jon got on the radio and asked for anyone in the nick to come out in the yard as we had a potentially violent prisoner. Fortunately, some people started to come out. I opened the rear van doors and then opened the cage door. I was in the process of pushing the door as far open as I could to give us plenty of room, and then the next thing I remember is coming round and sitting on the floor with my back up against a wall. As I came to, I could not move, had completely lost my sight and I was absolutely shitting myself!

A voice was talking to me that turned out to be an ambulance driver. I told him I was unable to see and that I could not feel my arms and legs. The next thing I knew, I was strapped to a trolley and heading off to hospital. It was initially thought my neck had been broken. After about two-and-a-half hours, the feeling started to come back to my arms and legs, with a really painful pins-and-needles sensation.

Over twenty-four hrs later I was eventually released from hospital, still with the imprint of the front of his right foot on my neck. I ended up off work for eight months, and it was the start of the next eleven years of awful head and neck problems! The kick had damaged ligaments, tendons, neck muscles and soft tissue. Many years later, a specialist discovered more serious damage that was to be the cause of all my problems over a period of years that still continues to this day. This moment of madness was to eventually finish my career a year earlier than intended.

While I was in hospital I discovered what had happened to me. The man I had arrested was called Richard Noel. He had recently been released from the government's infamous 'care in the community scheme' and was, in his younger days, a very intelligent man. He had also been a martial arts expert. Jon Godfrey told me that as I opened the gate to the cage, Noel had somehow managed to kick out with his right foot, wrapped his right shoe around my neck and pole-axed me completely. Jon said it happened so fast there was nothing he could do.

It was fortunate that as he kicked me, people started arriving in the back yard and there was a huge fight where Noel was eventually restrained. He kept shouting that he had been sent by God, and despite being handcuffed he was a real handful – very abusive and violent.

As I was taken off to hospital he was taken into the police station where he was so violent they had to call out the territorial support group in all their protective gear to go into his cell, restrain him and virtually truss him up like a chicken so he could be dealt with.

He was charged with a serious assault on me, and the next day, again with the help off the TSG, he was taken to the old West London court in Vernon Street. The magistrates wanted to deal with him in a civil manner and tried to deal with him in the dock. However, he had other ideas and went berserk, smashing up the lovely old court before again being trussed up by the TSG and taken to a cell. The magistrates sent him on remand to Wandsworth prison so his mental state could be assessed.

A week later he appeared at Horseferry Road magistrates and was placed in a mental hospital under a mental heath order for an indefinite period. As far as I am aware he is still there. I was later told that, during the week he was on remand in prison, he injured three prison officers. One of them was so badly injured he was in a wheelchair and not likely to recover or be able to work again.

I was very lucky. The specialist at the hospital later told me that with the amount of force Noel had kicked me with, if the kick had been to the front of my throat then he had no doubt my windpipe would have been crushed by the force and could have proved fatal.

The injury was to be the bane of my life for the rest of my service and was to seriously relapse on two more occasions causing me great problems and, even worse, a lot of time off work!

We finally catch one!

ONE OF THE CRIMES THAT all police officers hate is the crime of burglary artifice. This is, where criminals use distraction techniques or pose as water board or gas officials to gain entry into the home of elderly people in order to steal from them. It is a terrible crime and it always leaves the elderly feeling as though they were somehow responsible because they had let them into their home. It has on many occasions caused the death of the elderly person who has been on the receiving end of the con artist.

The main perpetrators of the offence are the travelling gypsy community. They are very callous in the way they go about this crime and even have their own code or mark such as an 'X' that they leave discreetly on or near an elderly person's house to give the next person that comes along an idea of what can be found in a certain house.

Because of the itinerant way of life, they lead and the way they all seem to have the name of either Ward, Smith or Doyle, it is a very difficult offence to deal with and it is very rare that one of these types are actually caught committing an offence.

One summer I was driving the area car on an early shift with Stuart Ryan as my operator. A 999 call was passed to us, sending us to a large block of flats situated in Linacre Court W14. The person calling was an elderly lady who was concerned about two men posing as water board officials. She had turned them away but had watched them enter her neighbour's flat. Her neighbour was also elderly and lived alone. She gave a description and stated they had deep Irish accents.

I raced down to the address. The entrance to the block of flats was in Linacre Court off Hammersmith Grove; the other side of the block faced directly onto the A4 Talgarth Road just east of Hammersmith flyover. I deliberately went with just the blue lights and headlamp flash on as I did not want to risk disturbing the suspects. As I pulled up outside the block I noticed a white transit van pull away slowly from a parking space about 200 yards up the road and head away from us.

This immediately rang alarm bells with me. Not wishing to risk the lady still being in the flat alone, I decided not to go after it but put the details of this van over the radio. Fortunately, another car on way to the flats to back us up had come in from the opposite direction and fell in right behind the van as it turned left onto the A4.

The crew immediately switched on their blue lights and pulled the van over. It actually stopped about 50 yards past the flats. As soon as it stopped the driver and passenger were out and running. The chase came over the radio so I called for Stuart to go on up to the flat to check on the lady and I ran around the side of the flats and, along with another officer, grabbed the passenger. He was nicked straight away and I then could hear that officers were chasing the driver, who was a lot younger than the passenger, along the A4 towards Barons Court.

I jumped into a marked car and raced off towards them. Ahead, I saw the officers with the suspect in front of them by some distance. The suspect was running down the centre of the road with cars travelling a speed towards him in three lanes of traffic, he seemed to have a death wish. He turned right into Barons Court and towards the tube station.

I got to the lights and by the time I got to the station bridge, the chasing officers were looking over the wall down at the tube line. I assumed the suspect had gone over the wall and was lying injured down on the track because it was one hell of a drop on the other side. Incredibly, I was told that he had in fact jumped the wall deliberately onto the roof of a passing tube train that was heading into town. It was something out of James Bond and he was now either going to get away or be found dead on the line.

Stuart dealt with the lady who was very distressed. She had let them in, as they had said there was a problem with the water and asked her to stand in the kitchen and turn the taps on and off while they checked other places. She became suspicious and found one of them in her bedroom going through her wardrobe. She screamed and the neighbour who had called us shouted out that she had called police and the two men had run out of the flat.

A great amount of forensic evidence was recovered from the flat, which helped us identify who they were. The man we had detained was John Doyle, who with his son, also John, was a part of a known artifice team which came back and forth from Ireland on a regular basis committing this type of crime. The son was wanted in Ireland for manslaughter after a pensioner died as the result of being knocked to the ground during one of their offences. That explained why he risked such a dangerous leap onto a moving tube train.

To my knowledge the son was never traced. The father received eight years in prison and was to be handed over to the Garda when his time was finished in this country. This was a very satisfying result to put at least one of these scum of the earth inside for this particularly horrible crime.

You always get one

There are times as a police officer when you despair at the people you come into contact with, and you would like nothing more than to take them to one side and quite happily punch their lights out. Unfortunately, this can no longer be done in the modern and politically correct police force. One of the strangest incidents took place one early shift at Hammersmith.

We received a call to a serious injury accident at Hammersmith Broadway bus station at the south entrance facing Fulham Palace Road. A lady of about thirty years of age was crossing between the up ramp and down ramp. She had jumped onto a very small kerb area between the two ramps. A bus coming down the ramp to leave the station came a bit close and caused her to lean backwards in surprise just as a single-decker bus entered the up ramp behind her. She lost her balance and fell back under the rear wheels of the bus. The wheels ran straight over her head, killing her instantly.

When I arrived with my operator, a foot-duty PC was already there. He was just about to cover up the lady with a blanket. Her injuries were horrific with her head completely squashed flat. Thankfully, almost immediately a traffic sergeant arrived on his bike and took over the handling of the scene.

I volunteered to go and deal with all the occupants of the bus. I went on and saw there were only about six people on it and explained that I needed them all to remain on the bus until I had all their details and a short statement from each of them. I asked them all to remain in their seats, as I needed to make a plan of where they were all sitting on the bus to show what sort of view they had of the incident.

Sitting almost at the front, on the right side of the bus, was a young lady who was heavily pregnant, and her mother. The young girl was very upset and had actually seen the woman fall backwards. Her mother was very worried about her as she was only two weeks away from giving birth and had just come from the hospital.

It was while I was talking to her I became aware of another man, in his fifties. He was eastern European and was very well-dressed. He had gone to the back of the bus and was looking down at the deceased on the floor. He then started telling everyone on the bus, in very graphic detail, what the woman looked like. I went to the back of the bus and saw that the ambulance crew had arrived and were examining the body of the woman. The bloke revelled in it and seemed to be taking great pleasure in describing everything. The other passengers were getting very distressed.

I spoke with him and told him to come away from the window as he was upsetting the other people on the bus. He then claimed he was Captain So-and-So from some country working here for the government. He kept going on about who he was and who he knew. I thought he was just a nutter and warned him to stay away from the window. He then produced documents with his name and title, etc on it and told me it was a free country and he could look if he wanted to.

I warned him not to and went back to finish taking the details of the young lady and her mum. Then the so-called Captain started again.

'Oh look at her head; it's flat, all squashed and all that blood. Oh God, come and see this…' He just kept going on and on. I could see that the young girl was getting very distressed. The other passengers were also getting very upset.

I went to the back of the bus and the man said, 'Look officer, look at her head; there is nothing left of it. I hope she is dead.' Well, that was it, before I knew it I had given him a short punch into his kidneys and he crumpled in a heap on the back seat puffing for air.

I leaned over him and told him if he said one more word without being spoken to first, I would arrest him, and that he should stay there until I was ready to deal with him. I went back to the young girl and her mother whispered to me, 'Thanks officer, nice touch!'

I eventually dealt with them all, leaving the man till last. He never mentioned the punch and sulked as I took all his details from his paperwork and a brief statement. I then allowed them all to leave telling them that someone would be in touch at a later stage for a full statement.

I gave everything to the traffic sergeant and told him all about the pain in the arse so-called captain. A few weeks later he got back in touch with me to tell me that all the paperwork the captain had appeared to be false as there was no records anywhere of him and he could not be traced. Very odd!

My biggest regret

There have only been a few occasions in all my service where I have regretted my actions, or have been bothered by the way I have dealt with an incident. There have been occasions where I have had problems sleeping because of having dealt with something very unpleasant or particularly upsetting.

I can say, however, without any doubt that the thing I most regretted in all my service, and the incident that gave me the most sleepless nights, was when I was involved with the initial investigation into the murder of a twelve-year-old girl in her own home in the middle of the afternoon.

My actions that day haunted me for years because I felt that if I had made the right decisions at the right time, although I could not have prevented her death, I might have been able to catch the person who murdered her. Instead, it took almost seven years to bring her murderer to justice. This is the story surrounding the murder of Katrina Koneva.

On 27th of May 1997, I was posted to drive the Hammersmith area car, call sign Foxtrot 2. My operator for the whole month was Katie Redhead. Katie at the time was still in her probation but was developing into an excellent officer. She was prepared to get stuck in, and I could rely on her totally. Some time just after 4.00 p.m. we were driving around the Brackenbury Village area of Hammersmith which runs between Paddenswick Road and Hammersmith Grove, W6. We received a call via our main radio set linked to information room at New Scotland Yard. The call related to a male armed with a knife chasing another male.

The location given was Amor Road towards Hammersmith Grove. When we received the call we were just turning onto Goldhawk Road from Brackenbury Road, less than half a mile from the call. We raced off along Goldhawk Road and turned right into Hammersmith Grove and within less than two minutes we were at the junction with Amor Road and Hammersmith Grove. At first everything seemed normal. Then Katie pointed out a member of the public waving to us a little further down to our left at the junction with Trussley Road.

There we found several people with a female who was very distressed. Katie spoke to her and discovered she had been forced to stop by a short fat bald man who pulled a knife and dragged her out of her car. He then drove off along Trussley Road under the arches towards Sulgrave Road.

The car was a small red vehicle – a Fiat I believe – and the lady told Katie the male appeared to have trouble driving it as the car jerked off along the road. Realising this was linked to the call we were dealing with, we informed other units and told the lady to remain there and someone would come to deal with her. She also told us we were only two or three minutes behind the man.

Trussley Road leads into Trussley Arches. The arches run under the tube line. When we got under the arches I had a choice to make: turn left into Sulgrave Road or right into Lena Gardens. Both roads eventually lead onto Shepherds Bush Road, a very busy main route between Hammersmith Broadway and Shepherds Bush Green.

I chose right because it was the quickest route to Shepherds Bush Road and if he knew the area he would take the shortest route. When I reached Shepherds Bush Road I pulled out into the junction looking left and right. Traffic was very heavy north towards Shepherds Bush Green but, unusually, lighter towards the Broadway. I could see no sign of a small red car. I decide to turn right and head south as there was less traffic and hoped he had thought the same. I raced to Hammersmith Broadway and was there in less than thirty seconds.

Having done a complete lap of the Broadway with no trace, I headed north back up Shepherds Bush Road towards the green. Katie saw it first and pointed out the small red Fiat parked half on and half off the pavement on the west footpath facing Shepherds Bush Green. It was five yards from the junction with Sulgrave Road; I had made the wrong choice! I was furious with myself for making the wrong decision.

The vehicle was empty and the key was in the ignition. Katie informed other units where we had found it and asked units to search the green for the male whose description was being circulated by an officer who was now with the lady owner. Why had he abandoned the car in such an odd place?

Almost immediately, we were joined by PC Shaun Dougherty. We were just about to start a search nearby, when suddenly over the radio came a request for urgent assistance from one of our sergeants, Steve Shearing. He gave an address in Iffley Road, which was very close to where all this had started. Steve was normally very cool in everything he did but there was something strange in his voice that worried me.

We tried calling him back as we made our way there, leaving Shaun with the red Fiat. This had to be linked and we were probably the nearest to Steve to help him. We knew he had requested an ambulance and when he did not answer his radio I was very concerned. We raced back through the arches to the address in Iffley Road.

As we arrived I saw the front door open, there was no noise coming from inside: another worry. The house was split into two flats. A door at the bottom of the stairs giving access to upstairs was also open. I ran up the first flight and, as I turned left onto the second flight of stairs, I could see a door open. Through the door I saw what looked like Steve's back. He appeared to be bent over. I could also see another male figure bent over him. It looked to me that the male was trying to strangle Steve from behind.

Without breaking stride I hit the door hard intending to hit the male as hard as possible with a full-blown rugby tackle to pull him off Steve. My second bad decision of the day! As I hit the room running I suddenly realised I had read the situation all wrong. Steve was in fact kneeling down over the lifeless body of Katrina Koneva, a twelve-year-old girl. Katrina was lying flat on her back in pyjamas and a cardigan and Steve was trying to revive her with mouth to mouth and cardiac massage. The male leaning over Steve was her father. Naturally things were all very mixed up.

Steve asked us to get the father away and find out exactly what had taken place; he continued working on Katrina and did so even when the ambulance service, including the air ambulance crews arrived. We managed to get Dad into another room; you can imagine the distress he was in but we needed to know what had taken place. The Dad was from Macedonia and his English was at times difficult to understand, but eventually the horror of what we were dealing with came out.

Katrina had returned home from school and changed out of her school clothes. Dad had to go out and collected Katrina's younger brother from a nearby school. He left Katrina, for the first time ever, alone in the flat to do her homework. On reaching the school he found his wife had already picked their son up and gone on to visit relatives.

Dad returned to the flat and entered to find the living room door blocked. He was unable to open it and started calling his daughter's name. He got no reply but could hear movement in the room. He then got on his hands and knees and looked under the door and could see a pair of feet. He tried forcing the living room door but could not do so.

He then heard one of the front windows being opened and he ran down the stairs and saw a male jumping down from the flat. He grabbed hold of the male believing him to be a burglar. The male pulled a knife out and threatened Mr Koneva and told him to stay away from him. The male ran off and Mr Koneva chased him, shouting for someone to call the police.

He chased the man from Iffley Road and right into Hebron Road. The man ran on into Amor Road and to the junction with Hammersmith Grove, where he tried to hide in a building site. At the site the male was challenged by several builders. He told them he was being chased by a man with the knife. When Mr Koneva came into the site looking for the male he was grabbed by the builders and ruffed up a little. While this was going on the suspect left and hijacked the lady with the car fifty yards away in Trussley Road. The builders also had dialled 999, which had led Kate and me there.

The immediate implications were horrendous. We were now all trampling over a major crime scene. I left Kate in charge of Dad and went in to Steve. The ambulance crew was trying to revive Katrina. At the time my daughter was not yet fifteen years old and seeing Katrina lying there suddenly hit me a little, and I struggled to get a grip on myself. I managed to quickly tell Steve the situation and left him to secure the room and to instruct the ambulance crew as to what was required to preserve the scene in the best way possible. They still had to work on Katrina but we badly need to make sure no evidence was lost.

I went downstairs to secure the front door and radioed to the nick that this was a major crime scene and requested the urgent attendance of the senior CID officer. This put the major incident process in motion but, more importantly, started the hunt for the man Katie and I had so narrowly missed. I was even more annoyed with myself now. The wrong choice had allowed the murderer of a twelve-year-old girl, in her own home, to escape. We were so close to catching him and I could not believe we had let him slip away. I really felt we had let little Katrina down and as time went on that afternoon and evening I could not get the thought of the murderer out of my mind.

Detective Chief Inspector Dick Quinn arrived with other CID officers and I briefed him on the situation. Despite all the best efforts of the ambulance crews it was plain to me that Katrina was already dead. I remained as controller at the front door for quite some time; the murder squad eventually arrived and I was relieved from my post as controller and told to return to Hammersmith to complete my reports on everything that had happened.

We all knew by now that Katrina had been pronounced dead at hospital and I was feeling very annoyed and angry with myself. A subsequent post mortem showed Katrina had been strangled.

At the station, Steve Shearing told me he had been walking nearby, when Mr Koneva had come running up to him very distressed. All Steve could really understand was the word burglar as Mr Koneva pleaded with Steve to follow him. He did so and when they went upstairs and found the door jammed shut, Steve forced it open. He was met with the sight of Katrina's lifeless body lying on her back on the floor, alongside the settee.

Steve, Katie and I were devastated by the incident. We had been so close to catching the person who had killed Katrina. Kate and I realised that we had been in Iffley Road just a short time before we received the 999 call and must have actually been in the street at the time the suspect was killing Katrina. I can only imagine what Steve was going through having actually physically tried to revive Katrina. We try to be big and macho about these things, but I know it affected Katie and it certainly affected me for quite a long time afterwards.

Police enquiries that night revealed the suspect had dumped the car where we had found it in Shepherds Bush Road and had ran across the road onto a bus heading for Hammersmith Broadway. I must have passed this bus at least twice while I was looking for the car. A video showing the suspect running in Trussley Road just before he hijacked the car was the only evidence we had of him. The video image was poor, but we knew we were looking for a very short, plump male who was balding.

As you can imagine, a massive murder enquiry swung into action. Everything possible was done to try to identify and find the murderer. Katie and I spent weeks and weeks afterwards touring the ground trying to spot the suspect, believing he must be local. We even actually arrested three people on suspicion. They all fitted the description but were eliminated by a palm print found at the scene which had been recovered from the window ledge which had been made as the suspect leapt from the window of the flat.

I found this event really difficult to deal with. I had dreams of bursting in the room and seeing Katrina's body lying there. On occasions I would see my daughter's face on the body instead of Katrina's. The number of times I relived the drive through the arches, even seeing the suspect on a bus laughing at me as I past. It really got to me and as time went on and the suspect was still free, I started worrying that if another young girl was murdered by him, then it would my fault because I failed to catch him on the day.

It literally took years to get rid of the dreams but I always had this feeling of failure about the whole incident. Despite numerous reviews of the murder and several *Crimewatch* reconstructions, it seemed that the suspect was never going to be found. The mother and father of Katrina suffered beyond belief and the stress of it eventually caused them to divorce.

Then suddenly, in the summer of 2003, I received a phone call from Katie Redhead. She said, 'Have you heard? They have arrested a man for killing Katrina; they have him on DNA.'

I was astounded, but naturally very elated and excited! How had he been caught after all this time? Katie was now a CID officer at

Hammersmith and the news was naturally all over the station! She did not have any other details about the arrest though. I just had to find out more. Fortunately, my very close friend, Andy Murphy was now a detective chief superintendent on the murder squad, he would know all about it. I called him and asked if he knew anything. He did... everything!

He told me the suspect was a Polish man in his late forties who was an illegal immigrant. He was a serial sex offender, wanted for many crimes in Poland and here in London. He had been arrested and convicted of a rape of a student in Acton. His DNA was taken following his subsequent charging with the offence. A sample piece of hair recovered from Katrina's cardigan had been developed by a new DNA procedure and a profile obtained.

When the DNA taken from the suspect was compared against the DNA national database it received a positive hit. He was the killer without a doubt! At last, a result for Katrina and her family. I called Katie and told her the good news; we were both chuffed to bits.

I was subsequently warned to give evidence at the trial of Andrezi Kunowski at the Old Bailey for the murder of Katrina. The trial was set to start on the 15 March 2003. Unfortunately, I was never called to give evidence. I really wanted to see the man I had so narrowly missed on the day of the murder. I wanted to look him in the eyes. I wanted to see what he looked like, to see if I recognised him at all. Unfortunately, I was not required to give evidence so never got the satisfaction!

On Wednesday 31 March 2003, Kunowski was found guilty of Katrina's murder and sentenced to life imprisonment. The full list of his horrendous crimes then came to public notice. The man was evil and no female of any age was safe from him. He had received his first prison sentence at the age of seventeen following the rape of a teenager in Poland. Detective Chief Inspector David Little described Kunowski as the most dangerous sex offender he had ever come across.

So finally Katrina can rest in peace. Her parents and brother have the satisfaction of seeing the man who killed their precious daughter go to prison for the rest of his life.

Personally, I think he should be given a lethal dose of something and removed from this earth. If they need a volunteer they only have to ask me. Although I am sure I am one of a long list of willing people to carry out the deed.

I WILL ALWAYS FEEL THIS was the most important thing I ever got wrong in my whole Police Service. A wrong decision to go left or right, that's all it took to let a murderer escape!

As a strange quirk to the ending of this story, in January 2005, I transferred onto the murder squad and was based at Barnes. The detective sergeant in charge of my team was Dave Standley. He was the DS who had dealt with Katrina's killer and who has since told me some further information. The man was a complete animal and deserves nothing more than to be put down like an animal, not living off the country for the rest of his life.

Summary justice

One night duty in August 1997, I was driving the area car at Shepherds Bush; we were really short on staff and I was in the car on my own. At about 1.00 a.m. we received a report of the sound of gunfire, at least three shots had been reported in the area of Erconwold Street and Wulfstan Street. This location was on a small estate just to the rear of Wormwood Scrubs prison.

I made my way there along with several others and we were told that there was an Armed Response Vehicle nearby and that they would also attend. The estate had a large mixture of people living on it. There were a lot of elderly people who had lived there for many years and who would always help the police. However, over the years a percentage of undesirables had been moved in by the council and they were a constant problem on the estate which was troubled by crime of all sorts.

As I arrived at the junction of Erconwold and Wulfstan I saw that the ARV was already on scene. I spoke with them briefly and then went and checked the street but found no trace of anything unusual. Other officers checked the surrounding streets but again nothing was found. I got the control room to call the informant back. They confirmed we were in the right place and that they were sure it was gunfire. But because they were scared of any possible recriminations they did not wish to come and speak with me.

With nothing positive to go on, the ARV decided to leave us to it. As they drove off I saw three shell cases lying on the road directly under where the ARV had been parked and immediately called them back. Having been a firearms officer I knew straightaway that they were real shells and I could also see the strike marks on the back of the shell made by a firing pin as it was fired. They returned, agreed with me and called for other ARV's to attend the scene. We put a cordon in around the streets and began a search of the area.

As I walked up Ercowold Street, towards Braybrook Street I was aware of a man, standing in an archway leading to a house. He was beckoning me towards him. When I went up to him he told me he had also heard the shots and when he looked out of the window he saw someone being dragged into a house across the road from him; he pointed out an address to me. He knew who lived at the address and he believed that one of the boys was the grandson of the occupier, who was an elderly lady.

I immediately informed everyone of the information and returned to my car, and an armed incident began to take shape. A full firearms team was called out from SO19 in order to deal with the premises. While we waited for them to arrive we discovered that the address was home to a well-known street robber called Jermaine Abbot. He was only about sixteen years of age but involved in serious crime on a regular basis. Also, while we were waiting for the SO19 team to arrive several witnesses came forward all confirming the sound of at least three gunshots.

By the time the firearms team arrived and were briefed, some two hours had passed since the initial call. Entry was eventually made into the premises by SO19 and they found a youth by the name of Jamic Alcondor lying on the settee, conscious, with three bullet wounds. Also hiding in the loft they found Jermaine Abbot, and in a bedroom, oblivious to everything, was his grandmother.

Alcondor was rushed from the house to a waiting ambulance and I followed behind to the West London Hospital, a very short distance away in Du Cane Road. In the emergency ward at the hospital I got details of the victim and was shocked to discover he was only just fourteen years of age; his physique belied his age and he could have easily passed as eighteen years old. As we stood in casualty, I was taking possession of the victim's cloths for forensics, when all hell broke loose with alarm bells sounding and doctors rushing to Alcondor's bed. He had suddenly gone into cardiac arrest and the next thing I knew they had cut open his chest and were rushing him off the surgery with a doctor manually massaging his heart to keep him alive.

Unbelievably, thanks to the skills of the doctors, Acondor survived and despite receiving three shots all at close range into his body, one in the chest close to his heart, within two weeks he was sitting up in bed at hospital demanding to be released. His recovery astounded everyone involved. It was only a very short time later he was out and about committing crime again.

The story of the shooting was told to police by Jermaine Abbot. He, Alcondor and two other teenagers were a team who together went out to places such as Knightsbridge and St Johns Wood, and they would target victims who were wearing Rolex watches. They had an agreement that all proceeds would always be shared between the four of them, so even if only two people actually committed a robbery, all four had to have a share. The other two member of the team were Aston Tew and Damien Hanson.

On the day of the shooting Alcondor had robbed a man of a Rolex watch on his own. He did not want to share the proceeds but needed Abbot's help to sell the watch. He phoned Abbot and told him he had a watch but not to tell the other two. Unfortunately for Alcondor, Abbot rang the others and told them that Alcondor had a watch he was trying to sell without telling them. They arranged for Abbot to tell Alcondor that he had a buyer for the watch and that they would be meeting them at the phone box in Wulfstan Street that night.

When they got to the phone box, the other two member of the team appeared. Hanson was armed with a gun and Tew had a knife. Hanson demanded that Alcondor hand over the watch to them, but he refused. Hanson then pulled out the gun and again demanded the watch. Alcondor had the watch hidden in his underpants and decided to make a run for it. As he tried to run Hanson shot him three times at close range and Alcondor fell to the ground.

Hanson took the watch and left with Tew. Abbot was unaware that the other two had weapons and had run off when the shooting started. He went back to help Alcondor and dragged him off to his grandmother's address. When they got there he laid him on the settee and tried to help him. He spent the next two hours giving Alcondor whisky and tea to try and keep him going. When the police came he tried to hide in the loft, which is where he was found.

A hunt for Tew and Hanson resulted in the fairly quick arrest of Tew in the Hammersmith area. Hanson disappeared but was eventually arrested at a flat on the south coast after he fell out of a second floor window as he tried to escape when police arrived. The three of them subsequently appeared at the Old Bailey charged with attempted murder, robbery and firearms offences. They were convicted of numerous offences and received lengthy prison sentences of twelve years.

Hanson was released from prison in August 2004 having served half of his sentence. Three months later he targeted a wealthy banker, John Monkton at his family home in Chelsea. With the aid of an accomplice who was dressed as a postman delivering a parcel, they forced their way in. Hanson had a gun in one hand and a knife in the other. He first stabbed Mrs Monkton in the back and demanded her jewellery. He then went over to where Mr Monkton was struggling with his accomplice. He stabbed Mr Monkton in the heart and lungs, the attack was so frenzied that at one point the knife went through Mr Monkton and stabbed his accomplice in the arm.

They left with just £3,000 pounds'-worth of jewellery leaving Mr Monkton dead and Mrs Monkton fighting for her life. The whole attack was witnessed by their nine-year-old daughter. Had it not been for her calling the emergency services then there is no doubt that Mrs Monkton would have died also.

By sheer coincidence, I was at the Old Bailey as exhibits officer in a murder trial in court two in November and December 2005. In court three was the trial of Hanson and his accomplice, White, for the murder of Mr Monkton and the attempted murder of Mrs Monkton. This was a very high-profile public trial. Mrs Monkton was still suffering from her injuries, and needed a walking stick to help her walk. God only knows what her nine-year-old daughter was going through, especially after having to give evidence at the trial because of Hanson taking the system as far as he could, pleading not guilty and denying that he had ever been there. Hanson was found guilty of the murder and attempted murder and sentenced to three life sentences…

At the time of writing, Aston Tew is still in prison serving his sentence for the attempted murder on Jamic Alcondor.

Jermaine Abbot was shot dead in 2003 a year after he himself was found not guilty of a murder charge. Alcondor has continued with a life of crime.

Mr and Mrs Monkton and their family have been failed by the judicial and prison systems, as Hanson should never have been released after just six years. Had he served the full length of his prison term Mr Monkton would still be alive today.

I ALSO MET JAMIC ALCONDOR again in April 2002. I was working on the crime squad at Hammersmith and sat in the office doing some paper work. A detective from the Central London Crime Squad came in and asked if anyone knew what Jamic Alcondor looked like.

He had a man in custody for a Rolex robbery and he had given a name that they believed was false. One of his colleagues thought his real name might be Alcondor but he was denying it. I told him I knew him and had a definite way of identifying him.

We went to the cells and I recognised Alcodor straight away but he claimed he was not Jamic. He was dressed in one of the white paper custody suits as all his clothes had been taken away by forensics. I asked him to undo the zip of the paper suit. He refused. I told him I knew he was Jamic, and I would prove it.

'You have a scar from your throat all the way down your stomach?' I said.

He looked a bit surprised and said, 'no.'

I told him I knew for a fact he did have a scar and to open his zip. He again refused. I took one arm and another officer the other and I undid the zip.

'There you go, exactly as I described!'

Alcondor said 'Ok I'm Jamic, how the hell did you know about the scar?'

When I told him I had been at the hospital with him, he was quite shocked especially after I told him that had I not found out where he was as quickly as I had done, he would be dead. I still did not get a thank you, but he did go to prison!

A VERY TRAGIC TIME

IT IS VERY DIFFICULT TO try to explain in a book just how stressful being a police officer can sometimes be. You see tragedy close up on a regular basis and have to put your feeling to one side to help the victims or relatives left behind to get through their ordeal. It is even worse when it is close to home and extremely hard to deal with.

On our sister team at Shepherds Bush was a WPC called Helen Johnson. Helen was a very quiet girl, almost shy really which is very unusual for a female officer! I did not know Helen that well, really. We would sit down and chat in the canteen but she was not a great conversationalist. She was very friendly with Steve and Sarah, a married couple who were on our team. She was single and lived alone in a flat in Greenford but spent a lot of time with Sarah and Steve.

In July 1998, we were night duty; Helen was acting very strangely and people and started to notice. Unknown to most of us, Helen had a history of bouts of depression and was receiving help for this problem. We were on nights for the week and Helen was posted as controller in the control room at Hammersmith.

Every night she sat there reading a book, stopping only to answer the radio. If you walked into the control room and tried to speak to her she would just swivel her chair and turn her back to you. People were starting to get a bit annoyed with her. Come the Friday night and the start of duty, there was no sign of Helen. We assumed she had gone sick or taken the night off.

However, what we did not know at first was that Sarah was very concerned as she had not been able to get hold of her on the phone. As the night went by Sarah's concerns were being echoed by several others on her team at Shepherds Bush. So, come the early hours of the morning, one of the team, Paul McRae, went to the nick local to her address and had a word with the inspector, and they decided to pay Helen a visit. Sarah had given Paul a spare key to Helen's flat that she had.

When they arrived there they knocked and found no reply. The inspector used to key to get in and was met with a terrible sight. On opening the door, the stairs went up immediately to the left. He saw straight away that Helen was hanging from the banister. She had committed suicide. The first we knew about it was when everyone was called back to Hammersmith in the middle of the night and Inspector Pat Baynon relayed the terrible news to us.

I cannot begin to explain what it did to the team. Everyone was in a state of shock and no one was in a fit state to go out and take any calls. Surrounding divisions were asked to cover for us for the rest of the night.

We managed to get through the last two nights, and come the Monday we were asked to come into work late afternoon where the Met were going to provide bereavement counselling for us. Now, we were all feeling some sort of grief; those that knew Helen really well were having a very hard time coming to terms with what had happened but counselling was really the last thing we needed.

We were all taken into the training room at Shepherds Bush police station. There were between twenty and thirty of us including all the civilian staff. Some very nice officers led by a female sergeant then sat us around in a big circle and started talking to us. I found this very difficult to deal with. They were trying to be very nice, pussyfooting around, telling us what we can expect to feel and how to deal with it. It went on and on I felt like a child being taught at school.

After about twenty minutes of this the sergeant said, 'If anyone is finding this too difficult, just raise your hand and step outside, we will give you a few minutes to compose yourself then one of us will join you and see you on a one to one basis.'

I looked around the room and I could see everyone getting frustrated, looking down at the floor, tapping their feet and generally not interested. There was complete silence in the room and I could stand it no more.

I looked at the sergeant and said, 'Please forgive me, but I would like to say something and I hope I do not offend you.'

She told me very nicely, 'No please say what you want.'

I said openly, 'I know you are trying to help the team and we are very grateful for you coming here, however, this is a complete and utter waste of time. You want us to deal with whatever grief or stress we are feeling, I'm sorry; this is not the way we deal with our stress. This team is very close, our stress-breaker is to all go on the piss together and that is what I suggest we go and do, go and get hammered and talk about Helen.'

The sergeant's face was a picture. Everyone clapped and agreed and that's exactly what we did: we all had a huge night on the piss, talked about Helen, had a great laugh and all felt better for it. I don't think I endeared myself to the lady sergeant, but it worked a damn sight better than her counselling could have ever done.

Because I had not known Helen very well, I volunteered to look after Helen's parents when they arrived from their home in Harrogate. I thought it was easier for me, than someone from her team, who knew her well to have to do it. It was still a very emotional time and I spent several days looking after them.

The worst part was taking them to the mortuary for them to see Helen. I never have any problems dealing with the deceased, but Helen's mum insisted I go in and see her. I cannot explain why, but doing so really got to me and I found it quite distressing. It bothered me for weeks afterwards and I have no idea why.

Helen had a full force funeral in her home town of Harrogate which we all travelled up in several coaches for; her mother who had once been a special constable was very proud of what Helen had achieved and was thrilled with the attendance of so many of her colleagues and it helped her family through a very painful time.

Helen was not the first officer I knew who committed suicide, nor was she the last, but it was her death that made me realise what doing the job can do to you if you are not able to control the extreme stress and pressures that come with certain aspect of life as a police officer.

Driving for the Flying Squad

Everyone knows of the world famous Flying Squad after the successful television series, *The Sweeney*. I had been very interested in the squad for years and my close friend Andy Murphy had served on the squad as a detective constable and a detective sergeant. It seemed a life far away from anything I had done or was ever likely to do. It was one of the most revered and formidable squads in the world and to be a part of one of the four squad offices in the Met was something many people strived for but very few achieved.

One of the things the squad was well-known for was its dedicated drivers. These were highly skilled advanced drivers and in 1999 there were about six drivers at each office. In addition to the drivers, each office ran a standby list of uniformed officers who had an interest in becoming a full-time driver. Although waiting was 'dead man's shoes', each office had a considerable list. These drivers were called 'strappers' and they would be called upon to fill in if the normal drivers were off on leave or extra drivers were needed for a particular reason.

In those days it was a case of 'who you knew' not 'what you knew' to get one of these posts. You had to be sponsored by a squad officer to stand any chance of getting on the strapping list. It had been something I was interested in very much and had mentioned it several times to Andy Murphy.

Then one day I got a call from him saying that a strappers vacancy was to come up at the Finchley office and did I fancy it? Too bloody right I did! So after getting permission from the divisional boss at Hammersmith, I applied and several weeks later got a call to go for a week's trial.

My first few days there were very odd; the squad is such a tight-knit group and the work they deal with is at times highly sensitive, and I just felt like a bit of a gopher. I was just given menial tasks of taking paperwork to Scotland Yard and other police premises. I did not really think I was going to like this, but then on the fourth day I was taken on a live operation and was immediately hooked on the work.

I was, however, well and truly set up for a joke before we left. One of the DCs came over to me and said, 'Have you made sure that the glove box is full?'

'Of what,' I asked.

He then said, 'Surely you know it is the driver's job to make sure the glove box is well stocked with chocolate, crisps and coke for the governor for when we are out on jobs.'

Well, I remembered seeing on *The Sweeney* on the television that there was always food in the car so I fell for it hook, line and sinker and dashed to the shop and bought a load of chocolate and crisps and coke and tucked it away in the glove box ready for the detective inspector.

The DI in my car was called Dave Ryan and it was the first time I had met him. He was a huge man with a big beard and he scared the life out of me. He was a bit like Giant Haystacks the wrestler. He got in the car and gave me a right hard look. The first thing he did was open the glove box. Boy, was I pleased I had filled it up!

Then he looked at me and roared, 'who the f*** is all this for? Where am I going to put all my papers?'

He looked at me and I mumbled, 'It's your chocolate and drinks for the job, guv.'

He roared even more and said, 'Are you trying to say that I am such a fat bastard that I need to keep eating? How dare you!'

I really thought I was in for it now and started to mutter some sort of apology. Then I looked outside the car and saw some of the squad absolutely wetting themselves with laughter. Mr Ryan then looked at me, smiled and said, 'Welcome to Finchley, young man.'

From then on I had a great time at Finchley and went there strapping as often as I was able to.

Long service and good conduct medal

Every police officer who gets to twenty-two years' service, provided he had not received any disciplinary procedures in that time, gets presented with the police long service and good conduct medal. This is usually presented to the officer at a mass ceremony at Hendon Training School, by the Commissioner of the Met. It is a time when you can take your family along and have a day out on the job!

My twenty-two years' service was completed in February 1999 and around that time I received a large envelope in dispatch at Hammersmith. I opened it to find instructions inside inviting me to a ceremony at Hendon in the July in order to receive my medal. Also inside was a strip of medal ribbon along with instructions on how to make a ribbon badge for attaching to my uniform tunic to show I was an officer with twenty-two years' service. What a load of bollocks. I also had to return a form to an office at New Scotland Yard accepting the invitation and stating how many guests I would be bringing with me.

I had already made up my mind a long time before this that I did not wish to attend a ceremony to collect my medal. I believed the commissioner at the time was destroying the Met with some of the things he was implementing and I had no desire to have my medal presented to me by someone I did not have any respect for. So I telephoned the office at the yard that dealt with the issue of the medals.

I spoke with a member of the civilian staff and told him I did not want to have it presented to me by the commissioner; he tried to tell me I had no choice and that I had to go. The more he told me I had to go, the more I was determined I was not going. He was a complete jobs-worth and sounded like a real anorak! After a very heated exchange he told me he would get back to me with an alternative.

A couple of days later he rang me and told me that he would allow the medal to be presented to me by my divisional chief superintendent. This annoyed me even more. Yes, I knew the chief superintendent; yes he was my boss, but I really did not like the attitude of the guy on the phone telling me who I had to have present me with my medal!

I said, 'No thank you,' and asked if it could be presented by either of my two close friends, Andy Murphy or Mick Wise. They both were now senior officers. He refused point black and said it had to be his way or not at all! So I basically told him what I thought of him and told him to stick to medal in dispatch and I would get the station cleaner to present it to me.

I thought no more about it until a few months later. I was called to the personnel office to collect a package. I signed for a small jiffy bag and walked out wondering what the hell it was. When I opened it, I found my medal inside. Well, I finally had it, and what a disappointment! My own fault, I know, for not wanting it to be presented to me by the commissioner. The medal now takes pride of place in a box, in a cupboard somewhere in my home.

A major change

After several different weeks of 'strapping' with Finchley Flying squad I suddenly found myself thinking of a change of direction in my career. I really thought that I would love to get onto the Flying Squad full-time as a driver. I loved the work and it was the first time I had ever really considered doing anything else other than uniformed policing.

With nearly twenty-one years' service under my belt, I was a bit unsure at first about doing something else, but the more I went and helped out with the squad, the more and more I felt it was the right thing to. The only problem was that I had a better chance of winning the lottery than getting a job as a driver on the squad.

You had to be a 'strapper' for quite some considerable time before you could even be considered for such a coveted job. Then you were on a waiting list of at least six people and I was bottom of the list as the new boy. The full-time drivers normally only left when they retired so vacancies did not come around very often. With only nine years left until I retired I was not likely to get a full-time post on the squad before retiring.

Then in the summer of 1997, Hammersmith started running a crime car to help combat the growing street robbery problem. This would be a large powerful unmarked car, fitted with a stick on blue light and two-tones. It was be crewed by a sergeant and two officers for twelve hours a day, working at times when the robbery offences were occurring. It meant being temporarily attached to the CID, and I put in an application for the first month's posting and got it. That month was exceptional, we had some great results and really got stuck into some well-known street robbers and got a lot them locked up.

During this month I was spoken to by the Detective Chief Inspector Dick Quinn. He was a former squad man at Finchley and he knew of my interest in getting in the squad. Over a period of a couple of weeks, he persuaded me that although I probably did not have enough time left to wait for a driver's job at Finchley, if I joined the CID I could get to become a CID officer and apply to join the squad as a detective rather than a driver. He told me that he was looking for new people to join the CID officer at Hammersmith as a trainee detectives and that I should apply. Well, after much thought and discussion I did apply and got one of the vacancies at Hammersmith, and in the latter part of 1997 I transferred into the CID.

This was very strange at first, but I soon got used to it. I first went onto the robbery squad where we dealt with all street robberies both by reactive investigations after offences had been committed and also by proactive operations against known offenders. I thoroughly enjoyed the work and the longer it went on the more I wondered why the hell I had taken so long to get around to doing it.

In early 1998, the robbery squad was merged with the burglary squad to form the Hammersmith crime squad and so started two years of very long hours and a lot of hard work. We were very fortunate to have two detective sergeants in charge us who brought out the best in the whole squad. They were perfect for this type of work. DS Jed Hodgson and DS Ian 'Dobbo' Dobson were infectious in their way of working and everyone else just got carried along with them.

In the first year, the crime squad was so successful that the crime figures for Hammersmith dropped and put the division at the top of the league for crime reduction in the whole of the Met. We put villains away who had plagued the division for the last few years. By carrying out proactive operations against them and catching those in the act of committing a crime meant the evidence was so good they were being locked up for fairly lengthy sentences.

We all worked really well as a team. It meant very long hours but it was really enjoyable and satisfying to be part of such a great team. There are so many great stories I could relate about the time I served on the crime squad – far too many to put in this book – but there is one story that I will tell because it does show how much hard work it can be doing this type of work; how dangerous it can be and also how much fun it can be.

There was a period of time in 1999, where it was noticed that street robbery in or around the Goldhawk Road area of Shepherds Bush was escalating. When research was done by members of the team, it was discovered that lone females, making their way home from the tube in the early evenings and late at night, were being targeted. The attacker was looking mainly for businesswomen carrying laptops and or handbags. He would follow the women as they left the tube and wait for them to walk down one of the many quite and often darker side streets off Goldhawk Road.

The number of offences was mounting up and despite us putting a lot of manpower out in the area to try to catch the person responsible, the offences continued. Then DS Hodgson put forward the idea of using a decoy officer in a pre-planned controlled situation to try at catch the suspect. This was a very risky idea because the suspect was prone to violence if any resistance was shown by the victim, and it meant putting a female officer on offer. However, after much discussion with senior officers and loads of paperwork, it was agreed that it was a sensible course of action to take. There had been a breakthrough in as much as we believed we knew now who the suspect was. He was a 6'2" black male who was well-known for this type of crime. He lived locally and fitted a very good description given to us by one of his latest victims. He had up to this point we believe, committed over thirty offences. Having identified a possible suspect, this made the decoy operation slightly easier and safer for the decoy officer as we knew who to look for. However, there was also the possibility that an opportunist thief might have a go so we still had to be on our guard.

COME THE NIGHT OF THE pre-planned operation, we attended a full briefing where we were to meet the two decoy officers who were to take it in turns to walk from the tube station in Goldhawk Road. When they arrived I was quite shocked because one of the decoys was a girl called Elaine.

Elaine and I had worked together at West Drayton. She joined my relief when she came out of training school and I had been involved in a lot of her original training when she joined us and we had become good friends. I did not even know she did this type of work and it made it even more worrying knowing she was going to be one of the targets. Also at the briefing we were joined by members of the central London crime squad who were there to beef up our numbers.

This was the plan. DS Dobson was going to be in a large white van with numerous officers from our crime squad tucked away south of the Goldhawk Road. Officers from the central London crime squad were in another van to the north of Goldhawk Road. Their job was to cover both ends of any street the decoy was to go down in case of any suspect following her and attacking her as she walked. Other officers would be deployed in the area to cover her on the route when she left the station.

It had been discovered, through research of the crimes, that a street called Sycamore Gardens was a potential hotspot… This street was very quiet and was in places quite dark as there were a lot of trees overhanging the pavements. The vast majority of the offences occurred in this street. It was approximately a 500-yard walk from the tube station and then a left turn off the main road into Sycamore Gardens. It was decided to make this the way the decoy would walk.

Opposite Sycamore Gardens, on the other side of the main road, is a public house. DC Russ Walker and I were to be in charge of the observation post situated on the first floor of the pub. We had a perfect view of the whole length of Sycamore Gardens and quite a lot of the route to be used by the girls, and we were to be responsible for calling in the 'strike' should the decoy be attacked.

Once everyone was in position, DS Hodgson, who was in a room at the tube station with the two decoys, was responsible for sending out one of them at irregular intervals. We started the operation just after 9.00 p.m. and things were very tense. The first decoy to come out was Elaine. She was dressed very smartly as a businesswoman carrying a laptop bag over her shoulder. Apart from a few glances from some several people as she walked the route nothing happened and she cleared the street at the far end of Sycamore Gardens and was picked up and returned to the tube station.

Nothing then happened for about half an hour. Then one of the team who was out on the street keeping an eye out for a suspect called up on the radio and said that our known suspect was stood under the bridge of the tube station talking to several other males. He also stated he was paying a lot of attention to females as they left the tube station. Five minutes later, DS Hodgson announced that the second decoy was about to leave the station.

As she came out and turned left towards Sycamore Gardens, the suspect immediately clocked her and started to follow her, walking at speed to close down the distance between them. A foot officer kept us informed of their progress and the suspect had obviously taken the bait. Once she reached the junction with Hammersmith Grove she was now in my sight and I took over the commentary of their progress. As they got closer to me, the suspect was only about ten feet behind her. Russ was able to positively identify the suspect as being the man we had previously suspected as being responsible for the other offences.

We thought this was it; he was definitely going for it. Then, as the decoy turned into Sycamore Gardens the suspect was just about to follow her into the road when suddenly two other black males ran across the road, whistling and shouting at out suspect to grab his attention. The noise they made attracted the attention of several people walking nearby and when the two males joined our suspect in the middle of the junction of Sycamore Gardens, he was furious.

He was jumping up and down and ranting at them both for spoiling his plans of attacking the lone female. After a very heated discussion they all walked off back towards the tube station. That was so close; we all just hoped that it did not put him off for the rest of the night. The suspect then disappeared off the street for about twenty minutes; we believed it was likely that he was taking his next drug fix somewhere.

Then he was spotted heading back to the tube station. Jed sent Elaine out straight away and she started the walk from the station. At first the suspect did not notice her, she had reached the junction with Hammersmith Grove before her spotted her. She was playing her part really well. It was now around 11.00 p.m. and she was walking along as if she was worse the wear for drink. As she crossed the junction at Hammersmith Grove, the suspect sprinted to try and catch up with her.

He got to within ten yards of Elaine and slowed down to match her pace. When she reached the junction with Sycamore, I knew that Dobbo's van was tucked away at the bottom end of Sycamore waiting to come around. The other van was on the main road, slowly moving forward towards Sycamore.

As Elaine turned the corner she started to cross over the centre of the road and head for the east pavement of Sycamore Gardens. All the time I gave a running commentary of exactly what was going on. The suspect walked straight across the junction and stopped in the middle of the road; he took a look down the road to make sure there was no one else in the street and picked up his pace and got on the pavement behind Elaine. He was now about five yards behind her. God knows what Elaine must have been thinking. She knew she was about to be attacked; how frightening would that be!

About halfway down the street, an overhanging tree made the pavement area quite dark. As Elaine reached this spot I saw the suspect start to run at her. This was it. Over the radio I called '**Attack attack attack**'. As I did I saw the suspect hit Elaine from behind knocking her to the ground. Almost immediately, I saw the van at the bottom of the street come screaming around then the other van arrived at the top of the street and about twelve squad guys jumped from the van and ran down the street towards Elaine.

The suspect had ripped the laptop from Elaine's grip and had started to run back up the road towards Goldhawk Road, as he came up the street I could see he was trying to hide the laptop bag under his coat. Suddenly, he looked up to see a dozen blokes running at him; he looked behind to see the same thing. He ran straight into the first squad guy, a big rugby player called Ian Warlow who floored him like a rag doll. He was then covered by a mass of bodies and eventually overpowered and arrested in possession of the laptop. The perfect evidence we required.

I immediately checked Elaine was OK, and apart from a sore back she was fine. She had done brilliantly. A very brave lady; her actions and courage helped to put away the attacker for nine years and instantly stopped that mini-crime wave that he had started. A subsequent search of his address, which was nearby, resulted in us finding items he had kept that belonged to other victims of similar attacks.

At court he pleaded not guilty and claimed we had set him up; he tried to play the race card and said we had picked on him because he was black. Fortunately, at the very same time as he attacked Elaine, a young black lady had turned into the street and had witnessed everything that had happened. Her statement blew his accusations out of the water and he was found guilty of several vicious robbery offences on lone females.

The one thing that came out of this operation that will always stick in my mind, apart from the great job done by the decoys, was something that happened to Dobbo. When we got back to the nick after the arrest, Dobbo was there with his entire left arm badly grazed as was his left leg and his jeans ripped.

The story then came out that Dobbo, who was well-known for being hyperactive, was being a real pain in the arse in the back of the van, chomping at the bit for some of the action and wanting to be first out of the van. The van had a side sliding door and his plan was to have the door slightly open with him holding it so that he could slide it back quickly and get out fast when the time came. The near miss on the first decoy had only served to get him more worked up.

When the hit was eventually called, the van speed around the corner, Dobbo swung open the sliding door and the momentum of the van pulled it out of his hand and as the van went around the corner he fell out head-first and tumbled along the pavement. Despite hurting himself, he still rolled into an upright position and went off up Sycamore Gardens like Forrest Gump and still managed to get a piece of the suspect being arrested.

The boys in the van with him said it was hysterical and it took ages for him to live it down. This was a great team effort, one of many that the squad were responsible for. We worked hard and also socially played hard together as a team. I loved it and this was a very special part of my service in the police.

DURING MY TIME ON THE crime squad, I started the procedure of becoming a fully qualified detective. The whole thing would take about two years to complete. It meant being able to evidence that you have carried out numerous criteria related to CID work and showing that you were competent in doing so. It covered the whole spectrum of CID work, but included things that you did on a daily basis as a matter of course.

So over that period I continued to cover everything I needed to do, which then left only a six-week course at the detective training school at Hendon to complete, and to pass an exam at the end of the course. I would then be made a substantive detective. There was a real problem here though, and it stemmed back to the serious injury I received in 1996.

I had been having some trouble with really severe headaches, especially when reading for any length of time. In 1997 I had studied for the sergeant's exam and this was when I first realised there was a problem. Apart from the headaches, I also found that I had a problem remembering anything I studied. While studying, the headaches got a lot worse causing my eyes to swell up on many occasions. (This problem, I was to later find out, was as a result of permanent damage caused by the injury and was to be with me for the rest of my life.)

This caused me concern because I knew there was an awful lot of studying to do on the CID course for the exam at the end. I knew that there was every chance that I would fail this exam just as I had the sergeant's exams in the March. This was a real bother to me and I was not sure what to do next. Then something happened that was a stroke of luck and changed everything for me. It meant me temporarily abandoning my plan to become a substantive detective, but it put me in a much better situation altogether.

The Flying Squad

In April 2000, the most unexpected thing happened to me. Out of the blue, vacancies occurred for advanced drivers on the world-famous Flying Squad. As I mentioned earlier in the book, I had experienced the squad as a 'strapper' for eighteen months, but here was a chance to work on the squad full-time. I just had to apply for it, as it was too good a chance to miss of a job that was highly coveted in the Met.

I took the interview board and was lucky enough to get accepted for one of the posts, so at the end of May 2000, I started what was to be the most unbelievable time in my career. The work carried out by the Flying Squad is amazing. My opening story in this book shows the great effort put in by squad officers. The hours the detectives on this squad work are unbelievable and their commitment to the cause is second to none.

I have never worked in such a highly pressurised role where you worked non-stop day and night to get the job done. The rewards were amazing and the buzz from taking out an armed robbery team just as they are about to or have just committed an armed robbery is fantastic. It is just not possible to describe in words how exciting it was to be a member of the Met Police Flying Squad.

The remit of the Flying Squad is to deal with all armed robbery offences against banks, building societies, and cash in transit vans, jewellers, betting shops and off licences. In addition, offences against any commercial premises that are open for business, if a firearm is seen or intimated.

The offences are dealt with by means of reactive enquiries and this leads on to proactive operations against the offenders to arrest them prior to them committing further offences or, if possible, as they do so.

The proactive operations normally involve weeks and weeks of tedious operational work for hours and hours on end which will lead us to several minutes of the biggest buzz in the world as we take out the armed criminals as they are about to commit another armed robbery.

This is then followed by weeks and weeks of tedious work on case papers to ensure a conviction at court. Not really like *The Sweeney* on the television. But let me tell you now, that in all the things I did in my police service, I have never felt a bigger buzz than I got at the end of a long operation against a team of armed robbers and taking them out 'across the pavement'. (This is the term used on the squad for taking a robbery team out as they commit or have just committed an offence.)

The feelings range from nerves to apprehension and even being slightly scared, through to a surge of adrenalin and a power rush as you move in and take them out at gunpoint. It was an amazing feeling and I loved it. It made everything worthwhile to see an armed blagger, cuffed and face down on the pavement, brilliant….

I do not intend going into the ways of the flying squad as these methods are highly confidential and would undermine the ability of the squad to work as well as they do. What I will do is try to give the factual stories and try to show the hard work that goes into arresting the armed robbery teams committing these serious crimes.

Firearms training

Within a month or so of joining the squad I was sent on a firearms course at the then Met police firearms training unit at Lippetts Hill. This was nothing new to me as I had done my previous firearms training there in 1983, and I had also spent a fair amount of time there when I was in the dog section and I was a firearms support handler. What was to be different was the type of firearm I was to be trained on, and also the tactical side of the training was something new to me.

The new weapon I was to be trained on was the Glock 9mm semi-automatic pistol. With a magazine of seventeen rounds of ammunition, this was a world apart from the Smith and Wesson revolver I had previously been used to carrying. The difference was amazing and I found this type of firearm extremely easy to use and got used to it very quickly. After passing the firearms course in July 2000, several weeks later I had to go off and do another week's course.

This was known as the Flying Squad tactical course and dealt with everything from prisoner-handling tactics to ambush tactics both on foot and from vehicles. There was scenario training using computer simulations, where a situation would develop on a screen in front of you and altered depending on the way you dealt with it. This was an excellent course. To make the training as real as possible we were armed with Glock training firearms. These were basically 9mm Glocks that had been adapted to fire simulation rounds of ammunition. They were 9mm rounds but instead of having a bullet head they had a paintball head attached.

During each exercise different incidents would be set up by the instructors and we would have to deal with them as they developed. The instructors would normally play the criminals with some of the students occasionally making up the numbers. We practised all sort of incidents: armed robbery on premises, armed robbers in cars and on foot – every possible scenario was covered and practised to great effect.

The training was very strict but occasionally things would degenerate into a fire fight and if you did not keep yourself in cover as the instructors taught you, then you would get shot. Even with heavy clothing, helmets, masks, etc, those bloody things hurt and left some nasty bruising. It did, however, give you an idea of what it was like to shoot at someone and be shot at. It certainly kept you switched on. The training was first-class and meant that everyone knew exactly what they and everyone else would be doing during any type of armed intervention.

A few senior officers from the squad were also on our course. They never carried guns but as they were the ones who were out on operations with us, and were responsible for controlling everything, it was essential they knew the tactics. This allowed them to deploy us as necessary. It was on their shoulders when to call the strike on any suspects and send the armed officers in to deal with the situation.

This was a very big responsibility. If they sent us in to early, we may lose the evidence to get a conviction at court. Leave it too late and a member of the public may get killed or injured. It was a very difficult decision for someone to have to make. So it was essential they knew exactly what we were capable of doing.

One such senior officer was a detective chief inspector from the squad office at Tower Bridge. He was fairly new there but, in the short space of time since his arrival, he had not gone down to well with some of the squad, making some decisions and changes that had upset the running of a very good office.

On one of the scenarios towards the end of the week, he was asked by the instructors to play the part of a driver of a security van delivering to a bank. All he had to do was to drive a van to the front of a building on the training area and act as a guard delivering cash in transit. The instructors were going to play the part of a team attacking the van and the rest of us were in vehicles and were to ambush the instructors as they attacked the van.

The DCI did as instructed and drove to the front of the building. As he arrived he was attacked by the baddies. As this occurred we all moved in when told to do so and ambushed them. There was a bit of a fire fight and after a few minutes all the baddies were either shot or arrested in a text book ambush by the rest of us. However, someone saw a chance to get even with the DCI.

As he sat hiding in the driving seat of the van during our ambush, in the confusion, someone slipped a 9mm Glock onto the passenger seat next to him. When the instruction called the exercise over, we were all gathered around the front of the van for a debrief. Now, it was not unusual for the instructors to try to catch us out with a sniper or something so we were always on our guard.

As we stood there the DCI was still sat in the front of the van. He must have suddenly seen the gun on the passenger seat and picked it up. He slid open the driver's door of the van and before he could actually say something, he held up the weapon and someone yelled: 'Gun.'

Including in training this was the warning shout you were taught to give if a gun was spotted and there was danger, and this let everyone know. On hearing the shout, all twenty-odd of us drew our weapons and suddenly the DCI was being shot at from all angles as he sat in the driver's seat. By the time everyone had emptied the magazines into him and we stopped firing, he looked like he had been doing battle with Rolf Harris as he had so much paint on him. The instructors gave us a bollocking, The DCI had the raving hump and the Tower Bridge guys had a great big smile on the faces. We never found out who planted the gun, though!

Following the completion of the course I was now authorised to carry a firearm on armed operations and surveillance. Despite drawing my firearms on many occasions, I never once had to use it. This was all down to the skill of the Flying Squad in the way we carried out our ambush tactics and were able to hit the baddies with such speed and surprise that they never once, in all the operations I took part in, had a chance to point a firearm back at us, thank God....

THE FIRST REAL ARMED OPERATION I was involved with was a planned robbery of a Texaco petrol station situated on the A4 at Brentford. The pagers all went off late one night calling us in for a briefing for 4.00 a.m. the next morning. Information from an informant had told us that a team of four to six Sri Lankan males were going to attack the petrol

Andy Vick

station, and take the manager at gunpoint as he arrived for work. It was believed the safe held a very large quantity of cash. The takings were boosted by a long bank holiday weekend.

No information was known about the suspects except they had hired a green Skoda to use to get to and from the petrol station. With very little to go on, and no real time to make further investigations, a plan was devised to control the petrol station and wait to see what happened. Also with us were officers from SO19 the specialist firearms unit as we did not know exactly how many suspects there were and how heavily armed they may be. The detective inspector in charge of the operation was Dave 'Tommo' Thompson. He was new to the squad and this was to be his first live armed operation.

After a briefing we were all deployed around the area of the petrol station with a view to hopefully identifying a possible suspect vehicle coming into the area. We had also managed to discreetly find out that the manager was expected to arrive between 8.30 a.m. and 9.30 a.m. We also had an officer in the CCTV room of the local council and he had control over the view of the petrol station forecourt from a local traffic camera.

We were all in position by about 5.30 a.m. and it was now a waiting game. At around 7.00 a.m. a green Skoda containing four Sri Lankan males was seen on the A4. It actually stopped on the petrol station forecourt and after a short period of time drove off again. It then remained in the area just driving around and occasionally coming back to the petrol station. Things were looking very good.

At around 8.30 a.m. the Skoda came onto the petrol station forecourt and parked up. One of the occupants got out and went into the pay area, looked around and eventually came back. We assumed he was checking to see if the manager had arrived and seeing he had not, the male returned to the car. As our info was that they were going to grab the manager as he arrived and force him to open the safe, the DI held us in position.

Suddenly an Indian male in a Texaco uniform appeared on the forecourt went in and behind the counter to the back office. This was obviously the manager and his arrival caused a stir in the suspect's vehicle and it was plainly obvious they had missed their chance to catch him as he entered the premises. What would they do now? Would they risk an attack on the premises or give up and go home?

This gave the DI a difficult choice now. Should he let them go and see what they did? Maybe they would try again another time. Or should did he call the attack now and hope that they did have firearms in the car, which would be enough evidence to charge them with a conspiracy to rob the petrol station?

Before he could make a decision the car left the forecourt. It was obvious that things inside the car were very agitated and so we carried out a mobile surveillance operation on them to see what they would do. We ended up doing a big circle of the area before they returned to the petrol station. This time they parked in a different place – on the car wash area – out of view of the cashier in the shop. This was looking good now and the DI put everyone on standby to go in.

They messed about a bit; one got out and back in again. Another got out and walked towards the shop area but turned around and went back to the car. It was all a bit nerve-wracking for them by the look of it. At the point when they were all back in the car the DI took the decision to take them out.

Over the radio the DI called: 'All units, **attack, attack, attack**.'

As per the plan, SO19 went in first; seconds later as I drove onto the forecourt I heard two loud bangs and knew it was shots being fired. I thought, as did most of us that it had all kicked off. However, I soon realised that an SO19 officer had fired Hatton rounds (a solid shotgun round) into the tyres of the suspect's car to stop them driving off. This was a bit worrying considering we were on the forecourt of a petrol station, with a very volatile explosive substance such a fuel all around us; all four suspects were dragged from the car at gunpoint and handcuffed.

A very tense few moments then dragged by for the DI as the car was searched. Much to his great relief, a search of the vehicle produced two loaded firearms as well as a large knife. This was a great result for Tommo on his first armed op. Our usual crime-scene controls then kicked in and the four suspects were taken off to various police stations. All four suspects later received lengthy prison sentences for their trouble.

Even more work to do

Towards the end of 2001, due to the serious rise of gun crime and, in particular, what was termed black-on-black shootings, firearms offences were getting out of hand! Operation Trident had been set up to deal with this matter but they were overwhelmed with so much work they were having difficulty keeping up with things.

It was decided that as well as the current terms of reference we dealt with on the Flying Squad, we were also to start dealing with all non-fatal, non-black-on-black incidents. On 30th January 2002 we were all at the office having just got back from a surveillance operation when we received information about a serious shooting incident in Shepherds Bush at Nando's chicken restaurant in Goldhawk Road. This place is about 200 yards from the local police station. Everyone scrambled from the office and we went on blues-and-twos in convoy to the scene.

When we arrived there it was total chaos. In the restaurant was a female waitress who had been shot in the arm. A short distance away was a car that had gone through the front window of an estate agent's shop. In this car was a seriously injured black male and close by on the road was a crashed moped with its rider on the ground, also seriously injured.

The London Ambulance services were working on both the driver of the car and the moped rider. Without really knowing what had actually taken place, I was instructed to go with a colleague, Martin Ainsworth, on the blues-and-twos to the Royal Free Hospital near Whitechapel and to get there before the air ambulance did in order to deal with the driver of the car. He was to be treated as a suspect until we knew the full story.

So we raced through the centre of London in the rush hour and into the city. As we arrived at the hospital we received a phone call to say the driver had in fact died at the scene and was now going to Charing Cross hospital mortuary. We then had a blues-and-twos run from the City back to Hammersmith to the hospital to deal with the deceased.

The deceased was Kieran Bernard, a well-known local man. At the mortuary we secured his body for continuity of evidence. It was plainly obvious that he had been shot in the chest as he had a hole there where the bullet went in and an even larger exit wound in his back. Having completed all we had to do, Martin and I returned to the scene to find out exactly what had taken place. Because this was classed as a black-on-black shooting, Operation Trident officers had arrived and they were to take over the investigation from us. This, however, is the story of what had happened.

The deceased was in Nando's restaurant with a group of people. It appears that they were being served by the female waitress when an argument started between Bernard and a second male. The argument had started over the man apparently 'dissing' (disrespecting) Bernard. As the argument escalated Bernard pulled a gun out and threatened this man.

In true Clint Eastwood style, the other male then produced an even bigger gun and threatened Bernard. Several shots then went off, one of which hit the female waitress in the arm. The whole incident was caught on the restaurants CCTV and looked like something out of the OK Corral gunfight.

Bernard had been shot in the thigh and in the chest. He ran from the restaurant and jumped into his car to drive off. As he did so he started to lose consciousness and he ploughed into a youth on a moped. This youth was seriously injured and, by a twist of fate, turned out to be a close cousin of Bernard's.

After colliding with the moped, the car veered across the road and ploughed straight through the front window of an estate agent, narrowly missing a man sitting at his desk. Despite all efforts by the ambulance crew, Bernard died at the scene.

The other male had left before police arrived, as did all of the witnesses. Very quickly a suspect was identified and police began looking for a black youth called Germaine Abbot. (This man has already appeared in a story in this book. He was involved in the shooting of fourteen-year-old Jamic Alcondor in Hammersmith 1998).

Abbot eventually did stand trial at the Old Bailey but was found not guilty of the murder of Bernard. However, several months later, in what appeared to be a revenge attack, Abbot himself was shot dead by an unknown gunman.

It was only a matter of months before the powers that be realised that the squad could not deal with the amount of firearms incidents that were occurring without impairing the squad's ability to carry out its core work of dealing with armed robberies. As a result, a new squad, known as the shootings team, was created to deal with all non-fatal, non-Trident shootings and we returned to our normal work.

Operation Juneberry

In April and July 2001 two armed robberies occurred in the South West London area. They were committed by two white males who used loaded firearms and violence to force post office staff to hand over large amounts of cash. In the two raids a total of £29,000.00 pounds was stolen.

DS Steve Alexander and DC Keith Lavallin were the officers dealing with the robberies. After a lot of hard work, and as the result of some great intelligence information, they had two suspects for these offences but no real proof. This resulted in Operation Juneberry, and so it was that another squad surveillance operation was put into action.

The operation ran for quite some time, but the case was no further forward. We had spent a fair bit of time on surveillance but it had not produced any real intelligence to help with proving that the two men were responsible for committing the offences. The men seemed to do very little work, but did appear to have money to spend.

Then on 9th October, things suddenly took a major turn. In the middle of the afternoon an armed robbery occurred at a post office in New Malden. Two men armed with revolvers entered the post office and one grabbed a customer by the neck and held a gun to her throat and demanded cash. The lady was held until the money was handed over. The two men then left the post office with £22,500 in cash and made off in VW Golf. They were spotted getting into the vehicle by some office workers and their description, and that of the vehicle, was circulated on police radios.

The squad received the details and everyone in the office scrambled towards New Malden. However, Steve Alexander and Keith Lavallin were already in the area doing some enquires on the Juneberry operation. They were at first unaware of the robbery, but spotted our two suspects passing them in the opposite direction coming away from New Malden in a VW Golf. They called up to get some troops to help them search for the vehicle and when told of the post office robbery realised that it was our two suspects who had committed the offence.

From all the work they had been doing Steve and Keith had a hunch where they might change over vehicles and directed several of us to a public house car park in the Raynes Park area. Sure enough, there was the VW Golf parked and unoccupied. Almost immediately, other officers spotted both suspects in a Ford Granada owned by one of the two men heading back towards an address where one of them lived.

As none of the squad officers were armed at the time, they just carried out a mobile surveillance operation on the Granada while awaiting armed back up. Sure enough, they drove back to a small estate where the one suspect lived and they were observed going into the house. A discreet containment was put in to secure the area and a full armed operation swung into gear.

Initially, I remained with the VW Golf until the arrival of a removal vehicle. I secured the vehicle with seals to protect the continuity of evidence, and after the vehicle was taken away, I joined everyone else at the rendezvous point just as the firearms teams entered the house in a rapid entry through windows and doors. As they went in, one of the men jumped out of a window, down onto a wall and, despite being challenged by armed police, he forced his way into the house next door and escaped out through the other side. He was found by armed police hiding in a rubbish chute.

The other man was detained inside the house straight away. The two men, Michael Reilly and Paul Rice, who were both in their forties, were arrested for the armed robbery in New Malden. I was to be the designated exhibits officer at the address, which meant I would be spending quite some time there over the next couple of days. The initial search with Rice being present was made with everything being videoed for evidential purposes.

We recovered a large quantity of the cash in the pocket of a pair of jeans and a large quantity of cash on a table. A revolver was also recovered along with live rounds. However, despite a thorough search of the house we were still missing about £18,000 pounds cash and also a second firearm. As it was getting very late it was decided to secure the house overnight with local officers remaining outside and then return the next morning with a specialist search team to do the rest of the house and the outside area, which included an outbuilding completely stacked full of rubbish of all sorts.

Early the next morning we made a start, a photographer as always videoing everything that went on. The search team carried out the search; anything found was videoed in place and then handed to me as the exhibits officers and bagged and sealed. Lots of evidence was recovered such as stolen car number plates, plans for further robbery offences as well as more ammunition. Then, during a search of the outbuilding, a member of the search team found a plastic container hidden underneath all the junk. In the container was another loaded firearm and also a large quantity of cash.

I dealt with the loaded gun first; it had to be preserved correctly for forensic purposes and also made it safe so it did not go off accidentally. While I was doing this I overheard someone on the search team commenting in a joking manner about the cash that had been recovered. He was laughing and saying that if this had been in the old squad days we would have had a good piss up on some of the proceeds of the crime.

He was not being nasty this was just a typical police sense of humour. However, I noticed that the sergeant in charge of the search team was a bit straight-faced and I immediately saw he was taking a keen interest in me and the large pile of cash I was holding.

Next, we came to counting the cash for evidential purposes. With me at the time was the photographer who was doing the videoing, Campbell McGee, who was the squad's scenes-of-crime officer and also the search team sergeant. I pulled a table into the centre of the living room and called Campbell and the sergeant over and said, 'Right, let's gets this money sorted then,' and I looked at Campbell and winked.

As the three of us stood around the table I started counting it out. One for you, one for you, one for me and one for the post office, and I carried on round again. After about ten times of going around the table, I finally looked up. The search team sergeant was slowly backing away from the table and looking very white in the face. As he reached the door Campbell and I looked at each other and started laughing. He then realised we were laughing at him and threw a wobbly, storming out very upset and not very happy with me. Even though everything was being videoed, he still thought I was serious and was not best pleased with me afterwards. Still, it brightened my day up.

At the end of it all every penny stolen was recovered, along with two firearms and ammunition. A great deal of effort was put into that operation by Steve and Keith and they were justly rewarded for all the hard work when, at the Old Bailey, Michael Reilly received a life sentence with a recommendation he serve at least seven years before he would be eligible for parole. He also received a further eight years for firearms offences.

Paul Rice received nine years for the robbery and eight years for firearms offences. They were told by the judge that he considered them ruthless armed robbers and a great danger to the public. Well, to their victims and members of the public caught up in their offences, let me just tell you, that after they had received some of their own treatment and had come face to face with a dozen or so armed police officers all screaming at them and forcing them to the floor, roughing them up a little, they were like most criminals, and shit themselves, they were so scared.

Operation Magician – The Millennium Dome Robbery

From around the middle of the summer of 2000, intelligence had been received that a highly organised gang of criminals were planning to pull off a spectacular robbery somewhere in the Met area. Following weeks and weeks of intensive investigation, and with the help of a major surveillance operation, senior officers on the Flying Squad were convinced that the intended target was the Millennium Dome at Greenwich.

Initially, it was not known what the intended target within the Dome might be. However, on 1st September 2000 the surveillance operation really paid off when one of the suspects was followed into the dome and observed by detectives to visit the De Beers diamond exhibition. There, the suspect was also seen to video the exhibition with a camcorder.

The suspect, later identified as William Cockram, then left the dome and met up with a second suspect, Raymond Betson, and together they went and videoed the surrounding river and jetty. These two were later joined by a third suspect, Aldo Ciarrocchi, and together the three of them were seen reviewing all the camcorder footage as well as studying a plan of the dome.

The De Beers diamond exhibition housed the 777-carat completely perfect millennium star diamond and 11 rare blue stone diamonds. Together, the total value of the collection was put at over £200 million pounds. This was to be an attempt to carry out the most audacious robbery ever and it resulted in the biggest operation ever undertaken by the Met flying squad. As a result Operation Magician commenced.

Over many months of surveillance and intelligence gathering, several more suspects were identified. Following more visits to the Dome, all under the ever-watchful eye of the Flying Squad, it became apparent that the gang were planning to use a speedboat at some stage of the getaway as they were observed testing one out on numerous occasions.

Through the month of October police identified an old coal yard near Plumstead, East London that was being used by the gang. In the coal yard was a yellow JCB digger, police saw members of the gang with this vehicle and discovered it had been stolen several months earlier. It was believed that this was also going to be used in an offence in some way or other.

It was during October that I first became aware of Operation Magician. While at work one day, I was warned to attend a briefing that night at a large police station in East London. Nearly the whole of the office were committed to this briefing but no one really knew what was actually going on. We duly arrived there to find that most of the officers from the other three squad offices were also there, along with many others officers from SO19, the surveillance teams, and plenty of other sections of the Met.

It was plainly obvious from the amount of us there all carrying firearms that this was something big, and we all thought at first that it might have been terrorist-related.

Eventually at around 3.00 a.m. we were briefed by Detective Superintendent John Shatford. His first words to us all were very strong. He warned everyone in the room as to the secrecy of this operation and that if anything of this was leaked out in any way, there would be very serious recriminations for the people responsible. He then went onto brief us about the operation and the current intelligence.

It was believed that the robbery was to be imminent and that tomorrow morning was a strong possibility due to the actions being taken by the suspects that day. We were told that the likely escape route would be via a speedboat on the Thames. The gang had on three previous occasions towed a speedboat to Greenwich and placed it in the river right opposite the Dome, this and other activates led the flying squad to believe that the offence was close to happening.

You're Nicked My Son

We were all given tasks to carry out if the offence should occur. The inside of the premises was being dealt with by SO19. The role of the Flying Squad was mainly to back up the specialist firearms officers. We were to move into pre-determined areas to assist SO19 when arrests were made and to take control of the prisoners from the firearms officers.

Following the briefing, we went to a small police station just on the outskirts of Greenwich to sit it out until we received further information. No radios were to be used as the gang had access to monitoring equipment and all communication was to be done by mobile telephone.

At around 7.30 the following morning we got the phone call that something was happening; all the suspects had met and then gone their separate ways. Then not long after 8.00 a.m. we were informed that the yellow JCB had left the coal yard at Plumstead and was heading towards Greenwich. We all thought this was looking good. With the help of traffic cameras and mobile and static surveillance officers, the JCB was followed. As it got closer to the Dome things started to get a bit tense; it really looked like this was going to come off.

Suddenly, we were informed of a lot of uniformed police activity in the area and we were aware of the sound of lots of sirens rushing about. All of this was a bit confusing and the next information we got was that the JCB had turned around and was heading back towards Plumstead. It appeared that the job had been called off. It was then discovered that an elderly tourist had been knocked down and killed by a car near to the Dome. The sirens had been police and ambulance going to the scene. The result was a huge traffic jam with nothing getting in or out of the Dome area. The villains had to call it off; it was very disappointing – so close, but there was sure to be another day.

As a result of all the observations and intelligence work, a study of the tides showed that the likely date for the next attempt was on the next high tide, which was Wednesday 7th November and a full pre-planned operation was prepared for that date. Again, most of the Flying Squad offices were involved. Unfortunately, I was assigned the task of being available to drive the chief superintendent of the squad, John Coles, should anything happen.

As a result, I watched and listened to the whole thing unfold from a room at New Scotland Yard. I cannot tell you how frustrating it was to be sitting there from about 7.30 a.m. when the gang started out in a white transit van towing the speedboat and just listening to everything as it started to piece together.

By 8.40 a.m. the speedboat was in the river and tied up in position. Then by 8.45 a.m. the JCB was on its way from the coal yard; it travelled to the Dome and then parked up out of sight. The cabin of the JCB had been altered to allow four people to fit inside and this is where the driver was joined by the three other member of the gang who were to carry out the robbery. The tension at Scotland Yard was unbelievable, so God knows what it must have been like for everyone down at the Dome itself.

At 9.30 a.m. the JCB crashed its way through the perimeter fence and headed towards the Dome. It then drove on and rammed open the double-locked gates at gate 4 and into the grounds of the Dome itself. At the same time the speedboat travelled across the Thames and waited at the Millennium pier.

At 9.35 a.m. the digger crashed through the side of the Dome and headed towards the diamond collection, stopping directly alongside the display. Three suspects wearing gas masks and body armour got down off the JCB. Two men entered the vault while one remained outside keeping watch.

Inside the Dome at the time were over 40 members of the specialist firearms teams from SO19. A few were deployed around the Dome in plain clothes posing as cleaners with their firearms hidden inside black rubbish bags and rubbish bins. Many others were hidden behind a secret wall within the Dome. All were waiting for the 'strike' call from Mr Shatford. Outside, a further 60 or more armed Flying Squad officers were deployed with even more officers deployed on the river itself.

Detective Superintendent Shatford was running the whole operation from the CCTV room within the Dome. He watched as one of the suspects attacked the display containing the millennium star diamond. The suspect was armed with a powerful Hilti nail gun and he fired at the glass several times. A second suspect then attacked the display with a sledge hammer. When he had broken through the glass he then started on the rest of the display. In the second cabinet were 11 rare blue diamonds. At this point Mr Shatford gave the order for officers to move in and arrest the suspects.

You're Nicked My Son

The suspect keeping watch outside the vault saw the officers approaching and threw a grenade at them. It exploded releasing a cloud of blue smoke. This suspect was immediately overpowered and arrested. He was found to be carrying further grenades, some fireworks and also ammonia.

SO19 then carried on through into the vault and they deployed distraction grenades to disorientate the two suspects in the vault. They were immediately over powered and arrested. In addition to the Hilti gun and sledgehammer, both men were also in possession of ammonia.

At the same time as all this happened, the driver of the JCB was arrested and armed officers deployed in three boats on the Thames moved in and cut off the escape of the speedboat and arrested the driver. Finally, a sixth suspect was arrested on the other side of the river where he was waiting in the Ford transit van used to tow the speedboat to the river. In all, six suspects were in custody

As the arrest took place I jumped into my car with Chief Superintendent Coles and we raced on blues-and-twos to the scene from Scotland Yard. I was very disappointed not to have been involved in any of the actual operation first-hand, but it was still very exciting to arrive at the Dome and see the results of all that had taken place

This was a fantastic result for the Flying Squad and SO19 after months and months of very hard work, involving long days and nights for the investigating team from Tower Bridge. But it had worked perfectly with no danger to members of the public or the police; a superb result all round for all, except for the bad guys, of course.

To make matters worse for them, what they did not know was that all the diamonds on display were in fake. A decision taken long ago by De Beers and the police had resulted in the real diamonds being replaced by fakes. Even if they had got away with the diamonds they were completely worthless.

The following day the six men arrested were charged with numerous offences relating to the robbery. Then on the 18th February 2002 at the Old Bailey, five of the gang were found guilty of the following offences.

Aldo Ciarrocchi, aged 33 years. He was the suspect outside the vault who threw the smoke grenade at police. He was convicted of conspiracy to commit robbery and received 15 years in prison.

William Thomas Cockram, aged 50 years. He was the suspect who attacked to diamond display with the Hilti nailgun. He received a sentence of 18 years for conspiracy to commit robbery.

Robert Alvin Adams, aged 59 years. This was the suspect armed with the sledgehammer who also attacked the displays. Adams received 15 years in prison for conspiracy to commit robbery.

Raymond John Betson, aged 41 years. Betson was the driver of the JCB. He received 18 years in prison for conspiracy to commit robbery.

Kevin Peter Meredith, aged 36 years. He was the driver of the speedboat to be used as the getaway across the Thames. He was sentenced to five years in prison for conspiracy to steal.

PROCEEDING AGAINST THE SIXTH MAN arrested, were dropped by the Crown Prosecution Service.

THE MILLENNIUM DOME ROBBERY MADE worldwide headlines and again brought to the attention of the public just how exceptional the world-famous Flying Squad were at doing what is a very hard job. This was all brought about by the sheer hard work and desire to prevent serious crime in the capital, something the squad was exceptionally good at, as the Dome robbery team found out to their disadvantage.

Operation Rockley

In the latter months of 1999 a sharp rise in instances of armed robbery offences against small corner-shops and other small commercial premises started to occur in the Lambeth borough of London. The offences were being committed around the edges of Brixton and Clapham. These offences became more frequent and a linked series was identified as being carried out by the same offender. The suspect was a white male and he would produce a firearm and demand money, very often leaving with very minor sums of cash.

The investigation was taken on by DC Sarah Staff. Sarah is a fantastic detective with endless drive and enthusiasm, and for the next three years she worked tirelessly to solve this series of offences. Every so often, the offences would stop for long periods of time, and then suddenly start up again. Every time they restarted, the type of premises being robbed changed and it seemed that the robber was working his was up to bigger and better things each time.

Although the offences were being committed exactly the same way, with the same MO (modus operandi), the description of the suspect always seemed to be changing. At one point Sarah was working on the possibility that there may be two or three people working together taking it in turns to commit the offences. To make matters more difficult the type of premises robbed seem to be chosen for the lack of or for the very poor-quality CCTV, so no decent photographic evidence was available to assist Sarah in identifying the suspect. Eventually as he got bolder, he got more careless, evidence then started to come together to assist Sarah in the investigation.

By the summer of 2002 the suspect had progressed onto robbing banks and betting shops. Finally, after extensive enquires by Sarah and other officers at Barnes flying squad, Sarah finally had a breakthrough and identified the suspect as Michael Beale.

A profile was built on this man who was 46 years old and who over the last couple of years had developed a major crack cocaine habit costing him hundreds of pounds a day. He had been a minor offender over the years but had obviously turned to armed robbery to fund his habit. The bigger his habit had got, the bolder he had got in his offences, working his way up to banks to obtain the funds he needed to pay for his fixes.

Sarah then had the problem of finding him. His lifestyle meant he never seemed to stay in one place longer than a night. Having lived most of his life in the Lambeth area he had plenty of places that he could stay if he needed to. Further investigation also showed that the times the offences seemed to stop for a while coincided with times that Beale was serving time in prison for drug-related offences.

The reason why the descriptions of the suspect had been so different was because of the amount of drugs he was using. He was so skinny and gaunt through the drug abuse that he looked nothing like he had done a few years earlier.

As we got towards July 2002, Beale was believed to be responsible for a total of over 45 armed robberies. Finally, after weeks of hard work Sarah and her team identified an address, Albert Square in Clapham, as being Beale's main address. A 24-hour observation post was set up in the square and once it was confirmed that he was using the address on a fairly regular basis, a major operation began to put Beale under surveillance with the intention of arresting him as he was about to commit an offence.

On a lot of the offences that Sarah believed Beale had committed, witnesses had given us two major pieces of information. The first was that the suspect had left on a pedal cycle and the second was that he wore a dark baseball cap, dark jacket, sunglasses, and he also had plastic surgical gloves on his hands.

The operation went on for a couple of weeks, Beale's lifestyle was awful and he spent so much of his time jumping on and off buses and in and out of cars and shops. This made it very difficult for the surveillance team to stay with him all the time. Beale was not doing this in case he was being followed – it was purely the fact that he was so hyperactive and in such a drugged state that he himself did not seem to know what he was doing.

Then on 1st August 2002, after weeks of surveillance, it finally paid off. At about 2.30 p.m. he was spotted leaving his house in a dark jacket and baseball cap. He was followed to a small red Fiat hatchback that he used occasionally. A mobile surveillance operation led us to a shop where Beale disappeared inside. He came out a few minutes later with a purple ladies' mountain bike and put it in the rear of his car.

With the surveillance team we followed him from the Clapham area through Brixton and to some narrow back street close to Camberwell Green. He was then observed by surveillance officers to park the car up on a small trading estate and take the bike out of the rear of his car. Then we knew it was game on, the surveillance officer came over the radio with the words, 'Subject one is wearing a black baseball cap, black jacket. He has put on a pair of sunglasses and is now also wearing white surgical gloves.'

The problem for us was, now where was he going. It was going to be very difficult to keep up with someone on a bike. There were several alleyways running from this trading estate, mainly out to Camberwell Green high street where there were several banks and betting offices.

The detective inspector in charge of the operation was Jon Boutcher. He decided to leave a couple of surveillance officers to keep an eye on the vehicle and sent the rest of the surveillance team around to the high street to see if they could locate Beale. The four Flying Squad gun ships (covert vehicles containing armed officers) were held in side streets to wait for the DI to call a strike on Beale if it looked like he was about to commit an offence. I was driving a vehicle with a DS and a DC with me. All the other cars also had three or four officers in them so we had plenty of manpower to deal with Beale.

After a couple of tense minutes, over the radio, one of the female surveillance officers said, 'Subject one is getting off the bike and leaning it against the front window of the Nat West bank. He is still dressed as previously described; he is now into the bank.'

The DI ordered all the gun ships to the vicinity. He also instructed the female surveillance officer to go into the bank to observe Beale and keep us informed of what he was doing. Tactics now dictated that he had to be allowed to come out of the bank to ensure the safety of staff and customers. If he committed an offence we would take him on the pavement. I was first into the high street and pulled up a few yards passed the bank.

The DI instructed everyone to take up a suitable position close to the venue. He also asked that someone take the responsibility of ensuring that Beale did not get onto the bike. I told him I would do that job and I left the car.

The bike was next to the doorway of the bank. To the right of the bank as you looked at it, was a jeweller's shop. The wall of the bank recessed towards the jewellers and I took up position there. The street was very busy with shoppers. A couple of squad officers were discreetly attempting to keep people away as much as possible from the front of the premises. At the opposite end of the bank I could see three of my colleagues tucked in by some scaffolding and others were dotted about near the roadway.

In the bank the surveillance officer was whispering details in her radio. Beale had actually joined a queue of people to get to a cashier. He must have looked very odd in his cap, sunglasses and surgical gloves, although compared to some of the sights you could see in this area on a daily basis, this was quite normal, really. Several minutes passed as he moved closer to the cashier.

Then very quietly over the radio came the words '**robbery, robbery, robbery**'. I put on my firearms officer's identifying baseball cap and drew my gun. I pulled a member of the public away from the cash machine just as the DI called the strike. Beale came out of the bank and from ten yards away, as I ran towards him, I yelled 'armed police' as loudly as I could several times.

He looked directly at me and his mouth just dropped wide open as I ran at him, arms at full stretch, with my gun pointing right between his eyes. He went rigid and I hit him hard from the front and the three guys on the other side of the bank hit him from behind. In less than a couple of seconds there were twelve of us pinning him to the ground and handcuffing him. Job done, and what a great buzz that was!

Having secured Beale we searched him and found the cash and his gun in the jacket pocket; off he went to be dealt with by Sarah and

Beale's run of crime was finally at an end. This brought to a conclusion a very long investigation by Sarah and her team and was a great result for the squad in general.

When finished, Sarah had amassed a total of over 600 exhibits relating to all the robbery offences over the three years. It was a superb investigation by her and her team, aided by the rest of the office and the surveillance teams. When interviewed by Sarah, Beale eventually admitted to a total of forty-eight armed robbery offences. He subsequently pleaded guilty to all matters at court and received fourteen years in prison.

Sarah is still a member of the Barnes Flying Squad and has in fact been promoted to detective sergeant running her own team.

The Great Train Robber Returns

As I mentioned at the start of this book one of my main influences as a kid, was the police series *Z Cars*. As I got into my teens I also had a real interest into the events surrounding the great train robbery. This was the most audacious crime this country had ever seen and netted the gang over £2.3 million pounds. The robbery occurred on 8th August 1963 and just fascinated me for some reason, and once one of the robbers, Ronnie Biggs, escaped from Wandsworth prison in July 1965 it just seemed to really capture my interest and has done so right up to this day.

The main reason for this was the constant struggle by Detective Chief Superintendent Jack Slipper from The Flying Squad to locate and arrest Biggs and return him to prison. The exploits of Jack Slipper are legendary among detectives in London and even after he retired in 1980, his famous attempts to track Biggs down in Brazil and bring him to justice had kept him in the spotlight of TV and radio every time something to do with the robbery or Ronnie Biggs came to light.

He became a bit of a hero of mine and another reason for me wanting to join the police. I believe that your life is all mapped out for you. I definitely believe that I was put on this earth to join the old bill. In May 2001, events occurred that confirmed that belief for me. On the Friday of the May bank holiday weekend I attended a friends wedding with my wife. While we were at the wedding my pager went off with a message to contact a Detective Sergeant from my office. I was astounded when he told me that there was a chance that Ronnie Biggs was going to return to this country on the Monday and would I work to help deal with him?

You're Nicked My Son

This was amazing. Here was a chance to be involved in the arrest of Ronnie Biggs, the great train robber. I said yes straight away. Having got all the details, I was told everything would be confirmed later that day and if he was coming back, I would definitely be one of the team dealing with Ronald Arthur Biggs.

On Monday 7th May 2001, along with the detective chief superintendent of the Flying Squad, John Coles, Detective Sergeant Terry Wilson, DC Debbie Ford and DC Mark Hellier, I travelled to RAF Northolt in West London to meet the private plane hired by the *Sun* newspaper, to bring Ronnie Biggs to the UK. Also with us was Detective Sergeant John Loudon from the Met police extradition squad based at Scotland Yard. When we arrived we were told that the plane had left Brazil and was expected on time at Northolt.

As you can imagine, the TV and press interest was massive and at all vantage points around the airport perimeter you would see camera crews and photographers trying to find the best view point. Fortunately, with it being a secure RAF base the media was forced to remain outside the airfield. The plan was for the aircraft to land and taxi to an area, which meant it was completely out of sight of the media.

We would then travel out to the aircraft and Mr Coles would board the plane and officially arrest Ronnie Biggs on warrant for being unlawfully at large following his escape from prison on 8th July 1965. He would then be placed in an unmarked secure prisoner transit van. I was to drive the van with DS Wilson and DC Ford in the back with Ronnie Biggs and his legal team. He would then be driven to Chiswick police station where the custody suite had been closed to deal with Ronnie and to then get him to West London Magistrates' Court as soon as possible. Well, as they say: all the best-laid plans!

Prior to the plane arriving we were joined by members of the Met police special escort group. These are the 'elite' drivers and motorcyclists who escort the royal family and members of parliament around London. They are very good at what they do but sometimes can be a little to full of their own importance. DS Wilson and I were approached by a sergeant from the SEG who told me that I would not be allowed to drive the van because I was not trained to drive within an SEG convoy. He said one of his men would have to drive or the convoy could not go ahead. Now, I have to say that I thought this was a load of bollocks but they insisted they do it their way or not at all.

I couldn't understand why they were there in the first place; it was as if we were not capable of getting him to Chiswick ourselves, but the powers that be decided that we needed an escort/convoy to ensure we evaded the media! They did, however, agree to let me sit in the front passenger seat of the van, oh what a thrill for me.

The plane arrived on time and we drove out to meet it once it had come to a stop at the pre-designated area. The other thing we had to conform with was to have an RAF military police vehicle lead us at all times when we travelled around the airfield. The driver of this vehicle was a bit of a 'jobs-worth' and kept on at us that we had to follow him and that he was to be lead vehicle at all times, which to us was no problem, but it did upset the SEG a little. So out to the plane we went.

We got to the plane to find a problem. Michael Biggs, Ronnie's son, was refusing to let his dad leave the plane. We felt this was a bit odd as it was Ronnie who had wanted to come back. Then we discovered that the *Sun* newspaper was trying to get Ronnie to leave the plane wearing a red *Sun* baseball cap and a red *Sun* T-shirt obviously for maximum publicity. Michael believed this would be disrespectful to his father, belittling him and making him look like a complete idiot. I agreed with this sentiment and eventually, after a bit of a stand-off, the newspaper backed down and we were allowed to approach the aircraft.

Chief Superintendent Coles went onto the plane introduced himself to Ronnie Biggs and shook his hand. At 9.05 a.m. Mr Coles formally arrested Ronnie as he sat in his seat on the plane. Ronnie smiled and said 'thank you.' Ronnie was then helped off the plane by his son Michael and came towards me. I was waiting at the side of the van with the door open, ready to put him inside. I was immediately struck by how weak and ill he looked. We knew he had decided to return because he had been ill for quite some time, but the last stroke he had suffered had obviously taken its toll on him.

As he got to the van I went to his left-hand side and helped him slowly into the van, and as I did so I told him to be careful not to bang his head as he was a tall man. As he got in he looked at me and mumbled quietly, 'Thank you, sonny.' He was joined in the back of the van by his

You're Nicked My Son

legal team and we prepared to leave. As we did so the RAF driver came and reminded me to follow him. In front of me was to be a very highly polished and gleaming, almost brand-new Volvo estate belonging to the SEG. He was to lead the convoy with motorcyclist going ahead to block junctions and traffic lights to allow us a clear run right through.

The RAF driver told me that he had agreed with the SEG driver of the Volvo that as we cleared the security gates of the base he would pull over to the right to allow the convoy to speed through and leave the camp at the roadside entrance, which was fifty yards or so from the security gates. The SEG driver of my vehicle had told me that when we left the entrance, the Volvo would take us on a diversionary route around the area before getting on the A40 and heading into London. This was to fool the chasing media pack, which might try to follow us. Operation Overkill yet again was my thoughts.

We set off across the base towards the main gates at a nice sedate pace as dictated by the RAF vehicle. I could see the SEG Volvo was itching to speed up as we approached the gates. I remembered that the RAF vehicle was going to pull over to the right to allow us through, so I was ready for a sharp burst of speed as we cleared the security gates.

Unfortunately, the driver of the very nice SEG Volvo did not remember this. As we cleared the gates the Volvo went to overtake at speed to the right of the RAF Land Rover just at the point the driver of the Land Rover pulled over to his right as he said he was going to do.

The SEG driver tried to avoid hitting the Land Rover but the large rear-nearside bumper of the Land Rover caught the offside wing of the Volvo and ripped it open like a can opener. It was hysterical, and all of it was caught on television by the waiting media. Oh, how I laughed as off we went on the merry-go-round trip around the houses and finally into Chiswick, West London. It was a good job they insisted the experts had to drive in their convoy…. I could not wait to tell this story back at the office!

We duly arrived at Chiswick police station and DS Wilson and I led Ronnie into the custody suite. We arrived there at 9.45 a.m. and the custody sergeant completed the custody sheet. How surreal was this, watching the great train robber, Ronnie Biggs, finally being booked back into police custody after thirty-years on the run. It really felt like I was taking part in a piece of Metropolitan police history. It felt very strange, especially because of my keen interest in the whole thing from my teenage years.

After he was booked in, we sat him down and offered him food and a drink. He asked for a cup of tea and he was given breakfast, brought in from McDonalds. I went and got the tea for him. It was then, I realised how very ill he was. He had terrible trouble holding his cup and when he tried to drink, because his face was drooping slightly on one side as a result of the stroke, he had trouble keeping the tea in his mouth, and I had to help him wipe up the tea that he had spilt down himself. He really was very frail but when he tried to speak to you there was still a sparkle in his eyes and a smile that made you think he was still quite sharp mentally.

There had been a doctor with him from the time he arrived at Northolt. The doctor was monitoring him constantly and was obviously concerned about his health. When I was talking with the doctor while at Chiswick, he told me he did not expect Ronnie to live longer than six months as he was very ill after his last stroke. I really did wonder if he had done the right thing coming back to Britain.

Terry Wilson and I then went with Ronnie to take his fingerprints; even though everyone knew he was Ronnie Biggs, we still had to take a set of prints as a matter of procedure to enable us to take him before a court in relation to the warrant issued for his arrest. In the paperwork was an original set of fingerprints taken from Ronnie at Wandsworth prison on 25th May 1956 when he was in custody for an offence of larceny. These were to be used by the fingerprint branch at New Scotland Yard to confirm that he was in fact Ronald Arthur Biggs. DS Wilson took Ronnie's prints while I completed the forms; because of his illness it was difficult for Terry to take the prints but he eventually managed to get a full set and following that, arrangements were made to get Ronnie to West London Magistrates Court in Hammersmith as soon as possible.

We got him to West London court just before lunchtime and he was to be dealt with as the last case before lunch. He was booked in with the usual grunts and groans you get from most of the private security staff at court now a day. After being booked in, despite his obvious ill health, he was made to walk to one of the farthest away cells from the booking-in area as was possible.

I went with him, as did his solicitor; he was shuffling along and the female prison guard looked at him in distaste and said, 'Bloody hurry up; I haven't got all day.'

The guard was in her late-twenties and obviously had better things to do than actually do her job. I stared at her at said, 'Haven't you got a cell closer to the booking-in desk? You can see he is not very well.'

She gave me a really dirty look and said, 'This is the one allocated for him; this is the one he goes in.'

'Thank you for being so helpful and polite,' I answered sarcastically. 'Manners cost nothing,' I added.

As Ronnie shuffled into the cell she slammed the door shut behind him and stormed off. I opened the little wicket on the front of the door in time to see Ronnie sit down on the bed. The look on his face told it all. He looked very close to tears and just kept looking all around him. I actually felt really very sorry for him.

A brief court appearance saw Ronnie remanded in custody to be taken to Bellmarsh high security prison to serve out the rest of his sentence or his life in prison. I rather suspected it would be the latter. I did not think he would last very long. However, as I write this in August 2008, Ronnie Biggs is still alive. He is very ill having suffered further strokes since being back in prison and he now is in the hospital wing of the prison being cared for. There has been big ongoing campaign running to get him released early on the grounds of his health. Despite this, the home secretary has refused to allow his early release and he still looks set to die in prison.

THERE IS ANOTHER SIDE TO this story. Following the return of Biggs, it was decided that it would be a good idea to have a photograph taken of the team that dealt with Ronnie Biggs as it was such an interesting part of the history of the Metropolitan police and the Flying Squad.

It was also decided by Chief Superintendent Coles that we should invite ex-Detective Chief Superintendent Jack Slipper along to the yard to be part of the photograph and take him out to lunch after having the picture taken. I was chuffed to bits as this meant I would finally get to meet him.

A date was arranged for the photograph to be taken at Scotland Yard and I was asked to go to Jack's house and pick him up and drive him to

Andy Vick

Scotland Yard. I was under strict instructions to have him in Mr Cole's office no later than one o'clock. I must admit to being slightly nervous as I arrived at his home in Sudbury but as soon as I met him and his wife I felt very at ease. He was a very tall man, of almost military bearing, but he put me at ease straight away.

We left for central London in plenty of time and on the journey into town I found it very easy to make conversation with Jack. He was really pleased by the invitation. I did not know at the time, but Jack had been ill with cancer; he made no mention of it except to say he had been ill and his short-term memory sometimes was not as good as it should be.

As I made my way towards central London the traffic, as normal, got slower and slower. I came off the main roads and tried to work my way through all the back streets. I came through Bayswater and Paddington and when we got to Marble Arch the traffic was absolutely at a standstill. I managed eventually to get onto Park Lane but time was getting on and it was getting close to 1.00 p.m.

The car we were in was my assigned car, a BMW530 fitted with all the equipment including a blue light for the roof, strobe lights in the grill and two tones. I told Jack we were running late and asked if he minded going a bit faster on blue lights and two-tones.

His eyes lit up and he said, 'That would be a great thrill for me, let's do it'

So I stuck everything on and we forced our way through traffic as quickly as possible down Park Lane to Hyde Park Corner. I looked at Jack several times and he had a great big grin on his face. At Hyde Park Corner, everything came to a complete halt with no sign of any likelihood of moving.

Unknown to me, there was a serious accident in Grosvenor Place and nothing was able to get around the system of Hyde Park Corner. There was no traffic coming around Hyde Park Corner from Grosvenor Place and suddenly I saw that the roundabout to the right was free of traffic. I pulled out and went around Hyde Park Corner the wrong way before the lights from Knightsbridge changed to green and let traffic come towards me.

Turning from Hyde Park Corner onto Grosvenor Place I saw the accident blocking the road ahead of me but with a couple of quick right and lefts I got around the scene of the accident coming back out onto Buckingham Palace Road. Minutes later we reached Scotland Yard. I switched off the blue lights and two-tones and parked the vehicle in the underground car park. I made it to Mr Cole's office with minutes to spare. On the way up in the lift Jack was saying how much he had enjoyed the blue-light run and I casually mentioned that it might be best if we kept it to ourselves.

I showed him into Mr Cole's office and slipped off to use the toilet; on my return I walked in to hear Jack retelling the story of how I had driven at great speed and with great skill the wrong way around Hyde Park Corner and raced to the yard to get here on time. Fortunately, Mr Coles was OK about it; at least I got him there on time...

After the photograph had been taken we made our way to a restaurant near Victoria coach station for lunch. The meal was excellent and then for hours we sat and listened as Jack told us some fantastic stories, giving us an insight into what really happened during the great train robbery investigation. He had an amazing recall for detail and before we knew it, over four hours had gone by. I could have sat and listened to him all night; I loved hearing all the old stories.

I am proud to say that this was the start of a friendship I maintained with Jack until he died in August 2005. In the short time I knew him, we met several times at further lunches arranged by Mr Coles.

I will never forget 11th September 2001, the day of the planes being flown into the World Trade Centre towers in New York. I went with Mr Coles to meet Jack for lunch at a favourite restaurant of his in Park Royal. A close friend of his, ex-Detective Chief Superintendent Mick McCadam had come along with Jack and we were sat in a four-seater booth.

I was sat opposite Jack when suddenly his jaw just dropped and his eyes went wide open. He just lifted his hand and pointed a finger over my head; we looked around and saw the TV screen, just as one of the hijacked planes hit into one of the towers. It really shook Jack and put him off his stride for a while as he was in the middle of telling one of his famous stories.

During one of the lunches I mentioned to Jack that I remembered reading his book *Slipper of the Yard*. He had written the book in 1981 and I had read it sometime after, when I found a copy in the police library, and really enjoyed the book. Jack told me that he funded it himself. I think he told me he had published 6,000 originally and they went so well he had a further 6,000 printed later in the year. They also sold out completely. His family had an original copy, but apart from that he did not think there was any still left in print.

I decided I would try and track down a copy if possible. I tried everywhere I could think of. One bookshop eventually gave me the details of a company that specialised in finding out of print books via the internet. I contacted them and they started a search for me.

A day or so later they informed me that they had located two copies. Both, strangely, were in America. I ordered one immediately and a week or so later received my copy at a cost of £38. It was in first-class condition and I was thrilled to bits.

The next day I rang Jack and asked if I could pop in and see him as I had something I wanted to show him. I duly arrived and his face was a picture. He was chuffed to bits I had found a copy and I explained to him where and how I had got it. He looked so pleased and I offered him the copy and said I would order the other one from America. He declined because they had the original family one.

'In that case then, will you sign it for me please?' I asked him. He faced beamed his great big smile and he took the book and wrote the following on the inside cover:

'To Andy –

With my best wishes. I can assure you that I will never forget that drive to Scotland Yard. You topped up my previous squad drivers, well and truly. Once again thanks.'

He then signed it Jack Slipper, ex-Detective Chief Supt of the Flying Squad. I was absolutely over the moon and it is a book I will cherish for the rest of my life...

As I said at the start of this story, it is amazing that the great train robbery and Jack Slipper were the sole reason in my teens for my wanting to be a police officer. Then some twenty-eight years later I became friends with Jack, who then went on to tell me so much more about the robbery. Like I said, I think fate plays a part of what happens to you in your life. I was extremely lucky and very privileged to have met and got to know Jack Slipper of the Yard.... Sadly Jack died in August 2005.

He once told me that he really wanted to outlive Ronnie Biggs and finally see the end of the train robbery saga. However, he did confide in me that he had recorded a television interview with his thoughts on Ronnie Biggs's return, which he believed will be aired on TV when Ronnie does pass away. We shall see....

Now this was a scary one!

On Monday 23rd December 2002, I arrived for work at about 8.00 a.m. and I was posted to the bank car for the day with DS Steve Coles and DC John Nolan. As the bank car we were there to respond to any armed robberies that happened in our area. I was really hoping for a quiet day as I had loads of work to sort out and with Christmas coming I needed to sort it all out before I went on annual leave.

At about 10.15 a.m. we were called out to an armed robbery in progress at a branch of HSBC in Regents Street, smack bang in the centre of London. We left the office and made our way at speed on blues-and-twos. When we arrived we then discovered that the robbery was not at a bank but in fact it was at a restaurant and club called 'Break for the Border'. The premises were situated next to the London Palladium and were below ground level with a lot of the rooms and corridors actually running underneath the theatre.

We soon discovered that the manager had been due to arrive at the premises at 9.00 a.m. that morning. He was, however, an hour late. When he did eventually arrive he had two different sets of delivery men waiting for him. He opened up the premises and went on down the steps into the club with one of the drivers. Unknown to the manager, lying in wait inside were three masked men armed with guns and knives.

They had gained entry overnight, intending to catch the manager when he opened up alone. These three men attacked the manager and the delivery driver when they entered the club. They were tied up or handcuffed and violence was then used on the manager to extract the codes to open up the safe in the manager's office. This safe contained over £46,000 in cash.

Unfortunately for the three robbers, the delivery driver had a mate waiting in the lorry; he realised something was wrong and called the police. As the police started to arrive the robbers had just cleared out the safe of the cash, when they saw the police outside on the club's CCTV system. Two of them attempted to escape by bursting out of a set of fire escape doors and running off. Both were captured after a foot chase in Oxford Street. However, no one knew what had happened to the third suspect. It was possible he had escaped during all the confusion or he may still have been hiding in the club somewhere.

While a full-scale operation swung into action to search the labyrinth of corridors in the club with armed officers and dogs, I went to deal with the manager. His name was Andy. He was in a terrible state and I felt really sorry for him. He had been beaten, threatened with being shot, almost stabbed with a knife, and it had really taken its toll on him. But I had to take a statement from him to find out exactly what had taken place. This took several hours and at the end of it all he was drained.

After three hours of searching the dogs had found no one; the firearms team had also been through double-checking that all was clear. They had found all the cash hidden in an alcove under the Palladium along with a firearm. They had left the items in place for retrieval by the forensic team and exhibit officer.

I then had to try to persuade Andy the manager to come back in the building with me. This was important, as we needed to know what things belonged in the club and what did not. It was vital that we retrieved all the forensic evidence of the suspects that we could. Andy was not very happy about this. He had been through a really horrific ordeal and did not want to go back into the club.

I told him how important it was and explained that if I was not confident that it was safe to go back in there, then I would not do so. I also explained that I had been a dog-handler and that I was certain that if anyone had been hiding down there then the dogs would have found him without fail. Eventually, he trusted me and down we went.

Now, I am not normally very nervous in situations like this, but by now it was late evening, dark outside and the club was very eerie and huge, with rooms and corridors off at all angles. We started the walk-through with Andy pointing out what belonged in the club and what did not. As we walked further away from the main bar area and into corridors under the pavements above Andy become more and more nervous and I could fully understand why. I kept reassuring him and we pressed on.

We eventually came to a corridor that was shared with the London Palladium which was mainly a fire escape route. There were stairs from the basement area up to ground level then further on up to the theatre. I discovered later that under these stairs was where the cash and gun were recovered from. When we reached these stairs Andy did not want to go any further.

The door was wedged open and I assured him it had been done so by the firearms teams and dogs as they searched. I told him they would have cleared it with the dogs and double-checked it manually. I was confident it was safe or I would not have gone on searching, especially as I had no gun, body armour, cuffs, asp (extendable baton) or even a radio with me.

This seemed to ease his mind and we moved forward. In front of us was a narrow corridor with a small wooden door at the end set into the wall. Above our heads was a two-foot square stainless steal air conditioning duct that appeared to turn left at the wall in front of us. I walked forward and at the wall I saw that to my left was a very dark hole with a two-foot wall preventing you from walking into it. The air-conditioning duct disappeared into the darkness above my head and I remember thinking, *My god I hope they have searched that properly!*

Andy was stood just slightly behind me. I was directly under the ducting and I pulled open the small wooden door and saw there was alight on inside. I could see it housed nothing more that two large gas pipes.

Suddenly, I jumped out of my skin as Andy screamed, 'It's a boot, it's a boot.'

I turned to face him with my heart pounding out of my chest he had scared me so much. As I turned he was off and running back through the building and out of my sight. All I could hear was him screaming, 'It's a boot,' over and over again.

I took a step back thinking, *what the hell is he on about?* I could see absolutely nothing. I thought about what I had just done and repeated it. This time as I opened the small door I stepped backwards. As I looked up towards the ducting, the light from the small room was lighting up the sole of a black training shoe. Oh shit! I knew the suspect must have known he had been discovered. Did he have a gun or maybe a knife? Was it better to back off and go and get help? No, of course not – this shit bag needing sorting out now, but how?

The only thing I had with me was my mobile phone; being a firearms officer I was trained to talk people out in armed situations, to control them using a loud aggressive voice. As it was quite dark with the little door now closed again, I knew he could not see me directly; I decided to take a risk and to act as if I was armed. Using the corner of the wall as protection, I put my phone in my hands, stretched out my arms in a classic firearms pose and yelled out as loud as I could, 'Armed police; stay still and do everything I say, do you understand me'?

There was no reply. I then screamed, 'You on the top of the air duct. I am an armed police officer, do you understand me'?

A shaky voice replied, 'Yeah, yeah; don't shoot, don't shoot'

Feeling more confident, I yelled instructions for him to drop down off the ducting with his back to me keeping his hands above his head as he dropped. He did as he was told. I told him to lie on the floor with his head furthest away from me and to put his hands on the back of his head and to interlock his fingers.

I said, 'Do you have any weapons on you'?

He answered, 'No, honest, nothing.'

As he lay there I could see he was a black male but he was covered from head to toe in thick grey-coloured dust. I then approached him from behind and took control of his hands and told him to lie perfectly still as I would have no worries about shooting him if he did not comply with my instructions. Then I thought *what the hell I do now?*

Fortunately, almost immediately a scene-of-crime officer appeared, having been alerted by Andy's screaming as he run back through the club. He duly got help in the way of a squad colleague, Caroline who arrived with handcuffs. The suspect was taken off to West End Central police station still convinced he had escaped been shot by an armed officer. If only he knew….

Armed officers eventually arrived after first refusing to come down until they knew it was clear and safe. Well, they should have bloody made sure it was safe and clear the first time they had searched. I lost it a bit with the sergeant on the firearms team as we went up the stairs and they were coming down. I told him exactly what I thought of him for refusing to come and help me. I will not repeat what I called him but it did seem to rhyme with the word 'tanker'.

I was even more furious when I discovered they found a loaded firearm some ten feet from where I found the suspect. I could make excuse for the dog not finding him on the air-con ducting, as all the suspects' scent would have been rising up through air holes in the pavement to the outside making it very difficult for the dog to catch the scent. As for the firearms team, well someone should have stepped up onto the small wall and checked the top of the ducting. I expect it was a bit too scary for them in the dark, bloody cowboys!

Andy the manager was never able to go back to work in the club as it affected him so much. I apologised to him for what happened the second time; he was fine with me but I know he made a big complaint about the firearms teams.

All three suspects arrested admitted the robbery and firearm offences at court and received sentences of nine, seven and five years for their trouble. I never trusted the firearms teams ever again, and after that little situation would have changed my vote to be armed all the time if I had the choice.

The skull cracker – Operation Rockley

Between June 2001 and September 2002 a linked series of violent armed robberies began to emerge. The offences took place in the Met and Home Counties and a lone robber targeted banks and building societies through five counties. During the raids he netted over £45,000 pounds in cash and left a trail of terrified victims behind him. As each offence was committed he seemed to get progressively more violent. As a result The Flying Squad at Barnes began a very difficult investigation to identify and arrest the offender before someone was badly injured or killed.

CCTV evidence clearly showed the suspect carrying out these offences. He would enter the premises dressed as a workman or similar, and approach the counter where he would grab hold of an elderly female customer and point a gun at her head. He would then demand cash and threaten to 'blow their heads off' if he was not given money. At one offence he pistol-whipped a seventy-three-year-old woman and a building society manager in order to force the cashier to hand over the money.

When the Flying Squad at Barnes took the linked series on, they discovered a total of thirteen offences spread across the south of England from Southampton to Royston in Hertfordshire. The investigation was led by Detective Sergeant Ian Dobson (Dobbo) and Detective Constable Sarah Staff. They very quickly identified the suspect as Michael Wheatley, a convicted armed robber. Wheatley had been paroled some twelve months earlier from prison where he had been serving a twenty-seven-year sentence for exactly the same type of offence he was now committing. He was also targeting exactly the same venues as before.

Because of the level of violence being used, the investigating officers took the decision to go to the national press with his photographs to try to locate his whereabouts as quickly as possible. The *Sun* newspaper was very interested in running a full-page story and it ran it in conjunction with the offer of a £25,000 reward from the bank and building societies who had been his victims.

There was a good response, most of which did not assist us. One bit of information we received was really useful and started a different line of enquiry that led us to the Limehouse area of East London. After a 4.00 a.m. briefing one September morning in 2002, four gun ships (covert armed cars) with fourteen armed officers were sitting up in and around the East India Dock Road. Other officers were in static observation posts nearby.

At about 8.00 a.m. the Observation Post (OP) put up a possible for Wheatley walking along East India Dock Road towards Burdett Road. They could not be certain that it was him, though. Someone from the nearest gunship got out to try and make a positive ID. Seconds later, it was confirmed it was him.

He was followed on foot to a newsagent in Burdett Road fifty yards from East India Dock Road. We all deployed on foot, in and around the footpath outside the shop. As soon as Wheatley stepped out, he was challenged by armed police and jumped on from behind by DS Dobson, who wrapped his arms around Wheatley to prevent him pulling his hands out of coat pockets where he may have had his gun.

Wheatley fell, face-first into the pavement, unable to put his arms out to stop his fall, his face smashed into the pavement, nose first. He was immediately arrested by DS Dobson and handcuffed on the floor. When we sat him up his face was covered in blood and his nose smashed from where he had hit the pavement. Straight away it was obvious that Wheatley was what we called an 'old-style villain'. He was not bothered in the least about his nose; as he put it: 'a hazard of the job'.

He was chuffed to beans it was the Flying Squad who had nicked him and straight away told us he was not carrying a gun, but that they were in his flat a short distance away. Officers were dispatched to deal with his flat. DS Dobson, DC Martin Ainsworth (Ainsy) and I put Wheatley in my car and headed of to Twickenham police station.

In the car, Wheatley was very talkative and was quite happy. He seemed actually pleased he had been arrested and it struck me as if he really wanted to go back into the prison system. We had given him first aid for his nose and had managed to stop it bleeding, but he did look a mess. Wheatley was quite proud of it and said it would stand him in good stead in prison, to have survived a hard-stop arrest by the squad. Once we were back at Twickenham he was led into the custody suite. It was here that one of the most bizarre incidents I have ever witnessed when dealing with a prisoner occurred.

We walked into the custody suite with Wheatley. I was on his right and DS Dobson was on his left. At the desks were two sergeants. On the right was a skipper I knew well, Mark Barrett. Mark was a very good old-style skipper who was ideal for dealing with our prisoner. Unfortunately, he was busy and nodded towards the other skipper who I did not know, and he looked a little inexperienced.

DS Dobson introduced himself and went into the details regarding the arrest. Now bear in mind that it is the custody sergeant who has the final say as to whether there is sufficient evidence to detain a person, and he normally only requires brief details as to the arrest. The custody sergeant looked at Wheatley's damaged face and I physically saw him swallow hard and I knew this was going to be a problem.

DS Dobson began: 'This is Michael Wheatley. He has been arrested today for thirteen offences of armed robbery and firearms offences. We have recovered two firearms from his address. Wheatley has been positively identified via forensics and CCTV as being the person responsible. The arrest took place in Burdett Road, E3 at 0800 hours, by armed officers from the Flying Squad at Barnes. He has been handcuffed and completely compliant.'

I saw the Custody Sergeant look towards DS Dobson and then look at Wheatley.

He said, 'How did you get your injuries?'

Wheatley said, 'It happened when I was arrested; I fell face first on the floor.'

The skipper said, 'Was it caused by these officers?' I looked at Dobbo and Ainsy in disbelief. He was actually accusing us directly of assaulting the prisoner.

Before we could say anything Wheatley said, 'don't be so f***ing stupid. What planet are you from? These guys are from the flying squad. They took me fair and square; at least they didn't f***ing shoot me. Let's get on with it.'

The skipper then said, 'If you wish to make a complaint you can do so later.

He then turned to Dobbo and said, 'Can I see some evidence please?'

Now let me say that in the twenty-six years I had at this time been a police officer, I had never known a custody sergeant ask to see evidence; it was not necessary. As long as he was given full details of why the person was in custody and that it met with the requirements of the law, then that was that. I looked at Dobbo and knew it was all about to start to go wrong. Dobbo was a very experienced CID officer and excellent at his job. He did not, however, suffer fools gladly. He had ginger hair and a fiery temper if upset.

Dobbo said, 'I beg your pardon, what did you say?'

The skipper repeated his request and Dobbo went very red in the face and said, 'I have just given the facts to you: the man is an armed robber, positively identified and arrested, and you do not need to see any evidence. Just book him in.'

The skipper replied, 'Unless I see some evidence against this man I am not prepared to accept him into custody.'

Next to him Sgt Barrett was holding his head in his hands in disbelief. I could also see Dobbo was about to explode and I was getting ready to intervene before he laid into the skipper.

Suddenly, Wheatley said, 'Wait a minute, I'll give you proof if that's what you need.'

He turned to Ainsy and said, 'Get my wallet out of my pocket for me mate (he was still handcuffed at this time).

Ainsy did as he asked and Wheatley said, 'Open it up and take out the folded bit of paper.'

You're Nicked My Son

When Ainsy opened it up it was the whole front page from the *Sun* newspaper with a full picture of Wheatley in the middle of a robbery. The headline said '**£25,000 price on the skull cracker's head**'.

Wheatley told Ainsy to hand it to the custody sergeant and said to him, 'There you are; there's your proof. See for yourself – that's me, I'm the skull cracker. Surely even you can see that?'

Well there were people biting their lips trying not to laugh. The skipper went white and did not know what to do next. He then said, 'Well yes, that is good evidence I suppose.'

He then started the booking-in procedure. He began ask Wheatley for his details and when he asked him for his occupation, Wheatley replied, 'Are you some kind of idiot? What do you think my job is? I'm a bloody armed robber.'

The skipper said, 'No I need your proper occupation.'

Wheatley said, 'That is my occupation; I'm a professional bank robber. When I'm not in prison, that's what I do for a living.'

This sparked off more laughter a little louder than before. When the booking in was finished, Wheatley was handed the arrest sheet to sign; he read it and said, 'What's this? You've shown me as refusing to give my occupation? What the f**k are you doing, trying to fit me up? I told you my job is an armed robber, now write it down.'

A very embarrassed skipper did as he was told and we got on with dealing with Wheatley.

We later discovered that the skipper was newly promoted and new to the Met having transferred from Surrey. He had obviously been a bit of a job's-worth and was trying to do what he thought was the right way to deal with the prisoner. I hope he learnt quickly, otherwise I could not see him surviving very long as a skipper in the Met.

When interviewed, Wheatley admitted all thirteen offences and also related firearms offences. On 1st October 2002, he appeared at the Old Bailey Crown Court and pleaded guilty to all offences. He was sentenced to life imprisonment.

He was described in court as a career criminal who spoke of each raid as no more than a trip to the corner shop. He accepted everything that was coming to him as an occupational hazard.

In my five years on the Flying Squad, Wheatley was the only 'old-style armed robber' that I had any involvement with. Thankfully, they are few and far between.

Heathrow airport (better known to police as thief row) – Operation Cartwright

One of the biggest problem areas for the Flying Squad grew to be Heathrow Airport. Crime was pretty rife all over the airport and most of it was dealt with by officers from Heathrow itself. However, it came under our area and from 2000 onwards Heathrow became the target of some very high-value crimes that came under our remit.

Because of this high level of crime, a separate arm of the squad was set up to look into the offences taking place and to try and identify the people who were organising and committing the crimes. This went under the name of Operation Grafton and was staffed by officers from the squad and from other agencies.

They were to look into the large amount of intelligence that we received regarding criminality at the airport. They would then put operations into plan, using the Flying Squad as the proactive wing to deal with the offenders. They did a fantastic job and soon identified a series of individuals who were masterminding all the serious crimes taken place in and around Heathrow. This was anything from hijacking lorries containing valuable computer equipment, attacking vehicles containing large quantities of cash, to attacking bonded warehouses. They were very well organised but eventually we knew, thanks to the team from Grafton, exactly who they were.

With the exception of one offence that occurred in March 2002 when a South African airways aircraft unloaded over £2.6 million cash in various currencies into a van that was attacked, virtually all the major crimes could be attributed to this one large group of suspects.

The South African airways offence was dealt with by the Flying Squad and in May 2002 following a protracted investigation and after weeks of surveillance on people suspected of committing the offence, a series of raids on 21st May resulted in their being arrested.

During the raids over £1.5 million pound was recovered. Over a £1 million was found in one rucksack alone at the home of one of the suspects. The suspects were under suspicion from a very early stage and watched closely for several weeks. A lot of the surveillance was filmed and some of the tapes were sent to a specialist in lip-reading who was able to produce some startling transcripts of what the suspects were saying to each other. She picked up one of them bragging how he was going to go to Hawaii and that the police hadn't sussed anything. Another was filmed saying 'Everybody will get £250,000.00; we have got it all over the place'.

One of the main suspects was an Indian male, Sundeep Singh, who had been the driver of the van and had claimed he had been attacked and robbed. His story was that two Asian males had appeared from nowhere at the back of the van, threatened him with knives and told him to drive the van out of the airport where the money was moved to another vehicle and the driver left tied up.

The investigating officers were immediately suspicious of him and looked at him as a possible inside agent. After his arrest he did admit everything and subsequently Sundeep Singh, his brother Harjit and a third male, Manish Bhadresa, all in their early twenties, all appeared at crown court. They all pleaded guilty to the theft and received a total of twenty-five years in prison between them.

WHILE THIS INVESTIGATION WAS GOING on, the offences, especially lorry hijacks were continuing and the Grafton team were kept very busy. We had several minor successes arresting some of the gang for some of the smaller crimes, but it was taking a while to get anywhere near the main organisers and planners of the offences.

Then around March 2004 we started getting hints at the office from the Grafton team that something big was looming. The main targets were under surveillance and it was looking like they were planning something major at the airport. The intelligence they were gathering was kept fairly close to their chests until they had a good idea that they knew exactly was the robbers were planning.

To go into the methods of how the intelligence was gathered would make really interesting reading, but I do not believe it is right to do so as some of it is very sensitive and would affect future actions the squad might take against serious targets; suffice to say it worked perfectly. As a result of all the intelligence, Operation Cartwright came into being.

The detective inspector in charge of the operation was Wilf Pickles. Wilf was born to be a flying squad detective. He had been a DS on the squad for quite a few years before being promoted, and stayed with us as DI. Even though he was in his last few years of service, this man had so much drive it was sometimes hard to keep up with him.

With all the long hours he worked he had the ability of surviving on a couple of hours sleep and then could return to work so fresh he looked like he had had twelve hours of sleep. The man was amazing and was a real inspiration. His main ability was his knack of doing the right thing and making exactly the right calls at the right time no matter how complicated the situation might be.

What I liked about him was that he was very old school in his ways. He expected loyalty and in return he would do anything for you and back you all the way. There was an expression used by people on the squad at Barnes and that is: 'I have just been Wilfed'. If that happened to you, it meant you had been working with Wilf either on an operation or enquiries of some sort, and he just keeps going and going day after day and never runs out of steam.

Everyone loved working with him but everyone dreaded being Wilfed as it took you days to recover from it. Unfortunately for the team of robbers, Wilf was on their tail.

In early April 2004, we got to finally find out what was taking place.

The intelligence showed that the known targets were going to attack a cargo warehouse situated on the south side of the airport perimeter. A very large quantity of cash was going to be arriving by plane sometime in the next few weeks and the gang would have had information from an inside agent as to when it would be arriving. Having been furnished with all the information they needed, the gang intended to attack the premises after it had been delivered and take the cash, rumoured to be in excess of £40 million in Swiss francs and US dollars.

Our information told us that a Monday was the day that this massive sum of money would be arriving. What we or the gang did not know was exactly which Monday it would be. So from the middle of April we started to cover the operation every Monday morning. The day would start at around 5.00 a.m. with a briefing at Staines police station. Staines is just to the south of the airport and part of Surrey police force.

We briefed there because the intelligence told us that the gang might have people out early in the morning watching our offices at Barnes to see if there was any activity, which might warn them we were onto them. We also knew that one of the main members of the gang would spend quite a long time driving around the immediate vicinity of the airport to see if there was any sign of possible police activity or surveillance.

Senior officers from the squad had approached the senior managers of the company the gang planned to rob, Swissport, and informed them of the intended attack on their premises. They cooperated fully keeping the information between several senior members of management.

As a result, every Monday morning, a member of the squad was sat in the CCTV/security office at Swissport with full control over their camera system. Outside, hidden in the back of a large van parked close to the premises, were officers from the SO19 specialist firearms teams. The vehicle was parked there from very early on and looked part of the surroundings.

From around 6.00 a.m. four gun ships from the flying squad were parked on a private business complex about a mile from Swissport. There were also a further four gun ships crewed by SO19 officers tucked well away from the Swissport premises. All the vehicles were well out of sight from where any member of the gang would be able to spot us when they did their drive around. Everyone had a designated job to do in the event of the offence taking place.

A surveillance team was also deployed at various addresses of the gang to give us an idea of what they were getting up to. On the first three Monday mornings, members of the gang were around the area, having a good look around and obviously planning their operation. We knew it really was just a matter of time before the money would arrive and the gang carried out the robbery.

Sure enough, on Monday 17th May we received word that the flight carrying the cash was due to arrive that morning. Very soon after we knew it was arriving, it was obvious that the gang also had the same information as they also started to organise themselves. With all of us in place it was now just a waiting game.

The plane landed at about 9.00 a.m. and a security van drove out to the plane. From a distance a surveillance officer watched as the cargo was unloaded and all the cash put into the security van. Again, under the watchful eye of a surveillance team, the van was carefully controlled from airside and the short distance to the cargo centre.

Entry to the cargo area is controlled by security gates and as the vehicle was let through, the tension was rising as we expected the attack to happen fairly quickly. The van reached Swissport and reversed up to a shuttered security area, which we knew allowed the van to enter a secure vault area and unload.

To our surprise nothing happened. We knew that the gang were close by. One of the robbers was floating around the area looking for police activity. We were certain that we had not been spotted, so what had gone wrong? About five or ten minutes later we were still in place when we received word that eight members of the gang had got into a stolen white van at a petrol station two miles away and were heading towards the venue.

Two were in the cab and six hidden in the rear. At the time, another security van had arrived at Swissport. This one was a lot bigger than the previous van and could not fit into the secure vaulted area and waited to reverse in through a set of larger shuttered doors. These doors let them into the large warehouse area of Swissport. We had no idea at the time that this vehicle was carrying over £40 million in gold bullion.

Just before 10.00 a.m. the stolen white van arrived at the security gate of the cargo area and the driver produced a set of legitimate paperwork they had acquired to allow them entry. The van then drove around the front of Swissport and appeared to take its place in a line of vehicles waiting entry into the secure area. We also were made aware by the surveillance team that another member of the gang was still floating around the airport perimeter road in a car watching for police activity.

Suddenly, the van pulled out from the line of vehicles and reversed at speed into the shutter door to the left of the secure vault area. The van smashed through the doors and the eight members of the gang jumped out armed with a pistol, knives and wooden bats they ran screaming into the warehouse yelling at members of staff.

The Flying Squad officer in the CCTV room yelled down the radio, '**attack, attack, attack**' and the firearms officers, armed with Heckler & Koch machine guns and shotguns leapt from the van and stormed the premises. At the same time we raced from our holding spot at breakneck speed and into the secure area. Our job, once inside, was to secure any prisoners.

The tyres of the stolen van had been shot out with special rounds called Hatton rounds. They are fired from a shotgun and they render the vehicle useless. As I entered the warehouses all hell had been let loose: four of the robbers were on the floor face-down, controlled by armed officers. Other armed officers were chasing two other suspects down the far end of the warehouse.

I immediately took control of a suspect on the floor. He was laying face-down, wearing a yellow fluorescent jacket and a full-face balaclava. It was immediately obvious that the attack had not gone completely to plan and at least two of the suspects had escaped. Unfortunately, the SO19 gun ships were slightly late in their arrival and had not got their outer cordons put in on time.

One of the fleeing suspects was armed with a firearm and hijacked a lorry and its driver, and rammed his way out of the security barrier. He was followed by surveillance officers until one of the late-arriving SO19 cars caught up with them. There was a chase for some miles before the stolen van crashed and the driver suspect ran off but was caught by the firearms team at a nearby address. The lorry driver was not hurt. The second missing suspect escaped over a fence and disappeared.

BACK AT THE WAREHOUSE, I discovered that another two of the suspects had been caught in the secure vault trying to get at the cash we knew they had intended to steal. It also then became obvious that they had almost had a massive stroke of luck. The second, larger truck to arrive had been carrying £40 million-worth of gold bullion.

Because the lorry was too big to reverse straight into the vault it had been taken into the warehouse. The pallet was in the process of being broken down into smaller pallets and taken by forklift truck into the vault when the robbers had struck. They had reversed through the door and stopped right next to the large pallet of boxes.

They realised very quickly what it was and while two of them went off to find the cash, the others had started throwing the boxes of bullion into the back of the stolen van. Then their world fell apart as the firearms teams charged in through the doors closely followed by the flying squad.

The CCTV footage from the warehouse is very dramatic and exciting to watch. Within minutes of entering the warehouse we were aware of a photographer taking lots of photographs. We then found out that the squad had allowed a reporter and photographer from the *Daily Mirror* to cover the story as part of a public relations exercise as they were doing a story on Operation Grafton. As a result, the next day there were a lot of pictures in the paper of the suspects in handcuffs at the warehouse.

The best one was a full front-page picture of one of the gang, James Fox. He was sat with his hands handcuffed behind his back and leaning against the large pallet of boxes containing the bullion. The look on his face said it all. I must say I did not think at the time that it was right to allow a reporter or photographer to be involved at the scene so quickly after the event, but I have to say the pictures were brilliant.

As things settled down I searched the prisoner I was looking after; he was moaning like a drain about his cuffs being tight and how uncomfortable he was. I removed his full-face balaclava and recognised the guy straight away. He was a black guy by the name of Tony Charles. I'd had dealings with him on several occasions during my Hammersmith crime squad days. He recognised me straight away and it broke the ice a bit; he started to see the funny side of things and chilled out realising he was deep in the shit, and there was nothing he could do about it. He turned out to have been the driver of the stolen van.

So this was a fantastic result: we had managed to arrest virtually all of the gang that had been causing so many problems at the airport.

A small team from Barnes led by DS Steve Coles then had the task of getting the case ready for court. The man who we knew to be the main organiser of the whole team, and someone we believed responsible for virtually all of the major crime that took place on or around the airport, was called John Beech. He was an ex-baggage handler who lived locally to Heathrow in Stanwell village. He was the mastermind behind it all.

He had made sure he was well away from Heathrow at the time of the robbery to disassociate himself from the team carrying out his plans. At the time of the robbery he was being followed by a surveillance team and just after we had all raced into the warehouse, Beech was videoed taking a phone call and judging by his very angry and animated reactions on the phone he was being informed of the failed robbery. He was subsequently arrested and charged with being involved in not only the attempted robbery at Swissport but also a £2.5 million robbery at Heathrow in 2003.

In March 2006 he was found guilty and received sixteen years in prison. All the other members of the gang received various lengthy sentences for their part in the attack on the Swissport premises.

A SLIGHTLY DIFFERENT STORY

As well as being known as one of the most successful squads in the Met, The Flying Squad is also one of the most charitable squads. Every year through the squad's rugby team, an amazing amount of cash is raised for good causes.

Every member of the squad is expected to generously donate when required to do so. It you are not forthcoming then you will be told in no uncertain terms to get your hand in your pocket and pay up. No matter what the charity was, if they could, the squad always did something to raise money, especially if the money being raised was going to help a badly injured or seriously ill colleague.

Although this story goes off track a little to what I have been writing about, I really want to tell it because it shows exactly what I mean about the squad.

In May 2004, a very dear friend and colleague of mine died. His name was Andrew Toole, Toolie to his friends. Toolie has been mentioned before in this book and at the time of his death he was one month away from retiring from the police service. He died tragically in a motorbike accident in Spain while on holiday, when a van that was out of control wiped him out. He had also helped out at Barnes as a 'strapper' whenever we needed extra drivers and was an absolute diamond. He was very well liked by all the squad at the office and had fitted in really well.

Andy had been due to travel to New Zealand with me on the British Lions rugby tour in July 2005 and other friends organised a black-tie memorial night for Toolie at an large airport hotel at Heathrow. I wanted to try and do something to help with it. It was decided to make it a fund-raising night in Toolies name. All money raised would go to the RNLI, of which Andy was a staunch supporter as his brother Jim was an RNLI crew member on the Isle of Mull. It was decided to have a sports memorabilia auction during the dinner as part of the fund-raising.

Lots of people managed to get their hands on loads of signed items for the auction. I wanted to do something a bit special. I remembered a contacted I had made on a recent job in Thames Valley. DS Russell Murden had a way to get to Sir Clive Woodward who was to be the British Lions team manager. With Russell's help I managed to get a British Lions rugby jersey, signed by Woodward, to put up in the auction and was really pleased as it was a great item to have. The dinner dance night was set for 21st May, a year after Andy died.

I picked up the signed jersey from Russell a few days before. To my horror, the shirt was signed **'TO THE FLYING SQUAD – Clive Woodward'**. This was a disaster and when I asked Russell why he had done that he explained that because so many people were asking for signed items and then putting them for sale on EBay, Woodward would only sign things if they were personal to someone in particular. This was a big problem as no one else was likely to bid on the shirt unless it was someone from the flying squad itself.

I went back to Barnes and went straight upstairs to the squad office (I had by this time moved one floor below onto a different squad). The first person I saw was Sarah Staff. I told her about the shirt, what it was for, etc, and asked her if she knew anyone who might want to buy it direct without it going in the auction as I felt this was the only chance of making any money for it. Sarah said to give her a little while and she would ask about.

About thirty minutes later she rang me and asked me to go back upstairs. When I did so Sarah told me that the whole office wanted to buy it between them and offered me £1,250 pounds for it. I was absolutely dumbstruck. This was far beyond what I had dared hoped we would have got in the auction. I accepted straight away and asked her would she mind if I presented it to her at the dinner dance to allow me to tell every one there of the squad's generosity. She agreed and I hurriedly went off to get the shirt framed so it looked top-notch for when I handed it over.

At the dinner, at the end of the auction, we had raised over £3,000, I was very proud to be able to stand up in front of about 250 people and tell them the story of how the squad had offered £1,250 for the shirt in less than thirty minutes of me offering it to them. The shirt now has pride of place on the wall of the Barnes Flying Squad office.

As an aside to this story, Clive Woodward got to hear how much the shirt had raised, and he asked, via Russ Murden, if he could have a much sought-after flying squad tie as a thank you for signing the shirt. I said I would get him one and take it with me to New Zealand to try and hand it to him personally to say thank you. Once in New Zealand, on the tour, I tried numerous times to make contact with Clive Woodward but could not get anywhere near him to give him the tie. Even using a contact with the Welsh RFU, I could not get to see him.

On the Saturday of the third and last test I decided to make one last attempt to get the tie to him at the team hotel. This was not to be a good idea, for two reasons. The first was that throughout the whole three weeks everyone had been suffering on and off with a horrendous 'flu bug and chest infection. We had all spent a small fortune at chemists in every place we stayed. You would think you had got rid of it, and bang, it was on you again. So on this Saturday morning I was up to my eyeballs in pills and cough medicine and not completely with it at all.

The second reason, which did not help the first, was that we had been involved in a very good night out on the Friday night which extended on in the hotel bar when we had returned. We were staying in the same hotel as the New Zealand side and there were a few of the players in the bar when we got back. (They were not playing the next day obviously!) An excellent social night was had until the very early hours of Saturday morning.

We got into a conversation with the players about the previous two tests and they all believed that Clive Woodward's team selection was the reason why the All Blacks had beaten us so easily. One of the players kept calling him Woodcock as a joke instead of Woodward, and in our drunken state we were soon using the same name as well.

When I eventually did get to bed I hardly slept due to all the coughing and sneezing. At about 9.30 a.m. on the Saturday morning I set off to walk the short distance to the Lions' team hotel and tried to get in to see Woodward. I soon wished I hadn't, as I felt like I had been hit by a bus. At the hotel it was like Fort Knox. I tried explaining to the security why I was there; I even tried showing my warrant card but it made no difference. And so I gave up and made my way back to my hotel.

As I passed through a shopping centre I saw Bill Beaumont, the former England and Lions player in a bookshop. He was part of Woodward's management team and I decided to approach him and ask him to give the tie to Clive Woodward. I must have looked a bit of a sight as I walked up to him, unshaven and dressed for the arctic. I introduced myself and told him briefly about Woodward wanting this tie and how I had not been able to get it to him, and asked him to give it to Mr Woodward for me.

Bill Beaumont is a huge figure of a man and looked down at me as if I was some sort of nutcase who had escaped from the asylum. I remember repeating my request: 'would you please give this to Mr Woodward and say thank you from the flying squad.'

He looked down at me and said, 'I'm sorry I don't know anybody called Woodcock.'

I looked and said, 'Of course you do, you know that so-called head coach Sir Clive.'

Beaumont then said, 'You said Woodcock.'

I replied, 'No I didn't I said Woodward.'

Beaumont replied, 'No you didn't, you said Woodcock.'

I then realised I probably had called Woodward Woodcock by mistake and got very embarrassed and thrust the tie at him and said, 'Well whatever his bloody name is please give it him and say thank you.'

I then looked at Beaumont; he had a bemused look on his face that was turning into a huge grin.

'Sorry to have disturbed you,' I said and left feeling very embarrassed.

All the way back to the hotel I could not stop giggling to myself; I can just imagine Bill Beaumont reliving that story at the end-of-tour dinner. When I told the boys when I got back to the hotel they fell about laughing and from then on Woodward has always been a Woodcock to me.

Andy Vick

After another trouncing by the All Blacks that Saturday, we were lucky enough to be in the hotel bar later that night when all the New Zealand side returned to the hotel. They were brilliant and really mixed in with us all signing anything you put in front of them. Shame the Lions side was not so friendly, but again that was all down to Woodcock… sorry, Woodward!

It was during my third year with the Flying Squad that the injury I had received at Hammersmith in 1996 started to cause me real problems again, Mainly, I think, due to some of the horrendous hours we worked. It was very difficult at times because we would get caught up in the enthusiasm everyone had for the work we did and the hours did not seem a problem.

I, however, at times had to spend the whole of a weekend off just sleeping or resting to try and get the headaches to a level where I could cope with working. I had been living with a constant headache of some sort since July 1996 but now they were so bad it would get to the point where my body would say 'that's enough' and put me to sleep for hours. This resulted in several months off sick in the latter part of 2004 and then when I did return to work I was advised that I really needed to get a less demanding job for the benefit of my health.

I really did not want to leave the squad, so I just tried to calm down a little and not work so many hours. Everyone on the squad was great about it and understood if I said no to working late or at weekends and I hoped that this would allow me to see the last three years of my service out on the flying squad. Unfortunately, things carried on getting worse and I was slowly realising I was going to have to leave.

Operation Poe

THE LAST PROPER OPERATION I was to get involved in before I left the squad was Operation Poe. A pair of young black guys had been carrying out armed robbery offences in North and West London. Their targets were small shops and betting offices and they had started a series of robberies and were getting more daring on each occasion.

After a few weeks my detective sergeant, Charlie Cairns had recovered some DNA and identified two suspects who were half-brothers. One of the suspects wore a very distinctive green and white baseball cap. Because of their unpredictability it was decided to put them under surveillance for a couple of day to see what their habits were and where they were living. When we had confirmed addresses then we would arrest them by means of a mobile ambush, taking them by surprise and hopefully catching them with firearms on them.

We did have a static video camera covering an address in Clapham twenty-four hours a day. Charlie knew they would be at this address at some point and, sure enough, a review of the video showed the one suspect coming in and out of the address on several occasions. However, we still did not know if this was his actual home address.

The next day we arrived at the Clapham address very early in the morning. When the videotape was reviewed the suspect was seen to leave there late the night before but did not appear to have returned. We sat up in various advantage points to see if he came back. Some time around mid-morning he returned in a green Mazda, with an unknown male.

Both entered the house and came back out having changed their clothes; they went back to the car and drove off. A mobile surveillance operation then swung into action and off we went. It was felt that they had changed their clothes and put on their robbing gear and as a result, a decision was taken to stay with them for a little while to see if they attempted to carry out another a robbery.

We followed them around and through the centre of London where they looked at a few places but appeared to bottle it because of the number of people in the premises. We carried on up around North London, all around Notting Hill, Maida Vale and the Harrow Road. Again, on a couple of occasions, they looked at a couple of shop premises but after hanging around for a little while, they would leave. DS Cairns was convinced they were desperate to do a robbery and that it was only a matter of time before they found the right place.

Late in the afternoon we ended up on the edges of Wembley where they went into a house and came out a while later with a third male and a girl. The third male was wearing the distinctive green and white hat we had been looking for. The vehicle drove off with us following and we waited to see what they would do next. After a while, a decision was taken by the governor (detective inspector) to put in a hard stop on the car and ambush them. We were certain we had the two main offenders in the car now and did not want to risk losing them.

We drove along the Harrow Road and the surveillance team had the suspect car well under control. As we got towards Westbourne Green, the DI informed the surveillance team we were going to move up on them and put in the attack.

We had three gun ships, with four squad offices in each, and a control vehicle. With the exception of me and one other, all the squad guys were armed. I was driving my BMW with Charlie Cairns, Neil Hanchett and Danny O'Sullivan in the car with me. I was to take the lead attack car position and it was my job to bring the Mazda to a halt in the right place and the right time, giving us the element of surprise.

With Charlie, Neil and Danny all armed, it was my job to put in a much distraction as I could. For this purpose I had one of the emergency window-breaking tools, such as you see on coaches and minibuses. The plan was for me to smash a few windows at the same time the others went at the car with guns drawn and making lots of noise. The whole idea being to put as much fear as possible into them and to distract them enough to drag them out of the car before they had time to go for any weapons.

The attack was called as we approached the slip road under the Paddington flyover. I moved up passed all the surveillance vehicles. The Mazda was in the outside lane and as we got onto the slip road approaching Paddington police station I made my move. I accelerated alongside and then edged past the Mazda. At exactly the right point I swung my car across the front of the Mazda, and we all piled out of our car as did the teams in the other three vehicles.

The Mazda had been forced into the kerb and had stalled. All the squad boys were out and yelling 'armed police; let me see your hands', etc. I reached the driver's door first and swung my left hand at the driver's window to break it, but unfortunately what I did not realise was that the window was already down and I hit the driver right in the centre of the forehead with the window breaker and instantly drew blood. The driver's door then swung open and two of the squad guys dragged him out.

I carried on attacking the windscreen to distract the others in the car until all four of them had been dragged out. With all three males out and secured on the floor, I had the task of calming down a hysterical female who turned out to be the girlfriend of our main suspect. As you can imagine, she was in a terrible state after experiencing the attack by the team on the car she was in. It took quite a while to calm her down and, thankfully, a WPC from the nearby nick arrived and took care of her for me.

The driver of the car was completely oblivious to the fact I had hit him in the head with the glass-breaking tool. He thought he had been hit by flying glass and it was not until I approached him to check on his welfare and give him some first aid did he realise I had accidentally hit him. He was quite cool about it really and said that he had more important things to worry about now than a little bash on the forehead. Thankfully, he made no more of it and was duly found guilty with the others of the robbery offences and sent to prison.

The murder squad

The injury that had caused me so many problems since 1996 finally forced me to leave the Flying Squad. I was warned that if I did not change my lifestyle as far as work was concerned, I could well find myself in a situation where I would be forced to take an office job for the last two years or so of my service. I could not stand the thought of being cooped up in some office and, much to my regret, I made the decision to look for another job, one that would still allow me to still do the type work that I really enjoyed.

I started looking around and was not really sure what I was going to do. I had informed the squad that I was looking to leave but was really struggling to figure out what I was going to do. It was looking like I would have to go back to a division and hopefully onto a crime squad; I really did not want to go back to uniform.

The main problem was that despite all that I had done over the last seven years I had, for various reasons, not gone on to finish the task of officially becoming a substantive detective and this made my choices few and far between. I was capable of doing all the work that any experienced detective had to do, but I did not have the official title and I was what was termed a 'branch detective'. This meant as long as I was on the squad I held the rank of detective but if I left I lost that and resumed to a PC rank.

Suddenly, out of the blue I got a call from my close friend, Andy Murphy. Andy was a detective chief superintendent on the murder squads at the time and told me he had heard a rumour that I was leaving the flying squad and was it right? Andy was well aware of my injury and the problems I had with it.

I told him it was true and that I was having trouble finding somewhere. He then asked me why I had not gone to ask him for a job. I explained that I had two reasons, one because I did not want to use our friendship to put him in a position of trying to find me a job, and the second being that as I was not a substantive detective I did not think I would be able to be employed on the murder squad.

Andy told me that as far as he was concerned I was more than qualified with all my experience to be on the squad and that, whether I was substantive or not, as far as he was concerned I was a DC. He also said he had a job for me on the murder team at Barnes if I wanted it. This was just one floor below where I was on the flying squad and for me was a perfect solution. Andy was particularly interested in using my exhibits officer skills as exhibits were a big part of all murder investigations. He told me to go and speak with the detective chief inspector, Dave Little, who was in charge of team 5 of the murder squad down stairs and then to let him know what I thought about it.

After speaking with Dave Little and several others downstairs I realised this was a fantastic chance for me. I would still be involved in some great work but not constantly doing the horrendous hours that were causing me the health problems. I called Andy and asked him when applications would be coming out for the job downstairs. This was my next piece of luck: Andy said that I should just put in a transfer request and to leave it with him and he would get his personnel office to sort it.

This was very unusual; normally you would have to sit an interview board but Andy had other plans. Sure enough, within a week it had been sorted. This was in November of 2004 and I was told that I would be starting on the murder squad on 5 January 2005.

AND SO IT WAS I started on the final two years of my career as a detective for SCD1 (2) the Met police murder squad. Now, over the years, especially in my first five years in Gwent, I had seen quite a lot of dead bodies in all sorts of different circumstances and had got used to dealing with them. It was normally the thought of what you might see or find that scared you; actually dealing with dead bodies are a lot easier.

In Gwent we used to get a lot of calls to premises where the elderly occupiers had not been seen for some time. It would mean breaking into the premises and searching for the person. It was always eerie entering a house where there may be a dead body. Your mind would play tricks on you, wondering what sort of state you would find the body in. Normally, they would be in the bed still under the blankets and provided the electric blanket was not on at the time they died it would not be that bad. But there were some strange ones as well.

I remember going to a bungalow one afternoon, called there by the home help of an elderly male. The dead-lock was on from the inside and she could not get in. I broke in through a rear window and made my way towards the front door. I checked the bedrooms as I did so but there was no sign of the man. Then I saw him: he was in the toilet stood up, totally naked as if he was having a pee.

The toilet room was very narrow and the man was leaning slightly to his right against the wall and he was dead. He had actually died while standing up, having a pee. How he did not fall on the floor, I do not know – very odd.

As a result, prior to leaving Gwent I had been to a few post mortems, normally just going in to identify the deceased to the pathologist. I did stay for one full post mortem but viewed it from a distance. Since joining the Met had I dealt with quite a few dead or dying people, but apart from initial contact with them I had nothing to do with them after that, certainly none of the gory side of it anyway.

So here I was on the murder squad, what was in store for me? It was here that I discovered that my team detective sergeant, Dave Standley had been the DS who dealt with the suspect for the murder of the twelve-year-old girl in Hammersmith in May 1997. It was very interesting to hear the intricate details all about the suspect who was arrested some six years later and found guilty of the murder.

Dave was a pleasure to work for and I really enjoyed working on his team. When I joined the team in January 2006, the system was that every nine weeks the team was on call to go to any murders that occurred on our respective area of west London. The team would go out and take control of the scene and witnesses, and, of course, the deceased and any suspects arrested. Then more often or not, within twelve hours it would be handed over the team who were in frame to actually deal with the next job. There were three categories of offences.

Category A offences were classed as high-profile murders, such as, for instance, the murder of the TV personality Jill Dando, or a murder that would have a huge public interest and where the suspects were not known. A serial killer would also come into this category

Category B offences were classed mainly as any stranger murders, where no suspect was known and required a full investigation to find the person responsible.

Category C offences were murders such as domestic-related matter, where the victim and suspect knew each other and the suspect was in custody or their identity was known.

If you happened to be the 'in frame' for the next job, then everyone would attend a full briefing given by the 'on call' team and the investigation would be handed over to us to deal with.

My first couple of months on the squad were fairly quiet; the team was already running several jobs and I just linked into them and took on the tasks assigned to me.

During a murder investigation, every single shred of information goes onto computer in the incident room and as a result, hundreds of actions come out. These are then allocated to officers to go out and complete the actions. The actions themselves could relate to anything at all that had to be done in relation to an enquiry. It meant an officer going out and completing the enquiry and returning the action with the result, for instance a statement taken from a witness. This in itself could then generate further actions; it seemed endless but was a very important part of the whole murder investigations.

Then one Monday in April 2005, we were in frame to pick up a new job when we all got called to go to Hendon to get briefed on one that had come in. Once we were all there, the duty team DCI briefed us all about what had occurred. The incident had taken place in the New Southgate area of North London. Some time around midnight between Sunday and Monday morning, a drug addict by the name of Stephen Cox had been in his bed-sit with has brother, Derek, also a drug addict. They had been paid a visit by another addict, Danny Cann and his girlfriend, Heidi.

Cann was an acquaintance of Stephen Cox. The bed-sit was in a house containing five other bed-sit. When Danny Cann knocked at the door that night he asked Stephen Cox if he and his girlfriend could spend the night there as they had nowhere to go. Stephen Cox agreed, providing they shared any drugs they had with him and his brother. Danny stated he was off to buy some and would return a little while later.

When they returned it was in the early hours of the morning, there was a bit of a commotion that woke up a few other occupiers, but things settled down and Stephen, Derek, Danny and Heidi remained in the flat smoking drugs.

At around 4.00 a.m. Stephen and Derek were sleeping on the bed and Danny and Heidi on the floor. Some music from another room annoyed Danny Cann and he banged on the floor with the heel of his foot to get them to turn the noise down. Stephen Cox took exception and remonstrated with Danny stating, 'This is my flat, if anyone is going to do any banging on floors it will be me.'

This caused Danny Cann to flare up and a confrontation and a tussle ensued between Stephen and Danny. Derek intervened, produced a hammer and threatened Danny and ordered him and Heidi to leave.

Danny was incensed and said to Stephen, 'This is brothers on brothers now.'

He then stormed out with Heidi. This all took place around 4.30 a.m.

Some thirty minutes later there was a loud bang on the front door and suddenly several men burst into the bedsit. At least two of them were armed with baseball bats and one with a hammer. Danny Cann was one of them and was armed with a baseball bat. All hell let loose for the next minute or so. Derek Cox found he was separated from his brother and he fell into a small toilet on the landing outside the flat and had to use a metal bedstead to protect himself from an attack by one of the males.

He could hear his brother screaming in the room next door. Derek received several blows from a hammer and his right arm was broken during the attack. Suddenly, the men ran off down the stairs. A couple living in another room had called police and had heard the attack taking place but did not actually see any of the attackers. When Derek went into the room he found Stephen on his knees with his torso lying face down across the bottom of the bed. His brother was hardly breathing and had a huge hole at the base of his skull. The couple from the other bed-sit came to his aid and helped him until police arrived. Stephen later died at 5.30 a.m. at hospital.

A murder investigation was started by the on-call team and Derek Cox stated that the people with Danny Cann were he believed his father, Gary and at least two brothers, Tommy and Alfie. Prior to us taking over the investigation the next day, all four members of the family had been arrested and they were in custody at various police stations in north London. A post mortem had already been carried out on Stephen Cox which showed he had died as a result of a severe blow to the back of the head. He also had numerous other serious injuries to his body.

The first day of the enquiry, I was tasked with a colleague to interview one of the brothers that were in custody. Because of the distance between the area where the murder took place and Barnes, it was decided to move the prisoners to stations in West London. I was sent to Hammersmith police station to deal with Alfie, who was the youngest of the three brothers. Following a lengthy interview it became obvious to my colleague and I that Alfie was probably not involved in the incident and had been wrongly identified by Derek Cox. We made some enquires with regards to his alibi and by the end of the second day were able to bail him from the police station, very confident he was not part of the offence.

Danny Cann was being held at Chiswick police station; he was admitting everything and claimed and had gone there with his father armed with two baseball bats for protection and that he had only returned to collect his clothes and some drugs he had left in the bed-sit. He claimed they were attacked by Stephen and Derek and that they had fought back in self-defence. He also claimed he did not hit Stephen Cox around the head at any time.

Gary was the father of the brothers. He admitted going to the flat, he claimed on his own, to retrieve his son's property. He said he took a baseball bat with him for self-protection as Danny had told him that the Cox brothers had a hammer and were not afraid to use it. He said that he was attacked by the Cox brothers and had defended himself. He also claimed that he never hit Stephen Cox around the head. He told the interviewing officers that he had hidden the baseball bat on top of a dog kennel at the Cann family home.

Tommy Cann denied all knowledge of the attack saying he had been out late drinking with a friend and had been home in bed with his girlfriend at the time of the attack. Eventually, all three were charged with the murder of Stephen Cox and remanded in custody. The team then set about getting the evidence to prove the offence.

I was tasked with organising the house-to-house enquiries and also helping out with retrieving any CCTV that might be useful. The other occupants of the house were, with the exception of the couple who called the police, very unhelpful and we were getting conflicting stories. The couple who did help us were very important witnesses.

They both heard the arrival of Danny and Heidi at the flat just after midnight and again their return later in the morning. When the row started around 4.00 a.m. the male from the flat went and knocked on Stephen Cox's door and complained about the noise. Stephen apologised and the man was aware of a male who he knew as Danny Cann and a female leaving the building. The couple were still awake about half hour later when they heard the front door being kicked in and the noise of several people running up stairs.

They then heard lots of screaming yelling and shouting and were so afraid of what was taking place they rang 999. When we later obtained a recording of the 999 call from Scotland Yard, the terrifying noise of the attack could be heard in the background. The incident lasted a minute or so and on the 999 tape you could hear the sound of several people running down the stairs and out of the house. Almost immediately there was banging on the door to the couple's flat and Derek Cox could be heard on the tape recording yelling, 'They've killed Stephen, they've f***ing killed him.'

The couple went into Stephen Cox's flat and found Stephen on his knees with his face and chest on the bed. He had a massive hole in the back of his head and was barely breathing. They put him in the recovery position on the floor and awaited the arrival of police and ambulance.

There was, however, a catch to this situation. The male from the flat was wanted by police at the time. He panicked and left prior to the first police officers arriving at the scene, and it was a couple of day or so later that we found out that he was an important witness. His girlfriend eventually told us the full story and they both became very important witnesses at the eventual trail of the Cann family.

During the investigation, among the evidence we were gathering came several important pieces of information. The first related to Tommy Cann. He was denying any involvement in the offence and denying any contact with his family at the relevant times. However, interrogation of all the phones, be it landline or mobile, relating to all of the members of the family, showed there was phone contact between Gary and Tommy from both the home landlines and mobiles at the relevant times to the murder.

Subsequent investigation and checking of Tommy's mobile also showed his phone moving around the relevant areas of New Southgate during the half-hour to forty minutes that the whole incident was spread over. All the phone evidence suggested that after leaving the flat, Danny telephoned his father and Tommy to join him at a phone box a short distance from where Stephen Cox lived.

The movements of Tommy's phone, using three different mobile phone mast sites, all centred on the probable journey from his home to the scene and onto his parents' address. This left us absolutely certain that despite his denials, Tommy was definitely involved in the attack on the Cox brothers. The mobile phone evidence given by an expert at court was going to be crucial to our case against Tommy.

Another important piece of evidence we discovered was that this was not the first time that the Cann brothers had been responsible for a vicious attack on another drug addict. Over a period of several years, Gary had become known for the handing out of punishment to dealers who he believed was responsible for getting Danny onto drugs.

One such attack several years before had left a friend of Danny's seriously injured from an attack on him with a baseball bat and a knife. He received a very bad stab wound and initially reported it to the police naming Gary and Tommy as two of his attackers. They were both arrested but the victim eventually refused to go to court and the police had to drop the case.

There was also another incident where Gary and Tommy were named after attacking a man in a local pub. They had used a baseball bat and a hammer on this occasion but although named by the victim, again it never went to court because the victim refused to make a statement against the Cann family. Unfortunately, this was not evidence that we could use in court to show their previous bad character as they had not be found guilty of any offence. This was really frustrating, but this is the stupidity of our laws.

The trial eventually came around to the Old Bailey at the beginning of November 2005. The trial lasted for six weeks. During the trial the defence prosecution did its best to paint the Cann family as good honest hard-working people who were being falsely accused.

Derek Cox gave evidence, and we knew because of his past being very chequered with a long list of previous convictions for all sorts of crime and his very heavy heroin addiction, that it was going to be a difficult time. Derek stood up in court and despite being bullied for a day-and-a-half by the defence, he completely stood his ground. He lost his temper a few times with the accusations thrown at him, but in general was a very good witness. He was totally honest about his life of crime and as he said in open court.

'I know I'm a druggie but no one deserves to watch their brother being beaten to death.' That really struck a cord with the jury.

The thing that really upset Derek was the inference by one of the defence barristers that he could have caused the death of his brother by accidentally hitting him with a hammer during the fight. Derek went absolutely mad at this. Swearing at the defence and getting extremely upset. Our two other main witnesses, the couple from the other room in the house also received the same treatment from the defence.

Again, the man had numerous convictions for drugs and his girlfriend a couple of minor cannabis convictions. The defence tried to discredit them totally but they both stood up in court and openly admitted their wrongdoings before standing up to the defence barristers and being very good witnesses. The defence tried to claim that when they lifted Stephen from the bed and lay him on the floor that they dropped him and that they had banged his head on a bedside cabinet and that this may have caused the injury that killed him.

Again it outraged both the male and his girlfriend when it was put to them in court. This actually did the defence no favours at all because when the pathologist and the forensic experts both gave their evidence they blew the defence suggestions of a hammer and or a bedside cabinet causing the injury completely out of the water. The pathologist was in no doubt whatsoever that the injury that killed Stephen was caused by an implement shaped like a baseball bat.

The defence tried on numerous occasions to get them to admit it was a possibility but both the pathologist and the forensic scientist stood firm. The forensic scientist also gave evidence of finding blood samples on one of the baseball bats recovered from the Cann home. DNA tests showed it was Stephen Cox's blood.

The jury showed great interest in their evidence and it was obvious they did not like the tactics of the defence barristers at all. Eventually, at the end of the trial and after three days of deliberation the jury found Gary and Danny Cann guilty of murdering Stephen Cox. They were also found guilty of the assault on Derek Cox.

To my surprise Tommy was found not guilty. I was watching Gary and his two sons closely as the verdicts were given, first Danny, then Gary. Neither of them showed any emotion. Tommy was a different matter he was in a right state and I am sure he was fully expecting a guilty verdict. The look of surprise on his face told it all. He knew he had just got away with murder.

Gary and Danny Cann were sentenced on Friday 9th December 2005 to life imprisonment with the judge recommending they serve at least fifteen years before they could become eligible for any parole.

THE JUSTICE SYSTEM, AND IN particular the crown courts, have for me become a joke. Police officers in this country work hard to get a case to trial. Just getting it there is difficult enough. When it does get to court there is so much legal arguing about what is evidence that can be heard and what cannot be heard by the jury.

Often crucial pieces of evidence are withheld from the jury because the defence has convinced the judge that it would be prejudicial to his client's case or is unfair to the defendant and it does not fit in the defence case to have it included (normally because it proves the case against his client); it makes a mockery of everything this country used to stand for.

How can you justify members of the public who give evidence for the Crown being literally torn apart by defence barristers in an attempt to get their client, who they know is guilty of an offence, no matter what crime he has committed, found not guilty? To both prosecution and defence it is just a big game, and at the end of it they come out with very large sums of money while normal everyday people have their lives torn apart.

Now police officers can be called to jury service. For me with my past experiences this can only mean one thing. It is so difficult now to get your evidence past the Crown Prosecution Service and to a court of law, as far as I am concerned, any defendant who finds he is actually sitting at court on trial has got to be guilty. If there was the slightest doubt then the CPS would have chucked the case out long before it got to court. So if I am called to jury service I can tell you now, that person is guilty. Decision made.

I know the twelve true persons of a jury are supposed to be the backbone of our legal system. However, with the very clever barristers now playing the games they play, doing their Perry Mason bit to the jury, it is more like theatre than a court of law and some of them are very good actors. Normal everyday people who sit on juries can very easily get taken in by the barristers and justice is very often not seen to be done correctly.

For me the time has come for serious matters at courts like the Old Bailey to be presided over by a trio of judges. They all know the score and can see right through the games of the barristers. But there you are. I am just a retired police officer – who is going to listen to me? They never paid any attention to me when I was serving so they are not likely to do so now!

Operation Achor

On 29th July 2005, Newton Murray Thompson, a sixty-one-year-old Australian booked into the Comfort Inn Hotel in Paddington. Mr Thompson was in the UK on a sixty-one-day tour of Britain and Ireland. He was halfway through his trip and had returned for a second visit to the Comfort Inn. He was due to stay one night after arriving from Ireland where he had visited relatives. He was booked into room 110, a small single room barely big enough to swing a cat in, and had in fact complained about the size of the room on his previous visit. The room was on a small separate area on the first floor with only three other rooms on the landing.

At around 9.30 a.m. the following morning, a housekeeper let herself into the room having got no reply when she knocked. Assuming the occupant had vacated the room, she intended to carry out the room change and clean as per normal after a guest leaves. As soon as she opened the door she realised that the guest had not left as there were things still in the room. She also noticed the front of a pair of black shoes tucked around the corner of a wall leading from the bathroom towards the bed; no one spoke but she backed out of the room and left to carry on with other rooms until the occupier of 110 left.

At around 11.00 a.m. the same housekeeper checked with reception to see if the occupier of room 110 had checked out. They realised he had not and the manager and the housekeeper went up to the room to speak with the guest. They knocked, got no reply and let themselves in. Around the corner of the wall where the maid had previously seen the pair of black shoes, the manager found Mr Thompson lying on the floor with his head on a pillow and he was fully covered head to toe by the top cover of the bed.

They called his name and got no reply from him. When the manager got closer and pulled the top cover back he was met with the horrendous sight of Mr Thompson lying dead with severe head and facial injuries.

The police were immediately called. The first to arrive were uniformed and CID officers from Paddington police station. Realising this was a murder, the on-call duty team were contacted and they took the initial enquiry. Later that day a post mortem revealed that Mr Thompson had died from severe head injuries caused by an assault of some kind. He also had severe injuries to the rest of his body, including broken ribs and damaged testicles. It was decided that the case would be handed over to my team and we were called in for a full briefing the next morning.

I was to be exhibits officer along with Pat Sales, another experienced detective. Pat and I had taken to working together as exhibits officer as it made the job so much easier to do as a pair. We were getting quite used to attending post mortems together and sharing the workload, which at a PM some times got a bit hectic, and having two people there to deal with the exhibits retrieved by the pathologist made the job easier as there was less chance of any potential serious mistakes being made.

After the briefing we linked up with the DC on the on-call team who had attended Mr Thompson's post mortem and took control of all the exhibits he had taken. Most special post mortems generate at least fifty items as exhibits. These are very important to the forensic side of the investigation. Having secured all of them we then made our first visit to the scene and met with Graham Owen who was going to be the crime scene manager. The room had been sealed since the initial investigation and local officers had remained there for security purposes.

The initial search of the crime scene by the duty team had revealed something quite unusual. We were told in the briefing that apart from a small suitcase and several items of clothing, the murderer had taken away with him all of Mr Thompson's possessions. This even included his wash bag, shoes and clothing.

Our first look at the scene showed exactly how small the room was. On opening the door there was a short hallway, about five feet long and three feet wide. On the left was a door into a very small bathroom. At the end of the short hallway the room opened up a little to the left becoming double the size of the hallway. The single bed was immediately in front of the end of the hallway and apart from the top cover being missing it looked like it had not been slept in.

Running down the left of the room was a small wardrobe, followed by a dressing table and a smaller unit with a television on top. Next was a small space below the only window in the room. Here, on top of a folding case stand was Mr Thompson's black suitcase, the lock of which had been forced open. Next to the bed was a small bedside cabinet with a lamp on it.

There were two main striking additions to the room. As you opened the bedroom door there was a very large area of bloodstained carpet. Then on the floor between the bed and the dressing table was also an area of carpet with bloodstains. This was where Mr Thompson's body had been found, his head on a pillow. The pillowcase was saturated in his blood. In addition there was a hole in the wall, about four inches in diameter. This was in the wall between 110 and 112 and the hole was about the right size to have been caused by Mr Thompson's head.

The plan of action was to let the Met forensic teams go in first and take any sets of fingerprints, DNA, etc they may find. They would then be followed by the specialist scientists who deal with the blood distribution areas, etc. Once they had all finished Pat and I would do our bit and take all the exhibits from the room that we decided were relevant and might yield some further evidence for us. The whole exercise was likely to take about a week.

Meanwhile, the rest of the team were in full flow. Search perimeters had been set up by the DCI and a trawl of the entire area for CCTV had begun. Each evening I would meet the team back in the basement of the hotel and take from them all the CCTV they had seized. Each would be sealed in property bags and it was my responsibility to ensure the continuity of evidence and take them back to Barnes to record and store them in the secure exhibits store.

Unfortunately, the hotel itself had no CCTV so we had nothing to work on from that point of view. Remarkably for Paddington, there was not any CCTV in the street where the hotel was either. We were really out of luck and the guys given the task of reviewing the CCTV really had their work cut out.

It was believed that Mr Thompson had arrived at the hotel at around 5.30 p.m. He was seen going out dressed in the same clothes shortly after. Staff said he was in the bar alone at around 8.30 p.m. that evening and then nothing was seen of him until he was found dead at around 11.00 a.m. the next morning. Our initial enquiries led us to believe that Mr Thompson may have been gay. A fellow guest, who had spoken to him the evening before he died, stated he certainly gave the impression that he was.

As a result the first theory was that he had gone out in the evening and met someone who he had brought back to his room. That person had then viciously assaulted him and left him to die on the floor of the room. This was believed to be the answer to the murder and all the teams efforts focused on finding him on CCTV in or around the Bayswater or Paddington area.

Eventually on day four, Pat and I commenced our retrieval of exhibits from the room. This took us two-and-a-half days. During the search we found several items we thought might help us forensically. The first was a plastic half-bottle of whisky. This was found on the floor next to the body. If the killer had drunk from this bottle there was a chance we could retrieve DNA from it.

Also on the windowsill behind the curtain was a half-drunk, large bottle of Bacardi Breezer. Again, this presented us with a good chance to obtain a DNA sample. We eventually left with over forty exhibits, which was quite a lot considering the size of the room. We had virtually stripped the room even removing the carpet from the floor and the lino from the bathroom.

During the search we recovered a ticket receipt from the bin. The receipt was for a bus ticket purchased from Kings Cross railway station just before 5.00 p.m. on the day Mr Thompson arrived back in London. An officer retrieved the CCTV from Kings Cross station, and at the time shown on the ticket Mr Thompson was identified as purchasing the ticket and his route to Paddington was then followed using CCTV images.

In the CCTV he is seen wearing a blue polo shirt and jeans along with sandals. He was pulling the black suitcase and also had a bag of some sort over his shoulder. This bag was also missing from the room. CCTV was eventually found of Mr Thompson walking down a street a few blocks from the hotel just shortly after he checked in and returning to the hotel via the same street some forty-five minutes later. There were no other sightings of him after that time.

Evidence from the post mortem suggested that in the forty-five minutes he was away from the hotel, Mr Thompson had eaten a small Chinese meal, probably somewhere in the Bayswater area.

Several days after the murder I went to Westminster mortuary, a second post mortem was to be carried out on Mr Thompson. This allowed the pathologist to have a look at further bruising and other related injuries that come out days after an attack. I had already viewed the original scene photographs and video and I had also received the photographs taken at the post mortem three days earlier.

I had not, however, realised just how severe the attack had been until I saw Mr Thompson's body. The pathologist pointed out several injuries to me that must have been caused by very severe blows. I realised then that we were dealing with not just someone who may have 'flipped' in a moment of madness. The person who was responsible for killing Mr Thompson had been extremely violent and could quite possibly have killed again with ease.

As well as the completion of all the forensic and exhibits side of the investigation, the whole team were working extremely hard to get a breakthrough, but there was just nothing forthcoming. No other CCTV evidence was found of Mr Thompson out and about in the area. We had absolutely nothing to go on and were desperate for something to come back on either DNA or fingerprints.

I really thought that our best chance was going to come from the Bacardi Breezer bottle we recovered from behind the curtain. I assumed that the room would have been cleaned after the previous occupant and that Mr Thompson and his killer might have shared a drink from the bottle. At worst, I thought we might get a fingerprint and at best DNA if they had drunk from the bottle. But this was going to start our run of bad luck on this job.

We got both prints and DNA from the bottle. The forensics told us the DNA was from a female. A check of the last person to use the room before Mr Thompson showed it was a female who had stayed there. In a telephone call to the lady she told us that she had left the

Bacardi bottle there during her stay. Subsequent DNA and fingerprint checks confirmed it.

The plastic whisky bottle found next to the body only had the victim's DNA and prints on it and slowly but surely every bit of forensic evidence came back with absolutely nothing to help us identify the suspect. Whoever was responsible for murdering Mr Thompson has gone to great lengths not to leave any forensic traces at all. In such a small room that really was quite a feat.

Obviously, officers from the team were in touch with Mr Thompson's family in Australia. He lived just outside Melbourne and they discovered he was estranged from his wife. He had grown-up children and it was discovered from his family that Mr Thompson was gay and in fact had a liking towards men much younger than him.

He was known for some very curious behaviour in his home area and his son believed he used gay internet chat sites to further his pursuits towards the younger man. This led us to believe that our first thoughts that he may have picked up his killer may well be correct. It was decided that officers should travel to Melbourne to speak personally with the family and to dig deeper into his lifestyle.

DI Steve Smith, who was the investigating officer, and DC Paul Webb, the family liaison officer, were originally set to go. It was also decided that Mr Thompson's computer might hold valuable information relating to his activities and soon I was also granted authority to go with them and deal with any exhibits we should recover.

So at the beginning of September all three of us flew out to Melbourne from Heathrow airport. In Melbourne we met up with officers from the Australian federal police and two officers were assigned to assist us during our 10-day trip. Andy and Gerrard really put themselves out to assist us in every way possible. Most days we would set out what had to be done in the day and then Gerrard and I would go off and do what had to be done on enquiries and exhibits, etc. Steve, Paul and Andy would go off and meet with the family and carry out the necessary enquires and take statements from them in relation to Mr Thompson.

Without going into too much detail, Mr Thompson's private life was very strange. He did seem to enjoy the company of men much younger than himself. This had on a few occasions brought him to the notice of the local and federal police. Our enquiries took us out and around all of Melbourne. At some time during the day we would then all meet up after our day's work, discuss what we had discovered and email anything relevant back to our office in Barnes to be added to the intelligence that the rest of the team was gathering.

After work, Andy and Gerrard gave up a lot of their spare time to show us the delights of their home city. Andy even invited us to his home one evening for a meal and we spent a very pleasant night with the whole of his family. It was not the first time I had been to Melbourne but having a local to show you around really made a big difference.

Everywhere we went on enquires; when people discovered we were detectives from London's Scotland Yard they were always impressed. I was astounded by how highly thought of the British police were, especially when you mentioned Scotland Yard. When they then learnt that we had come all that way to try and solve the murder of a fellow Australian citizen they were even more impressed and went out of their way to look after us. Mr Thompson's murder had made headlines in the local papers and everyone wanted to help us in any way they could; it was fantastic.

ONE SUCH ENQUIRY LED US to Melbourne's famous MCC ground, home of Australian rugby rules matches and the national cricket ground. Mr Thompson was a member there. One of the family mentioned he was hoping to visit Lords cricket ground while he was in London and had gone to the MCC in the hope of arranging some sort of contact there. We went and spoke with a very nice lady at the MCC about Mr Thompson.

After getting the information we needed from her, she then offered us a free tour of the MCC. We grateful accepted and later spent an hour or so there seeing the whole stadium both in front and behind the scenes. Steve is a massive cricket fan and it really made his trip. We all thoroughly enjoyed it though and even went to watch an Australian rules football game on the Saturday afternoon, an amazing experience.

Eventually, after a week of extensive enquiries and, of course, a little socialising with Andy and Gerrard, we had everything we could get and we returned to London and the investigation continued. Despite

Andy Vick

intensive investigations into the murder, Mr Thompson's killer still has not been caught. There are some leads that might eventually help to bring him to justice. It is not possible for me to write about these as it might hinder the investigation. To date although still being investigated Mr Thompson's murder has yet to be solved.

An ending I just did not want

It was following the six weeks at the trail of the Cann family at the Old Bailey that things started to go wrong for me. I realised in the run up to Christmas that the head and neck injury that had caused me problems since 1996 was starting to kick in again. This time however, it appeared to be a lot worse that the two previous relapses I had experienced.

As well as the headaches that some nights were so severe they left me scared to go to sleep in case I did not wake up again, I was finding myself very fatigued. Just a short walk left me absolutely knackered with blurred vision and so uncomfortable I could not sit down or stand up for more than a couple of minutes. I got to a point as we reached Christmas that I knew I was in serious trouble.

I decided to keep going and hope that the couple of weeks I had off over Christmas would, with a lot of rest, see me OK again. At work I was trying to get all the exhibits from the Cann trial boxed up and all listed correctly so that as soon as possible after Christmas I could get them moved to the central property store to make a bit of room in the exhibits store at Barnes. This meant a lot of computer work as well as packing and lifting of the sometimes heavy exhibit boxes.

I realised that something was very wrong when I just could not concentrate on what I was doing for more than a couple of minutes. Once distracted, I would then forget what I had been doing. My memory was a real problem; I started the same things over and over again. I later found that I had duplicated things on the computer many times and also I was making some horrendous mistakes in the detailed itemising of all the exhibits. I should have had it all completed before the Christmas break but when we finished on Christmas Eve my work was nowhere near complete.

I felt really sorry for my wife, Paula. That Christmas, I must have been a right pain in the arse to her. I don't really remember too much about that period as I was so ill and dosed up with pills for most of it. I decided that as soon as I started back at work I would try to get some treatment from the Met's occupational health department just as I had done previously. I was a bit apprehensive in doing so because I knew it was possible they would insist I went off sick. This is something I just did not want to do.

However, on 5th January 2006 I started back to work. On checking over the work I had been doing before the break I realised how much of a mess I had made of it and knew I had to get some treatment sorted out before it compromised a case. I filled out a form requesting for some treatment via the occupational health department and sent it by email to them. On the form you had to describe your symptoms and problems you were having.

Within half an hour I received a phone call from the occupational health department about my request. The lady I spoke with had looked at my previous file and was aware of my injury. She immediately told me that I should not be in work and that I was to take myself off sick straight away. I explained to her that I had some important work I had to finish but she insisted I was to leave work. We came to a compromise when I promised to be finished and on my way home within the hour. I really had no intention of going until my work was complete.

About an hour and a half later she rang one of my detective inspectors who unwittingly told her I was still in work. She went mad and told the DI that I was to be ordered out of the building immediately. I left feeling so ill I really should not have driven home myself. I knew the lady at occupational health was right; I just did not want to admit it.

This turned out to be the last time I ever worked as a police officer. And so, seventeen months later, exactly four months after my official retirement day I was retired from the service on an ill health.

With the last year of my service ruined by the reoccurrence of the 1996 injury, I found myself stuck at home and slowly but surely weaned off the police force, and the fear of retirement was no longer a concern. Though I was more than ready to go for numerous reasons, I did not want to be leaving under these circumstances, but it was out of my hands. And so on 24th June 2007, after thirty years and four months, I officially retired from the job I had loved doing so much.

BUT BEING RETIRED NOW FREES me from the mad world of political correctness that has overtaken this country and I can now to some extent speak my mind without fear of losing my job and my pension. I cannot end this book without trying to put into context exactly what I believe, and what many serving officers also believe but are not allowed to say.

Members of the public are getting no service at all from grass-roots policing. If you are in trouble and call for police it can take hours for them to arrive. This is not just happening to the public, though. In November 2006, several colleagues from my murder squad went out one morning to arrest a violent male for a murder he had committed the day before. He was traced to an address and when the officers tried to arrest him they had a violent fight before handcuffing and restraining him on the floor. They requested a van from the local station to attend to transport him to the police station. It took an hour and twenty minutes for the van to arrive! The situation is horrendous and can only get worse.

In the book written in 1982 by ex-Detective Chief Superintendent of the Flying Squad, Jack Slipper, he mentions in his final chapter his concern for the way things were turning for the worst in the country, I quote.

'I think there are a number of dangerous trends, particularly towards too many controls on the police; I don't think the members of the public realise just how much these controls hinder the police in their task of protecting them.'

His final paragraph then states:

'But I've always believed in the public's common sense and I'm sure there will be a place again for old-style coppering, at least I certainly hope so.'

Jack Slipper saw what was coming back in 1981 but unfortunately the public's common sense is now indoctrinated so badly against the police that it can only get worse. There are numerous reasons for this.

The very nice beanbag way of dealing with new recruits means that they no longer get the upbringing that used to form the stable ways of a probationer and that allowed them to develop into good officers. The recruitment of the ethnic minorities, some of whom struggle with even the basics of reading and writing of the English language, has become so important to the service and it has had a great detrimental effect on people who want to join up.

In 2005 a colleague of mine had a son wishing to join the job. With his dad a serving officer with over twenty years' service, he was a prime candidate. But no: he was told that there was a two-year waiting list. When his dad, rightly upset about this, made enquiries he was told that it was because they have so many ethnic minority people to get through the system first. I was also staggered to learn that ethnic candidates who were not able to pass the entrance exam were given extra lessons in order to reach the required standard to pass the exam.

In my experience there have been very few ethnic officers that I have met who were capable of being good effective police officers. The ones who were good were in fact very good, but I have to say a lot of them were bloody useless. Yes, you would get white officers who were also a bloody waste of time, but they hardly ever lasted in the job. The ethnic officers get pampered and looked after because of their origin and God help any supervisory officer who tried to get rid of them. They immediately played the race card to negate any attempt to get them to resign.

When I was on the Flying Squad, I once received a statement from a Nigerian officer with regards to his attendance at the scene of an armed robbery. The statement looked like it had been written by a child of about eight years of age. It was very difficult to read and was in large printed letters with many spelling mistakes. I tracked down his sergeant to have a bit of a go about it, thinking it was someone's idea of a joke but was told that it had been genuine. That was exactly how the officer wrote and because of his ethnic origin; despite trying, there was nothing that could be done about him.

The government have sold out this country and it is becoming lawless. The police no longer have the teeth or ability to deal with normal everyday policing. The only people still doing their job without too much interference are the specialist squads who work their arses off fighting major crime. They are doing a fantastic job keeping the lid on serious and organised crime in this country. Budgets and the wrong type of recruitment are selling the normal everyday British public a very poor service. I wish I could tell you more but there is no way this book would ever get published if I tried!

The papers constantly slag off the police saying the public are no longer behind them or support them. That, I believe, is totally wrong. Older generations of British people (whether they are white or not) are still behind the police. Unfortunately, so much of the country, particularly London, is no longer populated by British people. It is overrun with every type of nationality you can think of and with all but a few of those nationalities being lazy, money-grabbing and non-law-abiding.

It is the likes of these people who have comes from countries where violence and crime are part of life that are not behind the police. They are naturally anti-police because the police try to enforce the law. In the Met we were always being told by the media that we were racist and that we stopped more black people than white. Too bloody right we did; that is because there are so many black people in London now that they are in the majority for those committing crime. Hence, the figures will show that more black people are stopped and or arrested. If the politicians had to live in an area where the crime was rife they might understand but they don't. They would not dream of living in such an area so why expect British people to have to put up with it?

This country has to sort out its immigration policies and quickly, before the whole system collapses. You cannot go to hospital now without having to wait hours to be seen. Why is the waiting time to be seen so long? It is because A&E is full of people from every country but Britain. They demand everything and get it. Money that should be going into the national health system and towards policing this country is being used to pay for immigrants to live here in free housing and get paid large sums of money to do nothing but sit on their arses and produce children to put an even more of a drain on the country's finances.

If we went to their countries and tried the same we would probably disappear off the face of the earth and never be seen again. The do-gooders in this country need to wake up a see what is happening here or God help us.

Now I am sure all of this will have some people up in arms accusing me of being racist. I am not, far from it. I have many friends who are from ethnic backgrounds. I grew up with a very good friend who was black and I have never ever had a racist complaint made against me in thirty years of service despite dealing with every colour, race and creed you can imagine.

I am, however, against the scrounging, lawless and lazy good-for-nothing communities that are strangling this country with their attempts to bring us down to their way of life. The backlash we had in 2006 about Muslims and the wearing of veils covering the faces of females was a prime example. If we were to go to a Muslim country we would be forced to dress appropriately and behave in a way that showed respect to their religion or find ourselves in a dirty stinking prison. They should do the same in our country, but no – the government panders to their every whim to keep them happy.

As a result of our government giving them everything they want we now have them repaying us by producing home-grown British-born suicide bombers to kill and maim in our country, and we are still bending over backwards to keep them happy.

Unless the country gets to grip with the youngsters now and stamps out the yobbish and criminal culture that leaves old people afraid to go out, results in other youngsters who have disrespected them dead and parents letting their children run riot, then we are finished as a law-abiding country.

The past few years as a police officer have led me from someone who loved doing the job twenty-four hours a day to someone who could not wait to leave. That is now very common within the service. Where is it all leading to? For me it leads me to a life in another country where elders are given respect. Children have manners and respect the police and immigration is controlled correctly.

I am sorry to say that Britain will soon be an ethnic heaven for all the dross who wants to live here. I feel sorry for the decent hard-working people in this country who deserve better, and I am even sorrier to say that the British police force, unless some drastic measures are taken, will no longer be the envy of every other law enforcement agency around the globe.

Printed in the United Kingdom
by Lightning Source UK Ltd.
135700UK00001B/97/P